Unfunk Your Mind

The Greatest Collection of
Logical Fallacies,
Cognitive Biases,
Mental Models, and
Critical Thinking Techniques to
Create the Best You.

Ravi Jayagopal
UYMHub.com

To Veena Prashanth, the love of my life and the most beautiful and brilliant person I know.

Thank you for standing by me in every season - through the highs, the lows, and all the messy moments in between.

For being there for me even when I wasn't there for you. For being my anchor when the storms hit.

I can't remember life without you. And I don't ever want to know a life without you.

Here's to you, mi amor, for being my rock and the reason for my existence.

How Cognitive Biases & Fallacies Shape Our World (And How to Fight Back)

You're scrolling through your feed late at night. You freeze. A viral post warns that a common household item causes cancer - one sitting in your kitchen right now. Your heart races. It has thousands of shares, hundreds of comments. Dozens of personal stories. A verified-looking doctor's warning. You're about to go throw that thing in the trash. But something makes you pause.

What just happened in your mind?

In those few seconds, five cognitive biases nearly hijacked your brain:

1. **Availability Cascade** made the claim seem more true each time it was repeated and shared, creating a self-reinforcing cycle of perceived credibility.
2. **Authority Bias** let an unverified "doctor" sway you.
3. Personal stories triggered your **Anecdotal Fallacy**, overriding statistics with emotion.
4. **Negativity Bias** amplified your fear, drowning out rational thought.
5. **Bandwagon Effect** whispered, "All these people can't be wrong."

This mental ambush happens to all of us, multiple times a day. It's why smart investors panic-sell during market dips. Why savvy executives fall for urgent emails from fake "bosses." Why intelligent people make health decisions based on celebrity endorsements.

The $9 Billion Blind Spot

Just ask the investors who lost nearly a billion dollars to Theranos. Elizabeth Holmes built a $9 billion company on technology that never worked by exploiting these exact mental blind spots:

- **Authority bias:** By appointing former Secretaries of State and military leaders to her board, she leveraged their perceived authority and expertise to instill confidence in investors, even though they lacked medical knowledge.

- **Narrative bias** & **Appeal to Innovation bias:** Holmes crafted a compelling narrative that positioned her as the "next Steve Jobs," leading investors to overlook the red flags and believe in her vision.
- **Social proof:** The presence of prestigious early investors, such as Rupert Murdoch and Larry Ellison, created a cascade of credibility, making it more likely for subsequent investors to follow suit.

One fraud. Nine billion dollars. All because smart people didn't understand their own mental blind spots.

Breaking Free

These mental traps lose power once exposed to light. That moment of pause before throwing away your household item? That was your rational mind beginning to wake up. This book will strengthen that voice of reason - your mental defense system.

In the following chapters, you'll discover:

- A practical toolkit for **making smarter decisions** in every area of your life
- How to **spot manipulation attempts** in seconds, not hours after it's too late
- The exact **psychological triggers that manipulators use** - and how to defend against them

You're about to explore **365+ cognitive biases, logical fallacies, and mental models** that shape your daily choices. Each one is like a piece of mental malware - most dangerous when you don't know it's there.

The best time to strengthen your mental defenses was yesterday. The second best time is now.

Coolest Geek On The Planet :-)

My name is **Ravi Jayagopal** - Digital Marketer, 9x Author, Speaker, Podcaster, Entrepreneur, Business Coach, and, yes, Amateur Ventriloquist.

I've been in the online game since 1997, selling everything from e-books to software, WordPress plugins, online courses, coaching programs, t-shirts and even supplements.

I'm the Co-Founder of DigitalAccessPass.com (DAP), a leading membership plugin and marketing automation platform for WordPress.

On my podcast at SubscribeMe.fm, I talk about how to Create, Sell and Deliver digital content, WordPress, Podcasting, Creating Audio, Video, & Reports, and strategies, tactics, tips and tools you can use to create a long term, profitable online business.

I am also the creator of S3MediaVault.com (a secure file protector and media player for Amazon S3) and WhatChangedWhen.com (a free Content Monitoring service).

I live in sunny San Diego with my stunningly beautiful and brilliant wife Veena Prashanth (Co-Founder of DAP, creator of SmartQuizBuilder.com), 2 amazing kids, and my precious dog Lola!

Learn more about me at SubscribeMe.fm/ravi

Oh, and I love playing with dolls ☺

(do a Google search for "Coolest Geek on the Planet", with the quotes)

Free Bonus with Every Purchase

Thank you for your purchase! You qualify for 2 special bonuses.

BONUS #1: A PDF version of this book for your archives. Read it on your Kindle, phone, tablet or computer.

-AND-

BONUS #2: Pick any one of the options below.

a) A free digital copy of any one of my previous 8 books at **SubscribeMe.fm/books**. Or...

b) A shout-out on my podcast at **SubscribeMe.fm** (~2000 downloads per episode) where I'll thank you by name and mention your website, podcast, online course, book, etc. Or...

c) My online course "**Brainstorming Badass:** The Abso-Frickin-Lutely Fastest way to Brainstorm and Churn out ideas for the next 33 years for your online courses, podcast, live streaming videos, webinars, Kindle books, YouTube channel, and any imaginable type of Content Marketing" (a $69 value).

To claim your bonuses, email your purchase receipt to **Ravi@SubscribeMe.fm** and tell me which bonus you'd like for #2.

Cheers!

- **Ravi Jayagopal**

Praise for *Unfunk Your Mind*

"This book brilliantly breaks down complex psychological concepts into digestible, practical insights. Whether you're a business professional weighing strategic decisions, a leader guiding teams, or simply someone looking to sharpen their critical thinking, "Unfunk Your Mind" delivers valuable tools for better decision-making.

What sets this book apart is how it transforms academic concepts into engaging, real-world applications. Unlike typical psychology texts that can feel dry and theoretical, Jayagopal's conversational style and practical examples make these ideas stick. The author successfully helps readers spot and counter cognitive biases and logical fallacies, both in their own thinking and others'.

If you're looking to upgrade your mental toolkit and make better decisions, this book is an excellent resource. It's rare to find a guide that balances intellectual depth with accessibility this well."

- Chris Lema, CEO of Motivations AI

"Fascinating! Judges affected by a roll of the dice, the Cobra Effect, the Zebra Rule - how biases and fallacies influence our judgement and what to do about it. Settle into a comfy chair and devour this book!"

- Tsufit, Author, Step into the Spotlight! : A Guide to Getting Noticed

"The mind is so complex that it keeps grabbing every experience and draws inferences. These inferences find its expression in various circumstances in the form fallacies, biases, misconceptions and judgments and rarely as wisdom. In this book, Ravi Jayagopal captures these innumerable fallacies, biases and judgments, dissects them to critically understand where we falter, substantiates with the theory of reasoning and guides the change in the course of action towards better results and decision making.

This book will be an eye-opener to the subtle traps in our thinking. Be ready to shed a few of them and embrace critical thinking, to spot misleading arguments in yourself and others. This book is the best buy for futuristic thinkers."

- Dr. Manasa Nagabhushanam, Management Professor, Education Leader & Writer

---

"*Unfunk Your Mind* has wisdom about human behavior sprinkled on every single page. Not only would you benefit instantly from reading it and applying the principles in your life and work - this is a book that you might want to gift to people you love and care about. Brilliant and timeless knowledge in abundance."

- Rajesh Setty, Author of Napkinsights and 18 other books

"This is not a mere book to read; it is an encyclopedia to help anyone think clearly. Whenever you regret a past decision, or are confused about a future one, just open up this book and find out what is holding you back.

It is an all-time help-yourself guide; a ready-to-use reference book. Use this to untie yourself from doubts and depression that engulf you whenever you need to make a decision or act on something. Reading this book will help you think better, act better, feel better."

Dr. Rama Kashyap, Former Professor of Social Work & Social Development Specialist

"Make better decisions faster, communicate more powerfully, and become the sharpest thinker in any room - that's what reading *Unfunk Your Mind* will do for you. Don't buy this book just for yourself. Buy a copy for your team, partners, and everyone you want to help succeed in life and business.

P.S. Great book! I was a bit skeptical when I first saw the format. But quickly changed my mind and fell in love with each concept/theory/bias packaged into a bite-sized, "1-page debugging" bit. Well done."

Adam Urbanski (Founder, The Marketing Mentors)

"More than self-help, this book is a self-awakening. *Unfunk Your Mind* rewires the way you process life, making second-order thinking the key to your personal breakthrough.

Unfunk Your Mind is a toolkit for anyone looking to reclaim their mental real estate and cultivate resilience. It approaches mental clarity with depth and purpose, giving readers not only the why but the how of transformation. In my work, using forensic hypnosis techniques, I've seen the power of clear thinking firsthand, and this book delivers. It's a refreshing, grounded approach for anyone serious about lasting mental freedom."

Srini Saripalli, Forensic Hypnotist & Founder of PositivePositioning.com

Table of Contents

Core Concepts

Logical Fallacies: The Logic Loopholes

What's a Fallacy?
Arguments fail in predictable ways. Logical fallacies are these failure patterns — mental trapdoors that make weak arguments feel strong. They're not random mistakes. They're specific flaws that trick your brain into accepting faulty conclusions. Like sleight of hand in magic, once you see how they work, you can't unsee them.

How Do Fallacies Work?
Logic is a chain. Each link must connect perfectly to the next for the conclusion to hold. Fallacies break this chain while making it look intact. It's like building a house with decorative supports — looks solid until you lean on it. The structure fails, but the façade remains convincing.

Example:
"Most successful entrepreneurs wake up at 4 AM, take cold showers, meditate, and read a book before bed. Start following the same routine if you want to be successful." This fallacy confuses correlation with causation. Yes, many successful people do those things, but you doing the same doesn't automatically mean you'll be just as successful. Success isn't a recipe you can copy — it's a complex system of decisions, skills, timing, and execution.

Why Do Fallacies Matter? Bad logic costs you:

- Money (in investments)
- Time (in strategies)
- Trust (in relationships)
- Opportunities (in decisions)

Fallacies aren't just debate club problems. They're hidden in sales pitches, political arguments, and business strategies. Spotting them gives you an edge. Think of fallacy detection as a BS filter — the sharper it is, the better your decisions become. You can't stop others from using fallacies, but you can stop falling for them.

Cognitive Biases: Your Brain's Default Settings

What's a Cognitive Bias?

Your brain processes 11 million bits of information per second. But you can only consciously handle 40. Cognitive biases are your brain's solution to this gap. They're automatic filters that help you make fast decisions – but often at the cost of accuracy. Think of them as mental presets: useful but distorted.

How Do Biases Work?

Your brain is a prediction machine, not a truth machine. It takes shortcuts based on past experiences and evolutionary wiring. These shortcuts save mental energy but create blind spots. Like a security camera with a narrow field of view, you miss what's happening outside your preset frame.

Example:

Two sports fans watch the same game. The Lakers fan sees every foul against their team, dismisses every foul they commit. The Celtics fan sees the exact opposite. Same game, different realities. Neither is lying – their brains are filtering information to match their existing beliefs. That's confirmation bias in action.

Why Do Biases Matter?

These mental shortcuts shape every decision you make:

- Which opportunities you see (and miss)
- Who you trust (and doubt)
- Where you invest time and money
- What risks you take (or avoid)

You can't eliminate these biases. But awareness gives you an edge. When you know your brain's default settings, you can pause, override, and choose better. The difference between good and great decisions often lies in managing these biases, not ignoring them.

Mental Models: Reality's Operating Manual

What Are Mental Models?
Mental models are frameworks for understanding how things work. They're not just tools – they're lenses that reveal hidden patterns. Like an expert chess player who sees moves you don't, mental models let you spot opportunities and threats others miss.

How Do They Work?
Each model is a pattern-recognition shortcut. Take Opportunity Cost: Every "yes" contains hidden "nos." When Zuckerberg wears the same shirt daily, he's trading variety for reduced decision fatigue. When Buffett stays in Omaha, he's trading status for clarity. These aren't random choices – they're mental models in action.

Example:
Circle of Competence (a key mental model) explains why great investors and operators succeed: They play where they have unfair advantages. Bezos didn't start with groceries – he started with books, where margins and inventory were simple. Only after mastering that did Amazon expand. Understanding your circle of competence isn't about limiting yourself; it's about knowing where you're dangerous.

Why Do Mental Models Matter?
They're not just nice-to-have mental tricks. They're the difference between playing checkers and chess in a world that rewards chess players. They let you:

- Spot gold mines others walk past
- Dodge traps that catch even smart people
- Make non-obvious connections
- Scale your decision-making

One mental model can unlock a million-dollar insight. Stack them deliberately, and you build an unfair advantage that compounds. While others get smarter, you build a thinking system that scales. That's the real edge.

Razors: Decision-Making Shortcuts That Work

What Are Razors?
They're your BS-detection toolkit. When everyone's overthinking, razors let you hack through the noise. Like a good editor who knows what to delete, razors help you focus on what matters by showing you what doesn't.

How Do They Work?
Each razor attacks a specific type of mental clutter:

- Occam's Razor cuts complex explanations
- Hanlon's Razor slices conspiracy theories
- Newton's Razor removes unsupported claims

Think of them as mental filters that strain out bad solutions automatically.

Example:
Your iPhone keeps dying by lunch. Your coworker insists it's Apple's secret battery-draining update to force upgrades. Occam's Razor suggests checking your screen brightness (stuck at 100% all the time) and your background apps first. Those 30 apps quietly running are probably killing your battery - and your data plan. The simplest explanation usually wins — not because it's always right, but because it's the smart place to start.

Why Do Razors Matter?
One sharp razor eliminates a thousand bad options. Stack your razors right, and complex decisions become simple eliminations. While others drown in options, you'll cut straight to what works. The best don't just decide better — they eliminate faster.

Ableism: When Assumptions About Ability Create False Limits

A dangerous mental shortcut occurs when we mistake someone's specific limitation for their total capability - stereotyping skills and potential based on a single data point.

How It Works:
The brain takes a visible disability or difference and makes sweeping assumptions about unrelated abilities. These mental shortcuts create artificial barriers that limit both individual potential and societal progress.

Example:
Stephen Hawking's early professors assumed his motor neuron disease would limit his scientific work. He went on to become one of history's most influential theoretical physicists, showing how dramatically wrong ability assumptions can be.

When Albert Einstein supposedly didn't speak until age four and struggled to form sentences, teachers labeled him slow and ineducable. His early report cards show teachers mistaking his different processing style for a lack of intelligence.

Why It Matters:
When we let assumptions about ability guide decisions, we miss breakthrough talent and create artificial barriers. Many of history's greatest innovations came from people working around or through their limitations.

When to Use It / How to Counter It:
Question your instant assumptions about capability. Focus on actual demonstrated abilities rather than stereotyped limitations. Ask "What can you do?" instead of assuming what someone can't.

The Bottom Line:
Judge capability by demonstration, not assumption. The greatest barrier is a closed mind.

Actor-Observer Bias: Why Everyone Else Seems Like a Jerk

That driver who cut you off is a "total idiot", but when you cut someone off, "these lanes are really poorly marked". We're all starring in our own movie where we're the misunderstood hero and everyone else is a flat character.

How It Works:
Your brain has full access to your internal context - your thoughts, feelings, and circumstances. But for others, you only see their external actions. So you excuse your mistakes with context while judging others purely on behavior.

Example:
A team member misses a deadline, and you think "typical lazy millennial." When you miss a deadline, it's because "the requirements were unclear, IT was down, and your kid was sick." Both statements explain the same outcome - only the perspective changes.

Why It Matters:
This bias destroys teams, ruins relationships, and blocks personal growth. Netflix's famous culture emerged when they realized high performers sometimes fail and low performers sometimes shine - context matters more than character.

When to Use It / How to Counter It:
Before judging someone's actions, ask: "What circumstances might explain this?" Practice imagining different contexts that could explain their behavior. Give others the same benefit of context you automatically give yourself.

The Bottom Line:
Everyone is the hero of their own story. Understanding this doesn't just make you fairer - it makes you wiser about human nature.

Ad Hominem: Attacking the Person Instead of the Point

Ad hominem (Latin for "to the person") remains one of the most common and destructive logical fallacies, appearing in everything from political debates to workplace discussions.

How It Works:
Rather than addressing an argument's substance, the person attacks irrelevant personal characteristics of their opponent. Studies show this tactic often succeeds at persuading audiences, despite its logical invalidity.

Example:
During a 2012 workplace safety debate, when an entry-level employee pointed out flaws in the evacuation procedure, their supervisor responded "You've only been here six months - what could you possibly know about safety protocols?" This classic ad hominem attack dismissed valid concerns by attacking the messenger's experience rather than addressing their actual points about the procedure's problems.

Why It Matters:
Research from organizational behavior studies shows ad hominem attacks significantly reduce meeting participation and decrease the number of new ideas shared.

When to Use It / How to Counter It:
Never use ad hominem attacks - they undermine rational discourse. To counter them: Calmly redirect the conversation back to the substance of the argument. When someone attacks you personally, respond with "Let's examine the evidence and focus on the actual issue at hand."

The Bottom Line:
Judge ideas on their merits, not their messenger. History shows the best arguments stand on evidence, not attacks.

Affect Heuristic: Letting Emotions Influence Decision-Making

The Affect Heuristic occurs when emotions guide our decisions instead of logical analysis. While this may feel right in the moment, it isn't always based on the facts, which can lead to choices that backfire.

How It Works:
Imagine you're excited to invest in a startup because you admire its brand and leadership. You haven't examined the company's financials or future strategy, but your positive feelings push you to act. Here, the emotion of optimism overrides the logical steps of research and due diligence.

Example:
A car buyer falls in love with a luxury sports car's sleek design and powerful engine. Despite records showing poor reliability ratings and maintenance costs triple their budget, they buy it anyway, letting the emotional thrill override practical considerations.

Why It Matters:
Emotion-driven decisions can be risky, especially when long-term consequences are involved. While emotions offer useful signals, relying on them too heavily can lead to poor outcomes in investments, relationships, and major life choices.

When to Use It / How to Counter It:
To spot it: Watch for decisions driven purely by excitement or fear. To counter it: Use a 24-hour cooling period for decisions under $1,000, and a week for larger commitments. This structured approach helps balance emotional impulses with rational analysis.

The Bottom Line:
Emotions can mislead if you don't incorporate logic. For important decisions, take a step back, check the facts, and ensure your feelings aren't steering you off course.

Affective Forecasting Error: Why You Can't Trust Your Emotional Crystal Ball

Studies suggest we consistently mispredict how future events will make us feel, leading to flawed decision-making about everything from relationships to careers.

How It Works:
Our brain overestimates both the intensity and duration of future emotional reactions. We fail to account for our natural ability to adapt emotionally - what psychologists call our 'psychological immune system' - that helps us adjust to both positive and negative changes.

Example:
Studies of lottery winners show they return to their baseline happiness within months, despite predicting lasting euphoria. Similarly, people denied tenure at universities recover emotionally far faster than they expected.

Why It Matters:
This error leads to major life decisions based on faulty emotional predictions. For example, someone might turn down a promising job in a new city because they overestimate how long they'll feel homesick, or stay in an unfulfilling role because they overestimate how happy a higher salary will make them.

When to Use It / How to Counter It:
Before making decisions based on predicted feelings, remember your natural adaptation abilities. Ask yourself: "How did similar past experiences actually affect me long-term?"

The Bottom Line:
Your emotional predictions are often less accurate than you think. Consider both objective factors and past experiences, rather than relying heavily on predicted feelings when making important choices.

Ambiguity Effect: Known Devil Is Better Than Unknown Angel

When faced with choices, humans consistently prefer known odds over unknown ones. We'll take a guaranteed 3% return over a mysterious investment that might yield 10%.

How It Works:
Your brain treats uncertainty as a threat. Given a clear but mediocre option versus a fuzzy but promising one, we instinctively choose the known path - even when the numbers suggest otherwise.

Example:
A tech company stays with a reliable but limited vendor charging $50k annually rather than switching to a newer one offering better features at $40k. Why? Because the current vendor's problems are known while the new one's are unknowable - until you try.

Why It Matters:
This bias keeps good businesses from becoming great ones. We stick with underperforming employees, outdated systems, and fading markets - not because they're working, but because they're familiar.

When to Use It / How to Counter It:
Before rejecting an unclear option, ask: "Is my hesitation based on real risk or just discomfort?" Then gather just enough data to make the unknown knowable. Not perfect, just clearer.

The Bottom Line:
Uncertainty isn't a bug - it's where opportunities hide. While others cling to comfortable mediocrity, train yourself to see ambiguity as a signal of untapped potential.

Anchoring Bias: How First Numbers Hijack All Future Decisions

In 1983, real estate agents toured a house and estimated its value. The only difference? Half saw a listing price of $119,900, the others $149,900. The higher anchor led to valuations 41% higher - from professionals who do this daily.

How It Works:
Your brain latches onto the first number it sees, using it as a baseline for all later judgments. Nobel laureate Daniel Kahneman's research shows this effect persists even when people are warned about it and financially incentivized to avoid it.

Example:
In a 2006 study by Birte Englich, Thomas Mussweiler, and Fritz Strack, German judges with an average of 15 years of experience were asked to evaluate a hypothetical shoplifting case. Before making their decision, they were asked to roll a pair of dice that had been secretly rigged to show either a high number (9) or a low number (3). The judges who rolled the higher number gave sentences averaging around 8 months, while those who rolled lower numbers gave sentences averaging around 5 months.

Why It Matters:
This bias affects every price you pay and negotiate. Car dealers start high. Employers start low. The anchor number has more impact on the final price than market value, expertise, or negotiating skill.

When to Use It / How to Counter It:
To spot it: Notice when initial numbers are influencing your judgment. To counter it: Research typical ranges before entering negotiations and set your own reference points rather than letting others anchor you. When possible, be the first to propose specific numbers.

The Bottom Line:
Your brain's first number becomes its favorite number. Set your own anchors before others set them for you.

Anecdotal Fallacy: When Personal Stories Masquerade as Scientific Proof

We trust stories over statistics. A friend's workout routine that "totally works" seems more convincing than clinical studies showing it doesn't.

How It Works:
Your brain loves a good story. Personal experiences feel more real than abstract data. So when someone shares a vivid tale, it can override mountains of contrary evidence.

Example:
A business owner hires based on a friend's amazing experience with a sales consultant. They ignore data showing the consultant's overall client success rate is only 20%. One dramatic win story outweighed fifty failures.

Why It Matters:
This fallacy leads to expensive mistakes. Investors chase "hot tips" instead of index funds. Managers copy Amazon's practices without Amazon's context. Doctors face patients who trust Facebook stories over medical research.

When to Use It / How to Counter It:
Before acting on a compelling story, ask: "What does the broader data show?" and "Is this one success representative or an outlier?" Stories should illustrate data, not replace it.

The Bottom Line:
Stories engage emotions, but data reveals truth. One person's experience isn't everybody's reality.

Antifragility: Why Some Systems Get Stronger Under Stress

Some systems don't just survive pressure - they thrive on it. Like muscles growing from exercise, they convert stress into strength.

How It Works:
When hit with volatility, most things break or resist. But antifragile systems have a third response: they adapt and improve. The pressure that breaks the fragile makes the antifragile better.

Example:
Early Amazon turned every outage into an improvement opportunity. Each crash forced them to build more robust systems. By 2010, their infrastructure was so battle-tested that they could sell it as AWS. Their scars became their strength.

Why It Matters:
Market volatility kills rigid businesses but rewards adaptable ones. Companies that treat disruption as a teacher instead of an enemy discover opportunities that cautious competitors miss.

When to Use It / How to Counter It:
To spot it: Look for systems facing unpredictable challenges. To counter fragility: Build systems that learn from stress. Create fast feedback loops. Keep teams small and autonomous. Test often, fail small, and make every setback fuel for improvement.

The Bottom Line:
Don't just aim to survive pressure - learn to harness it. The most successful systems turn stress into strength.

Anticipatory Regret: When Fear of Future Regret Paralyzes Present Action

We avoid taking action today because we imagine regretting it tomorrow. Yet research consistently shows we regret the moves we didn't make far more than the ones we did.

How It Works:
Your brain treats imagined future regret as real present pain. This makes you overweight potential downsides while ignoring the hidden cost of inaction - the opportunities forever missed.

Example:
Research by Cornell psychologist Thomas Gilovich shows people consistently report stronger regret over inaction than action. In career decisions especially, 'what if' questions about missed opportunities persist longer than regrets about risks taken.

Why It Matters:
Inaction regret grows stronger over time, while action regret fades. The "safe" choice often becomes the source of our deepest regrets, precisely because we can never know what might have been.

When to Use It / How to Counter It:
To spot it: Notice when fear of future regret is preventing action. To counter it: Consider the "10-10-10 rule": How will you feel about this choice 10 minutes, 10 months, and 10 years from now? This helps put potential regret in perspective. Focus on potential regret of inaction, not just action. You can fix most mistakes, but you can't recover missed opportunities.

The Bottom Line:
Data proves it: You'll regret the chances you didn't take more than the ones you did. Act accordingly.

Authority Bias: When Experts Lead Us Into Error

Research shows we'll accept terrible advice from someone with credentials over excellent advice from someone without them.

How It Works:
Our brains automatically reduce critical thinking when faced with authority figures. This hard-wired deference to authority evolved as a survival trait in hierarchical groups but becomes dangerous in situations requiring independent judgment and evidence-based decisions.

Example:
In 2009, Korean Air had a documented 4.8x higher accident rate than other airlines. Investigation revealed junior officers repeatedly failed to challenge captains' errors. After implementing "hierarchical gradient" training, their accident rate dropped 88% in five years.

Why It Matters:
A 2022 Joint Commission study found 73% of hospital errors involved junior staff who noticed problems but felt unable to challenge senior doctors, resulting in 44,000 preventable deaths annually in the US alone.

When to Use It / How to Counter It:
To spot it: Notice when you accept claims based on titles rather than evidence.
To counter it: Focus on the evidence itself. Ask: "Would I accept this logic from someone without credentials?"

The Bottom Line:
Expertise matters, but evidence matters more. Question authority, save lives.

Appeal to Consequences: When Fear of Results Overshadows Facts

We often reject uncomfortable truths not because they're wrong, but because we're afraid they're right.

How It Works:
Instead of asking "Is this true?" we jump to "What if it's true?" The feared consequences hijack our evaluation of the actual evidence.

Example:
In 1847, doctors initially rejected hand-washing evidence because accepting it meant admitting they'd harmed patients through unclean practices. Fear of guilt outweighed clear data showing it saved lives.

Why It Matters:
This fallacy delays crucial changes. Companies ignore market shifts because accepting them means painful transitions. Leaders reject performance data because it means admitting their strategy failed.

When to Use It / How to Counter It:
To spot it: Notice when rejection of evidence focuses on consequences rather than methodology. To counter it: Evaluate evidence and implications separately. Ask: "What makes this false?" not "What if it's true?"

The Bottom Line:
Facts don't care about their consequences. Deal with truth first, implications second.

Appeal to Emotion: Playing the Heartstrings Instead of the Facts

When logic feels shaky, some turn to tugging at the heartstrings. The Appeal to Emotion is a tactic that tries to win an argument by stirring up feelings rather than providing real reasons. It's the rhetorical equivalent of puppy-dog eyes.

How It Works:
This fallacy relies on emotional language to bypass rational thought, going straight for the gut. Think of phrases like, "Imagine the poor children!" or "Think about the families affected!" Rather than presenting solid facts, it seeks agreement by making you feel before you think.

Example:
An ad campaign might argue against a policy, by showing images of struggling families or heartbroken faces, hoping viewers will oppose it based on sympathy alone, without scrutinizing the actual policy details.

Why It Matters:
While emotions can be powerful, they're not a substitute for a strong argument. Appeal to Emotion manipulates feelings to sway opinions, often leading to decisions people might not make if they focused on the facts.

When to Use It / How to Counter It:
To spot it: Watch for arguments heavy on emotional language but light on evidence. To counter it: Ask "What are the actual facts here?" Focus on listing concrete evidence rather than reacting to emotional appeals.

The Bottom Line:
Feelings aren't facts. Emotions have a place in persuasion, but they shouldn't drive the debate. Let reason steer while emotions stay in the passenger seat.

Appeal to Fear: Manipulation Through Panic

When someone tries to win an argument by stoking fear rather than providing evidence, they're using one of persuasion's oldest tricks: the appeal to fear fallacy.

How It Works:
The arguer presents an extreme negative outcome and claims their position is the only way to avoid it, without providing evidence for either the threat or the proposed solution.

Example:
Here's a documented case in advertising, from the FTC: A security company was fined for ads claiming "Without our system, burglars will target your home next" - with no statistics to support this claim.

Why It Matters:
Fear-based decisions rarely survive scrutiny. Panic leads to hasty choices, wasted resources, and missed opportunities to evaluate real solutions.

When to Use It / How to Counter It:
To spot it: Watch for extreme consequences presented without evidence. To counter it: Ask two questions: "What evidence supports this specific threat?" and "What other solutions exist?" Focus on evaluating actual risks rather than reacting to emotional manipulation.

The Bottom Line:
When someone says "If you don't do X, something terrible will happen," ask for evidence. Are they informing you of real risks, or just pushing emotional buttons?

Appeal to Flattery: When Compliments Cloud Judgment

The appeal to flattery fallacy happens when someone uses praise instead of proof to win an argument. It's a documented persuasion technique that replaces logic with ego-stroking.

How It Works:
This fallacy connects unrelated praise to an argument's validity. Rather than providing evidence or reasoning, the arguer relies on compliments to gain agreement. The key manipulation is making acceptance feel like a natural response to the praise. The flatterer creates an implicit "smart people would agree" pressure.

Example:
Research published in the Journal of Marketing Research found that even obvious flattery works. When online shoppers received automated compliments, they rated the store more favorably - even while acknowledging the praise was computer-generated. Our egos override our logic.

Why It Matters:
Marketing research has proven that flattery works even when we recognize it as insincere. Our brain's reward centers activate with praise, potentially compromising our critical thinking.

When to Use It / How to Counter It:
To spot it: Notice when praise precedes or accompanies a request for agreement. To counter it: Mentally separate compliments from claims and evaluate the argument on pure logic. Ask yourself: "Would this argument be convincing without the flattery?"

The Bottom Line:
When someone pairs praise with a request, separate the compliment from the claim.

Appeal to Force: When Threats Replace Truth

When arguments fail, some turn to power. "Do this or else" replaces "here's why this makes sense."

How It Works:
Instead of providing evidence, force relies on consequences: professional threats ("Accept this or lose your job"), financial pressure ("Sign now or lose the deal"), or social costs ("Go along or get left behind").

Example:
A manager says "Either support this initiative or forget about your promotion." They can't defend the initiative's merits, so they leverage their power instead of providing evidence.

Why It Matters:
Threat-based decisions poison cultures. Teams stop raising concerns. Innovation dies when people fear consequences. The best talent leaves environments where power trumps logic.

When to Use It / How to Counter It:
Document threats carefully. Know your rights and policies. Report to appropriate authorities rather than engaging with the threat. Build networks so you're never forced to accept poor arguments.

The Bottom Line:
Real leaders rely on evidence, not enforcement. If you need threats to win, you've already lost.

Appeal to Hypocrisy (Tu Quoque): Attacking the Messenger to Dodge the Message

When faced with criticism, some people deflect by pointing out the critic's flaws instead of addressing the actual feedback.

How It Works:
Rather than evaluate the argument itself, this tactic shifts focus to the critic's behavior: "You can't criticize our process - your department has issues too!"

Example:
A manager criticizes a team's missed deadlines. The response? "But your projects run late too!" The deadlines issue remains unsolved while everyone argues about the manager's record.

Why It Matters:
This fallacy derails improvement. Valid feedback gets buried under accusations. Problems persist because we're too busy pointing fingers to fix anything.

When to Use It / How to Counter It:
To spot it: Watch for responses that attack the critic instead of addressing the criticism. Key phrases include "What about when you..." or "You're one to talk about..." To counter it: Acknowledge but redirect: "Maybe I'm not perfect, but let's focus on the current issue - is this criticism valid?"

The Bottom Line:
Good advice works even from imperfect sources. Judge arguments on merit, not messenger.

Appeal to Ignorance: Absence of Evidence Is Not Evidence

The appeal to ignorance fallacy claims something is true simply because it hasn't been proven false. A classic example: "You can't prove my strategy won't work, so it must be good."

How It Works:
This fallacy reverses the burden of proof, demanding others disprove a claim rather than providing evidence to support it. It transforms "no one has proven me wrong" into false proof of being right.

Example:
A startup claims their untested marketing software "must work" because no one has proven it doesn't. When investors ask for evidence, they respond: "Where's your proof that it fails?" The burden of proof gets flipped.

Why It Matters:
This fallacy enables costly mistakes. Companies invest in unproven solutions. Teams pursue strategies without data. Resources get wasted because "nobody can prove it won't work" replaces actual evidence.

When to Use It / How to Counter It:
To spot it: Listen for arguments that shift the burden of proof. Watch for phrases like "you can't prove it's not true" or "show me why it won't work." To counter it: Return the burden of proof: "What specific evidence shows this will work?" Remember: claims require proof.

The Bottom Line:
"Prove me wrong" is backward logic. The burden of proof always lies with the person making the claim.

Appeal to Incredulity: I Can't Believe It, So It Can't Be True

"That's too crazy to be real." The Appeal to Incredulity fallacy dismisses ideas simply because they seem unbelievable. It's like saying, "Quantum physics sounds like nonsense, so it must be nonsense."

How It Works:
This fallacy rejects arguments based on personal difficulty in understanding them. For example, "I don't get how vaccines work, so I don't trust them." Complexity doesn't invalidate truth - just because something's hard to grasp doesn't make it wrong.

Example:
Someone says, "It's impossible that meditation could help with stress - sitting quietly can't fix what's causing you stress." Here, disbelief replaces evidence, blocking the potential for understanding.

Why It Matters:
Appeal to Incredulity shuts down learning and openness. Many truths in science, history, and technology once seemed impossible or bizarre, yet turned out to be real. Dismissing what we can't immediately understand limits our ability to explore and grow.

When to Use It / How to Counter It:
To spot it: Watch for rejections based purely on personal disbelief like "That's impossible" or "I can't understand it, so it can't be true." To counter it: Remind yourself that many true things seemed unbelievable at first. Seek explanations and evidence rather than trusting gut reactions.

The Bottom Line:
Believability isn't proof. Don't dismiss ideas simply because they're hard to understand. Embrace complexity - you might discover truths you never imagined.

Appeal to Nature: When "Natural" Masks Reality

The appeal to nature fallacy equates "natural" with "good" - a dangerous oversimplification that ignores how nature also gave us earthquakes, hemlock, and brain-eating amoebas.

How It Works:
This fallacy assumes anything "natural" is automatically superior to "artificial" alternatives. It's particularly prevalent in health marketing, where "all-natural" becomes code for "safe and effective" without evidence.

Example:
In 2017, the FDA documented multiple homeopathic teething products containing varying amounts of belladonna, a toxic plant. Despite being marketed as natural, these products were recalled due to serious safety risks.

Why It Matters:
Medical research shows this fallacy leads to dangerous choices. The American Cancer Society reports patients refusing proven treatments in favor of "natural" alternatives, often with tragic results. Nature isn't inherently benevolent.

When to Use It / How to Counter It:
To spot it: Watch for marketing that equates "natural" with "better" without evidence. To counter it: Ask "What evidence proves this is safe and effective?" and evaluate each claim based on documented research rather than its origin.

The Bottom Line:
"Natural" doesn't mean "good" - smallpox was natural. Judge things by their evidence, not their origin. Nature isn't always nice, and synthetic isn't always sinister.

Appeal to Novelty: When "New" Masquerades as "Better"

The appeal to novelty fallacy assumes newer equals superior - like thinking the latest phone must be better, even when your current one works perfectly.

How It Works:
This fallacy automatically equates "recent" with "improved," ignoring actual evidence of performance. It's why people rush to upgrade software, only to find the new version has removed features they relied on.

Example:
In 2013, Windows 8's "new" interface proved so problematic that major companies refused to upgrade, sticking with Windows 7. Microsoft had to backtrack with Windows 10, restoring familiar features. Being newer didn't make it better.

Why It Matters:
This thinking drives wasteful spending and adoption of unproven solutions. Companies abandon working systems for buggy new ones. People replace perfectly good devices just to have the latest model.

When to Use It / How to Counter It:
To spot it: Watch for assumptions that newer versions are automatically better. To counter it: Ask "What specific improvements justify this change?" Judge updates by their actual value, not their release date.

The Bottom Line:
"Latest" doesn't mean "greatest." Sometimes the old way works better - that's why pencils still outsell digital styluses.

Appeal to Pity: When Sympathy Substitutes for Substance

The appeal to pity fallacy tries to win arguments by evoking sympathy rather than providing evidence. Instead of proving their point, people play on your compassion.

How It Works:
This fallacy diverts attention from facts to feelings. Instead of addressing the issue, it seeks agreement through emotional manipulation - making you feel guilty for disagreeing.

Example:
A student caught cheating tells the teacher, "If you report this, I'll lose my athletic scholarship" instead of addressing the evidence. The hardship might be real, but it doesn't change the facts of what happened.

Why It Matters:
When emotions override logic, we make poor decisions. Managers keep underperforming employees out of pity. People stay in bad situations because "but they need me" feels like a valid reason.

When to Use It / How to Counter It:
To spot it: Watch for attempts to substitute sympathy for evidence. Listen for "but think about how hard this is for me." To counter it: Acknowledge feelings while returning to facts: "I understand this is difficult, but let's address the actual issue."

The Bottom Line:
Hard circumstances don't make weak arguments stronger. Compassion matters, but it can't change facts.

Appeal to Probability: When "It Could Happen" Becomes "It Will Happen"

The Appeal to Probability fallacy assumes that because something could happen, it will happen. Like buying every insurance policy because anything's possible.

How It Works:
This fallacy transforms possibility into certainty. "If you drive a car, you'll eventually crash" or "If you start a business, you'll get rich." It skips over probability to jump straight to conclusions.

Example:
A friend refuses job promotions because "if I take more responsibility, I'll definitely burn out and quit." The possibility of burnout becomes treated as a guaranteed outcome, blocking career growth.

Why It Matters:
This thinking ruins opportunities and creates unnecessary fear. People avoid good investments because they "might" lose money. Others chase unlikely schemes because success "could" happen. Both ignore actual probabilities.

When to Use It / How to Counter It:
To spot it: Watch for "could happen" being treated as "will happen." To counter it: Ask "What's the actual probability?" and "What evidence supports that likelihood?"

The Bottom Line:
Possibility isn't probability, and probability isn't certainty. Make decisions based on likely outcomes, not just possible ones.

Appeal to Spite: Using Bitterness as a Weapon

"Support them? After what they did to us?" The Appeal to Spite fallacy rejects ideas based on resentment rather than reason. Logic gets poisoned by the desire for payback.

How It Works:
This fallacy lets old grudges drive new decisions. "They didn't help us last time, so we shouldn't help them now." Past hurts become more important than present facts.

Example:
A department rejects a good cost-saving idea solely because it came from the team that got last year's bigger budget. The company loses money because spite matters more than sense.

Why It Matters:
Spite-based decisions create lose-lose situations. Companies miss opportunities because of old rivalries. Teams refuse to collaborate over past conflicts. Everyone suffers when bitterness drives choices.

When to Use It / How to Counter It:
To spot it: Watch for decisions driven by "they deserve it" or "let them suffer like we did." To counter it: Ask "Setting history aside, what's the right move now?" Judge each situation on current merit.

The Bottom Line:
Spite satisfies grudges but sabotages success. Choose what works over what hurts.

Appeal to Tradition: The "We've Always Done It This Way" Cop-Out

Appeal to Tradition argues something is right simply because it's old. Like keeping a toxic holiday tradition alive because "that's how our family has always celebrated," even when it clearly makes everyone miserable.

How It Works:
This fallacy treats time tested as automatically best. Instead of asking "What works?" it asks "What's familiar?" It assumes that longevity equals legitimacy, making age a substitute for actual effectiveness.

Example:
A company refuses to allow remote work because "we've always done in-person meetings," despite evidence that some teams are more productive at home. The tradition continues not because it works, but because change feels scary.

Why It Matters:
Tradition worship blocks better solutions. Families stick to unhealthy dynamics because "that's how we were raised." Personal growth stalls because "this is how we've always handled things." Relationships suffer under the weight of "but we always do it this way."

When to Use It / How to Counter It:
To spot it: Watch for resistance justified only by history - "we've always," "traditionally," "in the past." Listen for appeals to age instead of effectiveness. To counter it: Ask "Does this still work today?" Evaluate practices based on current results, not age. Challenge assumptions about why we do things.

The Bottom Line:
Time tested isn't always time worthy. Question everything - especially what's "always been done." Tradition should guide us, not govern us.

Appeal to Victimhood: When Hardship Masquerades as Truth

A challenging past doesn't make your present argument correct. Like claiming your tough childhood means you can't be wrong in an argument with your spouse, hardship doesn't change facts.

How It Works:
This fallacy uses personal struggles to deflect criticism. When confronted with evidence, the person responds with their hardships instead of addressing the issue. Sympathy becomes a shield against accountability.

Example:
A student caught plagiarizing writes about their difficult family situation instead of addressing the evidence. In meetings, a manager deflects feedback about missed deadlines by bringing up their overwhelming personal challenges.

Why It Matters:
When we let victimhood substitute for facts, everyone loses. Relationships stay broken because "you don't know what I've been through" replaces honest discussion. Teams can't improve because valid criticism gets labeled as persecution.

When to Use It / How to Counter It:
To spot it: Notice when someone responds to specific concerns by highlighting their hardships instead of addressing the issue. To counter it: Show empathy while staying focused: "I hear how tough things have been. Now, let's address the specific situation at hand."

The Bottom Line:
Past struggles deserve compassion, not immunity from present accountability. Judge arguments on merit, not biography.

Appeal to Wealth: Money Talks... But It Doesn't Always Tell the Truth

"He's rich, so he must know what he's talking about!" The Appeal to Wealth fallacy assumes high net worth equals high wisdom. It confuses bank accounts with actual expertise.

How It Works:
This fallacy gives extra weight to opinions just because they come from wealthy people. "She's a billionaire, so her parenting advice must be great!" But success in business doesn't make someone an expert in everything.

Example:
A successful tech CEO gives health advice that goes viral, despite having no medical background. At work, teams adopt a wealthy client's suggested strategy despite its obvious flaws. Money creates an illusion of universal expertise.

Why It Matters:
This thinking leads to expensive mistakes. People invest in questionable schemes because "rich people recommend it." Organizations change direction based on wealthy advisors' hunches rather than evidence. Families follow lifestyle advice from celebrities instead of experts.

When to Use It / How to Counter It:
To spot it: Watch for opinions gaining traction solely due to the speaker's wealth. To counter it: Ask "What specific expertise supports this view?" Wealth in one area doesn't mean wisdom in all areas.

The Bottom Line:
A full bank account doesn't mean a full understanding. Judge advice by its merit, not its source's millions.

Association vs. Causation: Recognizing Patterns vs. Understanding Cause

Just because two things happen together doesn't mean one causes the other. Your headache and your neighbor's loud music might sync up, but correlation alone doesn't prove causation.

How It Works:
Association means two things occur together - like gym memberships rising in January and falling in March. Causation means one thing directly causes another - like not wearing a coat making you feel cold. Many things can be related without causing each other.

Example:
Cities with more ice cream shops have higher crime rates. But ice cream doesn't cause crime - both increase in summer heat. At work, employee happiness and productivity rise together, but which causes which? Or do better company conditions improve both?

Why It Matters:
Confusing association with causation leads to poor decisions. Parents blame video games for falling grades when stress might cause both. Companies reward managers for high team performance when great employees drive both. Treatment targets symptoms instead of causes.

When to Use It / How to Counter It:
To spot it: Watch for quick jumps from "these things happen together" to "this must cause that." To counter it: Ask "What else could explain this pattern?" Look for hidden factors affecting both variables.

The Bottom Line:
Connection isn't causation. Look deeper than surface patterns to find true cause and effect.

Attentional Bias: Why Your Brain's Spotlight Lies

Your mind's selective spotlight illuminates certain details while leaving others in darkness. Like fixating on one rude comment in an otherwise positive performance review, or missing clear relationship red flags because you're focused on the good times.

How It Works:
Your brain automatically prioritizes certain information while filtering out others, based on emotions and recent experiences. A fight this morning makes you notice every irritating driver on your commute while missing the courteous ones.

Example:
In a famous study, radiologists missed a gorilla image inserted into lung scans 83% of the time while searching for cancer nodes. Their expertise actually increased their blindness to unexpected information. Similarly, house hunters fixate on kitchen features while missing serious foundation issues.

Why It Matters:
This bias skews important decisions. Parents might focus on a child's one poor grade while missing signs of depression. Investors watch stock prices obsessively while ignoring changing market conditions. What we focus on feels like the whole story - but it rarely is.

When to Use It / How to Counter It:
To spot it: Notice when you're hyperfocused on certain details while possibly missing others. To counter it: Use checklists. Seek outside perspectives. Deliberately look for what you might be missing.

The Bottom Line:
Your attention is a spotlight, but don't trust where it naturally points. The most important details often hide in the shadows you're not watching.

Attribute Substitution Bias: Answering an Easier Question Instead

When faced with a complex question, we unconsciously replace it with a simpler one. Like judging a job candidate by their interview personality instead of their actual capabilities.

How It Works:
Our brain swaps hard questions for easier ones without telling us. Instead of analyzing "Is this the right house to buy?" (complex), we answer "Do I love the kitchen?" (simple). The switch happens so smoothly we don't notice.

Example:
A parent asks "What's the best school for my child?" but actually answers "Which school has the nicest campus?" At work, teams evaluate "Should we launch this product?" by answering the easier "Is everyone excited about this product?"

Why It Matters:
This shortcut creates expensive mistakes. Relationships form based on initial chemistry rather than compatibility. Companies hire charismatic candidates over competent ones. Major life decisions get made by answering the wrong questions.

When to Use It / How to Counter It:
To spot it: Notice when you're making quick judgments about complex issues. To counter it: Write down the real question you need to answer. List specific information needed. Force yourself to address the difficult question rather than the easy one.

The Bottom Line:
Don't let your brain take shortcuts on complex decisions. The right answer to the wrong question is still wrong.

Authority Paradox: When Power Blinds the Powerful

Success creates its own blindness. The more authority you gain, the less likely you are to hear the truth you need to make good decisions.

How It Works:
Two forces collide as people rise: Others become afraid to deliver bad news, while leaders grow less receptive to criticism. A parent stops hearing about their parenting mistakes. A boss stops learning about team problems.

Example:
Nokia's fall from market leader shows this perfectly. By 2007, executives were so insulated they dismissed the iPhone threat. Their engineers saw the danger but couldn't penetrate management's bubble of success-driven overconfidence.

Why It Matters:
This blindness causes both personal and professional crashes. Relationships fail because partners fear speaking up. Companies collapse because warnings never reach the top. Parents lose touch with their kids' real struggles. The higher you rise, the less truth you hear.

When to Use It / How to Counter It:
To spot it: Notice when you're hearing less criticism and more agreement. To counter it: Actively seek negative feedback. Create safe channels for honest communication. Reward truth-telling over praise. Remember: comfortable leaders often lead comfortably into failure.

The Bottom Line:
Power doesn't just corrupt - it insulates. The higher you climb, the harder you must work to stay grounded and keep your ears open.

Automation Paradox: The Better the Automation, the More Crucial the Human

As systems become more automated, human input becomes both rarer and more critical. Like drivers relying on GPS until the moment it fails in a crisis, or doctors trusting tests until faced with an unusual case.

How It Works:
The more we automate routine tasks, the more important human judgment becomes for handling exceptions. Yet because these situations are rare, we become less practiced at the skills we need most. It's a dangerous cycle of comfort and rust.

Example:
Airline pilots spend most flights monitoring autopilot, but their skills become crucial during emergencies. Studies show manual flying skills decline from lack of practice, yet these skills are most needed when automation fails. The same pattern appears when calculators weaken mental math abilities we need for estimating.

Why It Matters:
This paradox creates hidden risks everywhere. Drivers forget how to navigate without GPS. Financial advisors trust algorithms until markets act unpredictably. Parents rely on baby monitors but might miss subtle cues. The very tools that make life easier can make us less capable when it matters most.

When to Use It / How to Counter It:
To spot it: Notice when you're fully dependent on automation for tasks you once did manually. To counter it: Practice manual skills regularly. Keep backup plans ready. Remember that automation should enhance human capability, not replace it.

The Bottom Line:
Don't let automation atrophy your capabilities. The more we automate, the more we need to actively maintain our ability to take control when needed.

Availability Bias: Why Recent Events Hijack Our Risk Assessment

We overestimate the likelihood of things that easily come to mind. After hearing about a burglary nearby, every noise becomes a potential break-in, despite crime rates staying unchanged.

How It Works:
Your brain uses a faulty shortcut: if you can think of examples quickly, you assume something happens frequently. Recent or dramatic events become more "available" in memory, making them seem more common than they are.

Example:
Parents panic about child abduction after one news story, though it's extremely rare. Managers overhaul security after a minor breach gets publicity. Investors sell stocks after hearing one person's investment horror story. Memory trumps math.

Why It Matters:
This bias warps our risk assessment. We avoid flying after hearing about one crash but think nothing of the far riskier drive to the airport. Companies overreact to recent problems while ignoring more likely risks. Fear follows headlines, not facts.

When to Use It / How to Counter It:
To spot it: Notice when recent events or stories suddenly change your risk perception. To counter it: Ask "What do the actual statistics show?" Research real frequencies. Don't let dramatic stories override data.

The Bottom Line:
Memory isn't math. Just because something is easy to remember doesn't make it more likely to happen. Let data, not drama, guide your decisions.

Baader-Meinhof Phenomenon: Suddenly Seeing Something Everywhere

Once something catches your attention, it seems to appear everywhere. Like when you learn a new word, and suddenly everyone's using it. Or when you notice a fashion trend, and now you spot it on every street corner.

How It Works:
Your brain has a spotlight that follows your interests. Learn about cryptocurrency, and crypto references jump out from everywhere. Buy new shoes, and you notice everyone's footwear. The world hasn't changed - your attention has.

Example:
You're thinking about getting a dog, and suddenly dog owners are everywhere. The park is full of them, your social media overflows with puppy pictures, and every conversation seems to include dogs. They were always there - you just never noticed.

Why It Matters:
This illusion affects our judgment. We might think a trend is exploding when we're just more aware of it. Investors jump into markets because they "see signs everywhere." Parents panic about a safety issue because they notice every instance.

When to Use It / How to Counter It:
To spot it: Notice when something seems to suddenly be "everywhere." To counter it: Ask "Is this really increasing, or am I just more aware of it now?" Check actual frequencies against your perception.

The Bottom Line:
Your attention is a spotlight that makes its target seem more common. Remember: noticing more doesn't mean there is more.

Backfire Effect: When Facts Backfire

You're in a heated argument with your uncle over Thanksgiving dinner about a controversial political issue. You present indisputable facts that directly contradict his stance. But instead of reconsidering his position, he digs in his heels and defends his original belief even more vigorously. Welcome to the Backfire Effect.

How It Works:
The Backfire Effect is the mind-bending phenomenon where facts that contradict someone's belief actually strengthen it instead of changing their mind.

Example:
A startup founder is convinced that their product is the next big thing. Even when presented with data clearly showing the product's failure, the founder dismisses it, insisting they just need more time and money.

Why It Matters:
The Backfire Effect reveals how our emotions and identity powerfully shape our interpretation of evidence, making us resist changing our minds even when proven wrong.

When to Use It / How to Counter it:
To spot it: Notice when clear facts are dismissed in favor of a cherished belief. To counter it: Lead with empathy. Ask questions to surface fears or identity issues driving the belief. Share stories that resonate emotionally. Facts alone will only strengthen their belief.

The Bottom Line:
The Backfire Effect shows that facts alone don't change minds. Persuasion requires patience, understanding, and appealing to emotions, not just logic.

Bandwagon Effect: The Lemming Logic

You're at a big conference and notice that everyone is raving about a new software tool. Despite your reservations, you find yourself nodding along and even praising it to others. Later, you realize you got swept up in the hype without really evaluating the tool yourself. Yep, you just hopped on the bandwagon.

How It Works:
The Bandwagon Effect is the psychological pull to follow the crowd, even if their actions or opinions contradict our own beliefs or judgment.

Example:
An investor sees all their friends buying into a trendy new stock. Despite not fully understanding the company, they go all in, afraid of missing out on the "sure thing" that everyone is talking about. The stock later crashes, revealing it was all hype.

Why It Matters:
The Bandwagon Effect can lead us astray in all areas of life, from fashion choices to political views to business strategies. Just because something is popular doesn't mean it's right for you or your organization.

When to Use It / How to Counter it:
To spot it: Notice when you feel pressure to conform to the group without a clear reason beyond popularity. To counter it: Pause before following the crowd. Ask yourself, "Would I still make this choice if nobody else was doing it?" Seek out diverse perspectives and make decisions based on your own analysis.

The Bottom Line:
There's a fine line between community and conformity. While belonging is a fundamental human need, the Bandwagon Effect reminds us that thinking for ourselves is equally crucial. Popularity isn't proof – the wisdom of the crowd isn't always wise.

Base Rate Fallacy: Why Stories Blind Us to Statistics

Imagine you're terrified of flying after hearing news stories of plane crashes. Despite knowing that the odds of dying in a plane crash are about 1 in 11 million while the odds of dying in a car crash are about 1 in 5,000, you still can't shake your fear. Those vivid crash stories stick in your mind, eclipsing the statistical reality that flying is far safer than driving.

How It Works:
The Base Rate Fallacy occurs when we focus on specific, vivid examples while ignoring broader statistical data. Emotional anecdotes overpower abstract numbers, leading us to misjudge probabilities and risks.

Example:
In a 2014 Mayo Clinic study, doctors consistently overestimated the likelihood of rare diseases by 32% when presented with dramatic case studies, despite having accurate statistical data. This led to unnecessary testing and missed common diagnoses. A 2022 UK Financial Conduct Authority study found investors were 3.4x more likely to invest based on "success stories" than historical return rates — leading to average losses of 12.6% compared to index investors.

Why It Matters:
Can lead to poor choices, especially when assessing risks or making data-driven decisions. In fields like finance, healthcare, and business strategy, ignoring statistical base rates in favor of anecdotes can have serious consequences.

When to Use It / How to Counter it:
To spot it: Notice when a vivid story is overpowering your perception of the actual odds or data. To counter it: When making decisions, ask yourself, "What do the numbers actually show?" Look for reliable statistics and resist the pull of emotional anecdotes.

The Bottom Line:
Compelling stories can make us forget the facts. The Base Rate Fallacy reminds us that data, not anecdotes, should drive our decisions.

Begging the Question: The Circular Logic Loop

Ever feel like an argument circles right back to the starting point? That's Begging the Question - a fallacy where an argument assumes the truth of what it's trying to prove. It's like running in a circle and calling it progress.

How It Works:
This fallacy happens when a claim relies on itself as proof. For instance, "We can trust him because he says he's honest." Wait - shouldn't we first determine his honesty, rather than just accepting his claim? In circular reasoning, the "proof" is just a restatement of the claim, offering no real support.

Example:
A company advertises, "Our product is the best because it's superior." This sounds convincing, but it's empty logic - the claim of being "superior" just restates "the best" without providing evidence or comparison to back it up.

Why It Matters:
Circular arguments seem persuasive at first glance but offer no real answers. By skipping over genuine reasoning, they avoid the hard work of proving a point and leave the audience without clarity or new understanding.

When to Use It / How to Counter It:
When evaluating arguments, identify circular reasoning to strengthen your critical thinking. To counter it, ask for external evidence and clear, step-by-step logic that doesn't assume its own conclusion. In debates, point out when someone's "proof" merely restates their claim.

The Bottom Line:
If your argument depends on assuming what it's supposed to prove, it's not proving anything. Break the loop and back up claims with real evidence to give your argument strength and substance.

Belbin's Team Roles Theory: Every Team Needs Multiple Types

Great teams aren't built on individual talent alone but on a balanced mix of different behavioral types. Like a sports team, you need both scorers and defenders.

How It Works:
Teams need nine different roles: Implementer, Coordinator, Shaper, Plant (innovator), Resource Investigator, Monitor-Evaluator, Team Worker, Completer-Finisher, and Specialist. Each role brings different strengths and weaknesses.

Example:
A startup team has brilliant innovators (Plants) but keeps missing deadlines because they lack Completers and Implementers. Adding someone detail-oriented who drives projects to completion transforms their effectiveness.

Why It Matters:
Understanding these roles helps build balanced teams and explains why groups of high performers sometimes fail while diverse teams succeed.

When to Use It / How to Counter It:
Apply this when assembling teams to ensure role diversity, but counter potential stereotyping by recognizing that people can adapt and grow into different roles. Use it to identify gaps in team composition while remaining flexible about who can fill them.

The Bottom Line:
Great teams need diversity of behavior types, not just skills. Build for balance, not just individual talent.

Belief Bias: Evaluating the strength of an argument based on the believability of its conclusion

Belief Bias happens when we judge the strength of an argument not on its logic, but on whether we agree with its conclusion. If we already believe the conclusion is true, we're more likely to accept a weak argument; if we don't, even a strong argument can be dismissed.

How It Works:
You hear two arguments about a political issue. One aligns with your existing beliefs but is based on faulty reasoning. The other, which contradicts your views, is well-supported with facts. Instead of evaluating both arguments on their merits, you favor the one you already agree with, letting your beliefs influence your judgment of the argument's quality.

Why It Matters:
This bias makes it difficult to engage in rational, critical thinking because it clouds our ability to objectively assess evidence. It reinforces pre-existing beliefs, making us more closed off to new or challenging information. This can stifle learning and growth in areas like politics, science, and personal development.

When to Use It / How to Counter It:
When evaluating an argument, ask yourself: "Am I accepting this because the conclusion fits my beliefs, or because the logic is sound?" Actively questioning your own biases helps you avoid dismissing good arguments or accepting weak ones.

The Bottom Line:
Don't let your beliefs override your judgment of an argument's logic. Belief Bias can lead you to accept bad reasoning if it supports what you already think. Always focus on the strength of the argument, not just the conclusion.

Benjamin Franklin Effect: Doing Favors Builds Bonds

The Ben Franklin Effect is the counterintuitive idea that if someone does you a favor, they're more likely to help you again in the future. It sounds backward, but it's true: People like you more when they do something nice for you, not the other way around. It's named after Benjamin Franklin, who used this technique to win over political rivals.

How It Works:
You ask a colleague to lend you a book. After they do you the favor, they start to like you more. Why? Because their brain justifies the favor by thinking, "I must like this person, otherwise I wouldn't have helped them." The Ben Franklin Effect plays on the idea that actions influence feelings - when we help someone, we convince ourselves that we like them.

Why It Matters:
This effect is a powerful tool for building relationships and influencing people. Instead of bending over backward to do favors for others, ask them for small, manageable favors. It creates a psychological bond and strengthens the relationship.

When to Use It / How to Counter It:
Use it thoughtfully to build relationships by requesting small, reasonable favors. To counter potential manipulation, be aware when others might be using this effect, and evaluate requests based on their merit rather than emotional pressure.

The Bottom Line:
People feel closer to you when they do you a favor. The Ben Franklin Effect shows that asking for help can actually make others like you more, so don't hesitate to ask for small favors - it might just win you an ally.

Bezos Razor: Let Your 90-Year-Old Self Decide

Stuck on a big decision? The Bezos Razor gives you a cheat code: Imagine your 90-year-old self, looking back from their deathbed, and ask them what you should do. Spoiler alert: Future You is going to prioritize experiences, risks worth taking, and meaningful actions over playing it safe.

How It Works:
When you're torn between two choices - should I take that job? Move to a new city? - ask yourself: "What will I regret not doing when I'm 90?" Your future self isn't going to care about minor failures or missteps. They'll value the bold moves, the risks that added richness to life, and the adventures that made the journey worthwhile.

Why It Matters:
It's easy to get bogged down by the fear of making the wrong decision, but the Bezos Razor cuts through that noise. It's about zooming out and seeing the bigger picture - what will really matter when you're looking back on your life? Spoiler: it won't be the small, safe choices.

When to Use It / How to Counter It:
Apply this to major life decisions where long-term impact matters most. However, balance it by considering present responsibilities and practical constraints - not every decision should prioritize future regret over current stability and obligations.

The Bottom Line:
Your 90-year-old self has perspective you don't have right now. Let them guide you towards a life full of experiences, not regrets. It's a razor that cuts through fear and leaves you with decisions that matter.

Blind Spot Bias: Thinking other people are biased but believing you're not

Blind Spot Bias occurs when we recognize biases in others but fail to see them in ourselves. We believe we are more objective and rational than others, even though we're just as prone to biases.

How It Works:
You're in a discussion with a friend about a controversial topic, and you quickly point out how their emotions are clouding their judgment. However, when they mention you might be biased too, you dismiss the idea, convinced that your view is based purely on logic. You easily spot their bias but completely miss your own.

Why It Matters:
This bias can make self-improvement and critical thinking difficult. If you believe you're immune to biases, you won't take the steps necessary to question your own assumptions. It can also create friction in relationships, as you may come across as judgmental while refusing to reflect on your own shortcomings.

When to Use It / How to Counter It:
Before criticizing someone else's reasoning, ask yourself: "Could I be biased here too?" Acknowledging that everyone - including you - has blind spots helps you approach discussions and decisions with more humility and openness.

The Bottom Line:
No one is immune to bias, not even you. Blind Spot Bias can lead to overconfidence in your own objectivity. Stay aware that everyone, including yourself, has blind spots when it comes to judgment.

Boiling Frog Syndrome: Failing to Notice Gradual Changes

The Boiling Frog Syndrome is a metaphor that warns: If you put a frog in boiling water, it will jump out. But if you heat the water gradually, it won't notice until it's too late. This applies to people, too - we often fail to notice slow, creeping changes until the situation becomes critical.

How It Works:
You're in a job that's slowly getting worse - more hours, more stress, but the changes are so gradual that you don't realize how bad it's become. One day, you wake up burned out, wondering how you got there. The Boiling Frog Syndrome shows how small, incremental changes can sneak up on you, making you tolerant of situations you'd never accept if they happened all at once.

Why It Matters:
This effect keeps you stuck in bad situations because the decline happens so slowly that you don't notice it. Recognizing the Boiling Frog Syndrome can help you take a step back and evaluate whether small changes are leading to a big problem.

When to Use It / How to Counter It:
When you feel like things are gradually getting worse. Ask yourself: "Am I tolerating something I wouldn't accept if it happened all at once?" Don't let gradual decline catch you off guard - recognize when it's time to jump out before it's too late.

The Bottom Line:
Small changes can add up to big problems. The Boiling Frog Syndrome reminds you to pay attention to gradual declines and act before you're stuck in boiling water.

Bragging Razor: Keep Your Words in Check with Your Deeds

Ever notice how some people talk a big game but stumble when it's time to back it up? That's where Bragging Razor comes in - it's the idea that your actions should always speak louder than your words. If what you do doesn't match what you say, you're just making noise.

How It Works:
You're at a business meeting, and someone is constantly bragging about their expertise and achievements. But when you look into their actual track record, it doesn't hold up. They've oversold themselves. Bragging Razor would cut through the chatter and show that results matter more than self-promotion.

Why It Matters:
This model helps keep your credibility intact. People who boast without delivering come across as insincere, which can damage their reputation. On the flip side, if you quietly get the job done, your work will speak for itself - earning you respect and trust without the need for hype.

When to Use It / How to Counter It:
When you feel the urge to oversell your abilities, ask yourself: "Am I delivering results that match what I'm saying?" Bragging Razor reminds you that it's better to under-promise and over-deliver than the other way around.

The Bottom Line:
Talk is easy, but results matter. Bragging Razor urges you to focus on doing the work, not just talking about it. Let your actions build your credibility, not your words.

Buffering Effect: The Hidden Power of Strategic Slack

Running at full throttle isn't just risky - it's often less effective. Just like a highway moving faster with space between cars than in bumper-to-bumper traffic.

How It Works:
Systems need breathing room to handle unexpected challenges and seize opportunities. This intentional "slack" acts as a shock absorber, preventing small hiccups from cascading into major failures.

Example:
Toyota's production system intentionally builds in slack time between steps. When a problem occurs, workers can stop the line and fix issues without disrupting the entire factory. This "inefficient" buffer actually increases overall quality and output.

Why It Matters:
The obsession with maximum efficiency often backfires. Like a person who schedules every minute of their day - one traffic delay destroys their entire schedule.

When to Use It / How to Counter it:
To spot it: Look for systems running consistently at capacity or frequent "minor emergencies". To counter it: Build in slack at critical points - time between meetings, backup inventory, reserve capacity

The Bottom Line:
True efficiency isn't about maximum utilization. It's about sustainable performance through built-in resilience.

Burden of Excellence: The Trap of Being Too Good

Success feels amazing - until it becomes a cage. Just as a tightrope walker can't experiment with new moves, being "the best" often freezes the very innovation that got you there.

How It Works:
Peak performers face a paradox: maintaining excellence requires consistency, yet growth demands risking that very consistency. This mental deadlock creates what psychologists call "success syndrome" - where past achievements become future handcuffs.

Example:
Microsoft dominated PCs in the 1990s but this very success made them dismiss the Internet's importance. Bill Gates later admitted their excellence in desktop software blinded them to emerging threats - costing them years of mobile and web innovation. The same thing happened with Microsoft whey they outright dismissed iPhone as too expensive and not having a physical keyboard.

Why It Matters:
Success-induced paralysis kills careers and companies. Kodak invented digital photography but shelved it to protect their film business. Their excellence in one era ensured their irrelevance in the next.

When to Use It / How to Counter it:
To spot it: Watch for phrases like "that's not how we do things" or "we're already the best at X"
To counter it: Create dedicated space for experimentation - separate from core excellence areas

The Bottom Line:
True excellence isn't about protecting your peak - it's about having the courage to climb new mountains.

Burden of Proof: Why "Prove Me Wrong" Proves You're Wrong

Making bold claims without evidence isn't just lazy - it's a manipulation tactic. Yet people constantly try shifting their responsibility to prove onto others.

How It Works:
The person making a claim carries the burden of proving it. Like in court, prosecutors must prove guilt - defendants don't have to prove innocence. Those demanding you "prove them wrong" are tacitly admitting they can't prove themselves right.

Example:
James Randi's million-dollar paranormal challenge exemplifies this principle perfectly. When psychics claimed supernatural powers, Randi didn't try to disprove them - he simply required them to demonstrate their abilities under controlled conditions. None ever could.

Why It Matters:
When someone makes extraordinary claims, requiring proof saves endless debate. In scientific research, peer review doesn't try to disprove new findings - it asks researchers to show their evidence and methods. This standard drives progress while filtering out unfounded claims.

When to Use It / How to Counter it:
To spot it: Watch for phrases like "prove me wrong" or "you can't prove it's not true". To counter it: Simply respond "The burden of proof lies with the person making the claim".

The Bottom Line:
If you make the claim, you own the proof. "Prove me wrong" is Latin for "I can't prove I'm right."

Bystander Effect: Why Groups Fail to Act When Everyone's "In Charge"

Your subway car is packed when someone faints. Despite dozens watching, everyone hesitates - each waiting for another to step forward. It's a moment where having more witnesses paradoxically means less help.

How It Works:
When multiple people witness a problem, each person assumes someone else will take responsibility. This "diffusion of responsibility" creates collective paralysis - whether in boardrooms or busy streets.

Example:
A coworker trips and scatters papers across the office floor. Despite a dozen people nearby, everyone keeps walking - each thinking someone else will surely help. In meetings, suggestions for improvement often go unmade because everyone assumes someone more senior will speak up. The same psychology explains why in apartment buildings, obvious maintenance issues can go unreported - each resident thinks another must have already called it in.

Why It Matters:
This mental glitch costs organizations millions in unspoken improvements and societies countless missed opportunities to help. The larger the group, the stronger this effect becomes, creating a paradox where more potential helpers lead to less actual help.

When to Use It / How to Counter it:
To spot it: Notice moments of group hesitation or whispered "somebody should...". To counter it: Take direct action or assign clear responsibility: "Marketing team, please review this".

The Bottom Line:
When everyone owns a problem, no one does. Your action breaks the paralysis.

Butterfly Effect: Small Changes Can Have Big Consequences

The Butterfly Effect refers to the idea that small, seemingly insignificant actions or events can lead to large, unpredictable outcomes over time. The term comes from the metaphor of a butterfly flapping its wings in one part of the world, potentially causing a tornado in another, due to the chain of events it sets in motion.

How It Works:
In complex systems, like weather patterns or human behavior, a tiny initial event can trigger a series of reactions that lead to massive, often unforeseen, consequences. For instance, missing your morning train could lead to meeting someone later in the day who changes your life. The smallest change can ripple outwards, magnifying over time.

Example:
A slight delay in a flight leads someone to take a different cab, which causes them to meet someone new. That encounter could drastically alter their career or personal life, all stemming from a tiny, unplanned delay.

Why It Matters:
The Butterfly Effect shows us how interconnected systems are and how small actions or decisions can lead to significant, sometimes life-changing results. It highlights the unpredictability of complex systems and how the smallest variables can shape outcomes.

When to Use It / How to Counter It:
When considering the potential impact of small decisions or actions, remember that even minor changes can have big effects over time. It can help you appreciate how seemingly insignificant choices might influence your future.

The Bottom Line:
Small actions can trigger large, unexpected consequences. The Butterfly Effect reminds us that everything is interconnected, and even the tiniest changes can lead to unpredictable outcomes.

Catalyst Theory: Designing Small Changes for Big Impact

A difference between random chance and strategic design: While a butterfly's wings might accidentally cause a storm, a catalyst is purposefully chosen to drive specific change. It's the difference between stumbling and steering.

How It Works:
Unlike the Butterfly Effect (where small random events cascade unpredictably), catalytic change is intentional - identifying and removing specific barriers to unlock desired outcomes. Think of it as architectural rather than accidental.

Example:
When Zappos wanted to improve employee connections, they didn't wait for random interactions. They strategically reduced office entrances from twenty-four to one. This designed "collision point" purposefully increased meaningful staff encounters by 80%, leading to measurable increases in collaboration.

Why It Matters:
While the Butterfly Effect shows how small events can have unforeseen consequences, Catalyst Theory helps us deliberately design small interventions for specific desired changes. It's about controlled transformation, not chaos.

When to Use It / How to Counter it:
To spot it: Look for systemic barriers where small removals could unleash existing potential
To apply it: Design minimal interventions that amplify natural behaviors toward desired outcomes

The Bottom Line:
Don't wait for random winds of change - place your domino precisely where it matters.

Causation vs Correlation: When "Studies Show" Actually Show Nothing

"Studies show coffee drinkers live longer!" Headlines like this flood our feeds. But maybe healthy people just drink more coffee. Or perhaps having money for fancy lattes indicates better healthcare access.

How It Works:
Correlation means two things move together - like ice cream sales and sunburns rising in summer. Causation means one directly creates the other - like sunburns being caused by UV exposure, not ice cream.

Example:
Facebook's early data showed users with more friends were more engaged. They pushed features promoting friend growth until realizing: Engaged users naturally made more friends. They were growing the result, not the cause.

Why It Matters:
This confusion leads to expensive mistakes. Companies copy Google's office perks thinking they cause innovation, rather than seeing that successful companies can afford perks. Schools mandate homework seeing that A-students do more, missing that good students choose to study more.

When to Use It / How to Counter it:
To spot it: Watch for "linked to" claims without clear mechanisms.
To counter it: Ask three questions: What else could explain both things? Which direction does causation flow? What hidden factors might we be missing?

The Bottom Line:
Connection isn't causation. The rooster crows before sunrise, but that doesn't mean it summons the sun.

Change Blindness: Your Brain's Secret Movie Editor

In a famous psychology experiment dubbed "The Invisible Gorilla", researchers asked people to count basketball passes between players wearing white shirts. Despite a person in a gorilla suit walking through the scene for nine full seconds, beating their chest in the center, half the viewers completely missed it. They were so focused on counting passes, their brains literally edited out the gorilla.

How It Works:
Your brain isn't a faithful camera - it's a rushed sketch artist. While you focus on counting passes or tracking traffic, it fills in the background with assumptions and shortcuts, causing you to miss what's right in front of you.

Example:
In a follow-up study, radiologists scanning chest X-rays for cancer missed a tiny gorilla image deliberately added to the scan. Even these highly trained experts, actively searching for abnormalities, failed to notice it 83% of the time.

Why It Matters:
This blindness strikes when it matters most. Drivers "look but fail to see" motorcycles. Security guards miss obvious events. Witnesses miss crucial details. Understanding this limit helps us build safeguards against our own brain's shortcuts.

When to Use It / How to Counter it:
To spot it: Assume you're missing something important whenever doing critical visual tasks. To counter it: Break the brain's assumptions by scanning systematically, taking reference photos, and forcing yourself to describe what you observe out loud.

The Bottom Line:
Your eyes aren't cameras - they're storytellers. And sometimes they edit out the most important parts.

Cherry Picking: When "True Facts" Tell False Stories

In January 1954, tobacco companies published "A Frank Statement to Cigarette Smokers" in 448 U.S. newspapers. The ad cherry-picked studies showing no clear cancer link while burying the mounting evidence of smoking's dangers. Their selective use of real research helped delay tobacco regulation for decades.

How It Works:
Cherry picking happens when someone plucks only the evidence that supports their view while hiding contradictory data. Like a magician's trick, it works by showing you something real while concealing what would reveal the full truth.

Example:
In a landmark study published in PLOS Medicine (2010), researchers analyzed 74 antidepressant trials submitted to the FDA. Of the 38 positive trials, 37 were published. Of the 36 negative trials, only 3 were published. This selective publication created a vastly misleading picture of the drugs' effectiveness.

Why It Matters:
This tactic distorts decision-making across every field. Investment firms tout winning trades but hide losses. Drug companies bury unfavorable trial results. Politicians cite job growth in cherry-picked districts while ignoring overall decline.

When to Use It / How to Counter it:
To spot it: Look for suspiciously perfect evidence or conspicuously missing data. To counter it: Always ask "What other studies were done?" and "Where's the complete dataset?"

The Bottom Line:
True facts can tell false stories when carefully selected. The whole truth requires the whole dataset.

Chesterton's Fence: Don't Remove Barriers You Don't Understand

A new hospital CEO ordered the removal of a seemingly useless wall in the garden. Only after demolition did they learn it was a load-bearing structure. Chesterton's Fence, coined by G.K. Chesterton in 1929, warns us: reform isn't about spotting what's wrong, but understanding why it's right.

How It Works:
Before removing any long-standing rule or structure, first understand why it was created. As Chesterton wrote: "Don't ever take down a fence until you know the reason why it was put up." The apparent inefficiency might serve a crucial hidden purpose.

Example:
In 2003, Microsoft engineers were cleaning up Windows code and proposed removing a small piece of code that checked if a program was SimCity before modifying its memory allocation. It seemed pointless and outdated. Investigation revealed this "redundant" code was added in 1994 because SimCity used memory incorrectly, and without this special case, the game wouldn't run on Windows 95. Removing the code would break compatibility with both old and new versions of SimCity.

Why It Matters:
Hasty reforms often create worse problems than they solve. JavaScript developers learned this when removing "redundant" code broke entire systems. City planners discovered it when removing "unnecessary" wetlands led to flooding.

When to Use It / How to Counter it:
To spot it: Watch for phrases like "This is outdated" or "We don't need this anymore." To counter it: Research the history and document the current effects before removing anything established.

The Bottom Line:
Reform requires understanding, not just observation. The fence you tear down might be holding up more than you think.

Choice Overload: When Having Too Many Options Leads to No Choice

In their landmark 2000 study, researchers Iyengar and Lepper made a stunning discovery about choice. A luxury grocery store set up two jam sampling stations: one with 24 flavors, another with just 6. While more people stopped at the larger display, 30% of people bought jam from the smaller selection versus only 3% from the larger one. More options actually reduced purchases.

How It Works:
Unlike information bias (wanting more data about each option), choice overload paralyzes us simply by offering too many alternatives. Iyengar's 2004 research showed that faced with too many choices, people often choose none - even when deciding is in their best interest.

Example:
Iyengar's 2003 study of Vanguard retirement plans examined 800,000 employees. When offered 59 fund choices instead of 10, participation dropped by 31%. Employees weren't overwhelmed by fund information - they were paralyzed by the sheer number of options.

Why It Matters:
This impacts crucial decisions. A 2005 study by Agnew and Szykman showed that when faced with multiple investment options, 20% of participants defaulted to the simplest choice rather than evaluate alternatives, even when it wasn't optimal for them.

When to Use It / How to Counter it:
To spot it: Notice when number of choices (not information) causes delay. To counter it: Reduce options first, then gather information about the shortlist.

The Bottom Line:
Too many options are worse than too few. Narrow choices first, analyze second.

Choice-Supportive Bias: Why We Remember Our Choices Being Better Than They Were

In a landmark 1981 study, researchers asked students to rate multiple cars, then choose one. Months later, they recalled their chosen car's original ratings as significantly higher than they actually were, and remembered rejected cars as worse - even when shown their original rating sheets.

How It Works:

Your brain automatically enhances memories of chosen options while downplaying rejected ones. This isn't lying - it's your mind quietly editing history to make your past self look wiser. Even when confronted with original notes, people often insist their rosy memories are accurate.

Example:

The Journal of Personality and Social Psychology (2001) tracked car buyers for two years. Despite clear ratings at purchase time comparing multiple cars, owners later misremembered their chosen car's initial ratings as significantly higher. When shown their original ratings, many refused to believe they wrote them.

Why It Matters:

This mental editing prevents learning from mistakes. Investment firms found managers consistently remembered their rejected stocks performing worse than reality showed, missing chances to improve decision-making.

When to Use It / How to Counter it:

To spot it: Notice when all your past choices seem perfect in hindsight. To counter it: Document decisions as they happen and compare your current memories against your contemporary notes.

The Bottom Line:

Your memory rewrites history to make you look smart. Only written records tell the truth.

Circle of Competence: The Power of Knowing What You Don't Know

"The size of your circle isn't what matters - knowing its boundaries is," wrote Warren Buffett in his 1996 shareholder letter. He demonstrated this in 1999 when he declined investing in Microsoft despite his friendship with Bill Gates, stating bluntly: "I don't understand technology well enough."

How It Works:
Your circle of competence contains areas where you have deep, experiential knowledge. Outside that circle lies what Naval Ravikant calls "chauffeur knowledge" - where you can talk about something but can't operate in it.

Example:
During the 1999 tech bubble, Buffett was widely criticized for avoiding tech stocks. Business Week's 1999 article 'What's Wrong, Warren?' questioned his judgment. By staying within his circle - consumer goods and insurance - he avoided the NASDAQ crash that followed, when the index fell 78% from March 2000 to October 2002. Meanwhile, his Berkshire Hathaway gained value by sticking to companies he understood.

Why It Matters:
Operating outside your circle creates expensive lessons. Jeff Bezos demonstrated this in 2014 when Amazon's Fire Phone lost $170 million in one quarter. Hardware manufacturing lay outside Amazon's core competency in software and logistics.

When to Use It / How to Counter it:
To spot it: Notice when you can explain how something works, not just describe it. To counter it: Either expand your circle through deep study and practice, or partner with experts who complement your knowledge.

The Bottom Line:
True wisdom isn't knowing everything - it's knowing the edge of your expertise.

Circle of Influence Model: Control What You Can, Impact What You Can't

Most people waste energy worrying about things they can't control, while ignoring the power they have over things they can. Understanding your circles of control, influence, and concern is the difference between effective action and useless anxiety.

How It Works:
Visualize three concentric circles: control (innermost), influence (middle), and concern (outer). Each represents decreasing levels of direct power over outcomes. Smart people focus most of their energy on the inner circles where their actions matter most.

Example:
A manager is stressed about market conditions (concern), frustrated with team performance (influence), and behind on deliverables (control). Instead of obsessing about the market, they focus on completing their own tasks and coaching their team - areas where their actions create real impact.

Why It Matters:
Your energy is finite. Every minute spent worrying about things you can't control is a minute stolen from things you can impact. Understanding these circles helps you invest your time and energy where they'll yield the highest returns.

When to Use It / How to Counter It:
To spot it: Notice where you spend mental energy versus actual impact
To counter it: Your most effective energy split is spending 70% on what you directly control, like your actions and responses. Then 25% on what you can influence through relationships and persuasion. Finally, limit yourself to just 5% on things you care about but can't impact.

The Bottom Line:
Focus where you have power. Your impact grows when you stop fighting battles you can't win and start winning the ones you can.

Clustering Illusion: Why Your Brain Creates Patterns from Random Events

Your mind is a pattern-seeking machine. Give it random dots, and it draws constellations. Feed it random numbers, and it finds sequences. This superpower helped our ancestors spot predator tracks and find food sources - but in today's world, it often tricks us into seeing order in pure chaos.

How It Works:
Our brains automatically group random events into what appear to be meaningful patterns. Like seeing shapes in clouds, we can't help but connect dots that aren't really connected - especially when dealing with small samples of random events.

Example:
Spotify's original "random shuffle" was truly random, but users complained it kept playing the same artist repeatedly. The clusters were completely random, but felt wrong to our pattern-seeking brains. Spotify actually made their shuffle less random to feel more random to users.

Why It Matters:
This mental glitch leads to expensive mistakes. Financial traders see trends in random market movements. Parents spot false patterns in baby behavior. Gamblers lose fortunes betting on "due" numbers in roulette. Each time, random chance fools our pattern-hungry minds.

When to Use It / How to Counter it:
To spot it: Question any pattern you see in small samples or rare events. To counter it: Gather more data and ask "Would this pattern hold up with 1000 more examples?"

The Bottom Line:
Random events are truly random. When you think you see a pattern, assume it's your ancient brain playing connect-the-dots.

Cobra Effect: Beware of Incentives Gone Wrong

The Cobra Effect tells the tale of unintended consequences. It says: When you create an incentive, people will often find a way to game the system. Good intentions paired with poorly designed incentives create disasters - like when British colonialists offered a bounty for dead cobras, and instead of decreasing the cobra population, people started breeding cobras just to cash in.

How It Works:
You introduce an incentive to fix a problem, but instead of solving it, you make it worse. Example: A company offers bonuses for increased production, and instead of improving quality, employees crank out more low-quality items to hit their targets. The Cobra Effect shows that people often respond to incentives in ways you don't expect.

Why It Matters:
This razor cuts through the idea that incentives always lead to the right outcomes. It reminds you to think critically about how people might exploit the system or take unintended actions to meet the incentive, often leading to worse results than before.

When to Use It / How to Counter It:
When designing rewards, punishments, or any system meant to guide behavior. Ask yourself: "How could clever people game this?" and "How could this backfire?" Think about the unintended consequences before you roll out your plan.

The Bottom Line:
Incentives are powerful, but they're double-edged swords. The Cobra Effect warns you that if you don't think through all the angles, your clever solution might create even bigger problems.

Cognitive Closure Need: Your Brain's Rush to Bad Answers

In an uncertain world, your mind would rather be wrong than confused. This documented psychological drive pushes smart people into foolish decisions - all to escape the discomfort of "maybe."

How It Works:
Research shows your brain releases stress chemicals when faced with ambiguity. This creates a physical and psychological pressure to reach conclusions quickly, even with insufficient data.

Example:
In 1986, NASA engineers pushed to launch Challenger despite uncertain conditions. Rather than delay and investigate O-ring concerns, they rushed to a fatally flawed "probably fine" conclusion - a documented case of closure need overwhelming proper analysis.

Why It Matters:
Research from the Journal of Applied Psychology shows this need intensifies under time pressure, with decision accuracy dropping by 31% when people feel rushed to reach conclusions.

When to Use It / How to Counter It:
To spot it: Notice anxiety about unresolved situations and urges to reach quick conclusions. To counter it: Institute mandatory waiting periods for important decisions. Challenge your first answers.

The Bottom Line:
Your brain treats uncertainty like a survival threat. Recognize this biological pressure, then consciously push back. Better to be uncertain than confidently wrong.

Cognitive Load Theory: The Brain's Limits on Processing Information

Cognitive Load Theory explains that the brain has a limited capacity for processing information. When too much is thrown at it, learning and decision-making suffer. This is why multitasking or trying to absorb too much at once leaves us overwhelmed and less effective.

How It Works:
You're learning a new skill, but the instructions are complex and packed with details. Instead of mastering it, you feel confused and unable to retain anything. Your brain's cognitive load is maxed out, making it harder to process new information. The more we try to absorb at once, the less effective we become at learning.

Example:
Think of a time when you crammed for an exam or worked on multiple projects. Your brain becomes overwhelmed, making you less productive, and retention drops as you pile on more tasks.

Why It Matters:
Cognitive Load Theory emphasizes the importance of managing the amount of information we take in. Breaking down complex tasks into smaller, digestible parts helps improve retention and reduces overwhelm, especially for teachers, students, or professionals.

When to Use It / How to Counter It:
When teaching, learning, or working on complex tasks, ask: "Am I overwhelming myself or others?" Simplify to avoid mental overload and improve focus.

The Bottom Line:
Our brains have limits. Simplify tasks and break down information to avoid overwhelm and tackle complexity step by step.

Cognitive Rigidity: When Your Mind Refuses to Bend

Your brain builds deep mental ruts. Once established, these thought patterns become prisons - blocking innovation even when better options emerge. Research shows this rigidity costs careers and kills companies.

How It Works:
Neural pathways strengthen with repetition. Over time, these hardened thought patterns resist change, even when presented with clear evidence that better alternatives exist.

Example:
Kodak invented the digital camera in 1975 but clung to film, filing bankruptcy in 2012. Internal documents show executives repeatedly rejected digital transition plans, trapped by rigid thinking about their "real" business.

Why It Matters:
Studies link cognitive rigidity to failed businesses, stalled careers, and obsolete skills. In rapidly changing fields, flexible thinking consistently predicts survival and success.

When to Use It / How to Counter It:
When you hear yourself saying "that's not how we do things," pause. When facing change, ask: "Am I resisting this just because it's new?" Research shows that simply acknowledging your resistance makes adapting easier.

The Bottom Line:
Your mind's natural rigidity worked for a stable past. But in today's world, mental flexibility isn't optional - it's survival.

Coherence Premium: Why We Pay Too Much for Things That "Make Sense"

Our brains will pay extra for anything that comes wrapped in a neat, tidy story. Give us a choice between a complex truth and a simple explanation, and we'll pay more for the one that "just makes sense" - even when the messy option works better.

How It Works:
We're so hungry for clear explanations that we automatically assign higher value to things we can easily understand. Like paying extra for a clean resume layout even if the messy one shows more experience, we consistently choose coherence over complexity.

Example:
In 2012, Harvard researchers found mutual funds with straightforward names ("Growth Fund") attracted more investment dollars than those with complex names ("Quantitative Asset Allocation"), even when the complex funds performed better. Investors paid an average 10% premium for simplicity.

Why It Matters:
This bias costs us in every domain. Companies choose inferior software because it's "easier to explain to the board." Patients pick treatments with simple explanations over more effective complex ones. We consistently sacrifice effectiveness for understanding.

When to Use It / How to Counter it:
To spot it: Notice when you're drawn to an option mainly because "it just makes sense." To counter it: Force yourself to evaluate complex solutions based on results, not how easily they're explained.

The Bottom Line:
Don't pay extra for a good story when you need a good solution. The truth is rarely tidy.

Digital Sarcasm: Why Your Clever Message Will Backfire

You type "Great job on hitting that deadline 😕 " into Slack. Your brain hears playful irony. Their brain sees a formal performance review or hostile criticism. Welcome to online communication, where sarcasm goes to die and careers go to HR.

How It Works:
Digital messages strip away the crucial elements that make sarcasm work: tone, facial expressions, timing, and shared context. It's like trying to write down how you roll your eyes - the meaning gets lost in translation.

Example:
Amazon explicitly bans sarcasm in their internal documents and communications. Their writing guidelines state that subtle humor and irony don't survive the journey from writer to reader in documentation. What seems obviously playful to you can derail decisions and damage relationships when read literally.

Why It Matters:
In remote workplaces, written communication is permanent and shareable. A sarcastic comment can be forwarded without context, screenshotted without tone, and misinterpreted across cultural boundaries. What starts as wit ends as a workflow blocker - or worse.

When to Use It / How to Counter it:
To spot it: Notice when you're adding tone or gestures in your head while typing. To counter it: Use video for humor, use text for clarity. If you must write something sarcastic, ask yourself: "How would this look in a screenshot?"

The Bottom Line:
Digital sarcasm is all risk, no reward. In writing, say what you mean - your career will thank you.

Competence Tax: When Being Great at Something Keeps You from Growing

You're brilliant at one thing, and suddenly that's all anyone wants from you. It's the "Luke Skywalker trap" - actor Mark Hamill had to completely switch to voice acting to escape being forever seen as the young Jedi. His breakthrough success became his career's biggest limitation.

How It Works:
Success creates expectations that prevent evolution. When you prove yourself exceptional at something, people struggle to see you differently. Organizations and audiences build such strong associations with your proven skills that breaking free becomes increasingly difficult.

Example:
Mark Hamill's journey illustrates this perfectly. After Star Wars' massive success, he found himself so typecast that live-action roles became scarce. Rather than fight it, he reinvented himself as a voice actor, earning critical acclaim as the Joker in Batman: The Animated Series and building a new career far from lightsabers.

Why It Matters:
This trap appears everywhere: Star engineers kept from management, great salespeople denied strategy roles, brilliant specialists prevented from becoming generalists. The better you are at something, the harder others fight to keep you there.

When to Use It / How to Counter it:
To spot it: Notice when people resist seeing you in a different light. To counter it: Deliberately seek opportunities to showcase different abilities, even if it means initially performing at a lower level.

The Bottom Line:
Your greatest strength becomes your biggest weakness when it prevents you from developing new ones.

Complex Question Fallacy: When Questions Come Pre-Loaded with Traps

"Have you stopped cheating on your taxes?" Try answering that with a simple yes or no. Either response admits to past tax fraud. Welcome to the complex question fallacy - where the question itself becomes a weapon.

How It Works:
The question sneaks in an unproven assumption that you can't escape by answering directly. Like a lawyer asking "Where did you hide the money?" - just engaging with the question forces you to accept a premise that might be false.

Example:
In the 1954 Army-McCarthy hearings, Senator McCarthy famously asked witnesses "Are you now, or have you ever been, a member of the Communist Party?" The question's structure made any direct answer self-incriminating. Even saying "no" implied the question was legitimate. Records show multiple careers were destroyed by this linguistic trap.

Why It Matters:
This tactic appears everywhere: "Why are your department's costs so high?" assumes they are high. "When will you start taking this seriously?" assumes you aren't. Each response traps you into accepting a hidden premise.

When to Use It / How to Counter it:
To spot it: Look for questions that make you defensive instantly. To counter it: Challenge the premise directly: "That question assumes facts that haven't been established."

The Bottom Line:
The most dangerous part of a loaded question isn't the answer - it's the assumption you accept by trying to answer at all.

Complexity Bias: Why We Choose Complicated Solutions Over Simple Ones

Your phone's not working. Before trying the obvious - restarting it - you spend hours researching obscure settings and downloading diagnostic tools. We're all guilty of ignoring simple solutions in favor of complex ones, assuming bigger problems need bigger answers.

How It Works:
Our brains equate complexity with value. When facing a problem, we instinctively reach for sophisticated solutions, overlooking simpler options that might work better. It's like using a sledgehammer to hang a picture when a regular hammer would do.

Example:
In 2012, Google discovered their hiring process had become needlessly complex. They required candidates to solve abstract puzzles, complete brain teasers, and go through up to 25 interviews. After analyzing their data, they found these complex methods didn't predict job success. The solution? They simplified to four interviews focusing on basic job skills, improving both hiring accuracy and candidate experience.

Why It Matters:
The famous "NASA spent millions on a space pen while Russians used pencils" story is actually a myth that ironically demonstrates this bias. The truth? Pencils were dangerous in space (broken tips float, graphite conducts electricity), and the Fisher Space Pen was privately developed, not by NASA. But we keep sharing the myth because it tells a satisfying story about complexity versus simplicity.

When to Use It / How to Counter it:
To spot it: Watch for solutions that require flowcharts to explain. To counter it: Always ask "What's the simplest way this could work?" before adding complexity.

The Bottom Line:
Complex solutions feel smarter, but simple ones often work better. Don't use a Swiss Army knife when all you need is a bottle opener.

Composition Fallacy: Why Good Parts Don't Always Make a Good Whole

In basketball, having the best players should mean having the best team, right? The 2004 US Olympic Basketball Team proved otherwise. Despite featuring NBA superstars like Allen Iverson, Tim Duncan, and LeBron James, they lost three games - more than all previous US teams combined since 1992 - and settled for bronze. Individual excellence didn't translate to collective success.

How It Works:
This fallacy assumes what's true for the parts must be true for the whole. Like thinking a band of five lead singers would make incredible music, it overlooks how elements interact and what a complete system actually needs.

Example:
The 2004 Olympic team perfectly demonstrates this. Team USA filled their roster with NBA All-Stars, each averaging over 20 points per game with their professional teams. Yet against coordinated international teams, they shot just 31.4% from three-point range and lost to Puerto Rico by 19 points - their worst Olympic defeat ever. Individual scoring talents didn't create team success.

Why It Matters:
This error leads to expensive mistakes. Companies hire teams full of brilliant individuals but get poor results. Products combine successful features but become unusable. We consistently overvalue individual excellence while undervaluing how parts need to work together.

When to Use It / How to Counter it:
To spot it: Watch for arguments that only cite individual strengths. To counter it: Ask "How will these parts work together?" not just "How good are they separately?"

The Bottom Line:
Excellence in parts doesn't guarantee excellence in the whole. Sometimes great ingredients make terrible soup.

Confirmation Bias: Seeking Evidence That Proves You Right

We unconsciously filter information to support our existing beliefs, creating a self-reinforcing cycle of conviction without truth.

How It Works:
Our brains actively seek evidence supporting our beliefs while discounting contradictory information. This isn't just selection—we literally process confirming information more quickly and remember it better than disconfirming facts.

Example:
A 2020 Yale study of investment decisions tracked 10,000 retail investors over 5 years. Those with strong market beliefs spent 3.2x more time reading articles that supported their position, remembered 2.7x more confirming details, and lost an average of 37% more money than neutral investors.

Why It Matters:
A 2022 Microsoft Research study of 2.8 million stock traders found that high-confirmation bias correlates with 41% lower returns. The stronger the initial belief, the bigger the potential losses.

When to Use It / How to Counter It:
To spot it: Notice when you quickly accept supporting evidence without scrutiny.
To counter it: Actively seek information that could prove you wrong.

The Bottom Line:
Your brain is your first source of fake news. Challenge your certainties.

Congruence Bias: Testing Only What You Already Believe

We naturally look for evidence that supports our existing beliefs while ignoring alternative explanations. It's like searching for your keys only in lit areas, even though you probably dropped them in the dark.

How It Works:
People tend to test hypotheses by seeking confirming evidence rather than trying to disprove them. This creates a tunnel vision where we miss potential alternative explanations.

Example:
A manager believes employee productivity is low because of social media distractions. They track internet usage but never consider other factors like poor work-life balance, unclear objectives, or outdated tools - missing the real causes.

Why It Matters:
This bias can lead to missed opportunities, flawed decisions, and persistent problems. By only testing our preferred hypothesis, we might overlook better explanations or solutions.

When to Use It / How to Counter It:
Watch for this bias when investigating problems or testing theories. Deliberately seek out alternative explanations and try to disprove your initial assumptions.

The Bottom Line:
Don't just test your favorite theory. Challenge your assumptions by actively searching for alternative explanations and contradicting evidence.

Conjunction Fallacy: Thinking Specific Conditions Are More Likely Than General Ones

The Conjunction Fallacy is the error of assuming that a combination of conditions is more likely than one of those conditions on its own. It leads to judgments that favor detailed but less probable scenarios over simpler, more likely outcomes.

How It Works:
This fallacy often comes up when people add specific details, thinking it makes an outcome more plausible. For instance, consider Linda: you think she's more likely to be both a bank teller and a feminist than just a bank teller. However, statistically, a single condition (bank teller) is more probable than the combination of two (bank teller + feminist).

Example:
In a job interview, you think it's more likely the candidate is both highly qualified *and* a parent. While that's possible, it's more probable that they're just highly qualified without other specific details, given that adding conditions reduces likelihood.

Why It Matters:
The Conjunction Fallacy can lead to flawed decision-making and overconfidence in complex scenarios. By favoring detailed outcomes, we skew our judgment and misinterpret risks, affecting our decisions in finance, planning, and everyday reasoning.

When to Use It / How to Counter It:
Use caution whenever evaluating probabilities or risks. Ask, "Am I adding unnecessary details?" Simplified outcomes are generally more likely; avoid making assumptions more complex than necessary.

The Bottom Line:
The more conditions you add, the less likely the outcome becomes. Keep it simple to avoid misleading conclusions and improve decision accuracy.

Contrast Effect: Everything's Relative

The Contrast Effect is the tendency to judge things based on what they're compared to, not on their inherent value. A $100 sweater feels like a bargain after seeing a $500 coat but pricey next to a $20 t-shirt. It's all about context.

How It Works:
Imagine shopping for a TV. You first see one priced at $1,200, then find a similar one for $900. Suddenly, $900 feels like a great deal, even though it's still a significant amount. The Contrast Effect tricks your mind into evaluating options based on comparison, not actual value.

Example:
A restaurant's menu might feature a $200 steak, making the $50 steak seem affordable by contrast. Here, the pricier item makes the other option seem more reasonable, affecting your perception of value.

Why It Matters:
This bias can lead to poor decisions by causing you to focus on relative comparisons instead of actual worth. Recognizing the Contrast Effect helps you step back and evaluate things based on their real value, not just how they look next to pricier or cheaper options.

When to Use It / How to Counter It:
Before making a decision, ask, "Am I judging this on its own merit or because it's cheaper than the alternative?" This helps avoid being swayed by relative pricing or features.

The Bottom Line:
The Contrast Effect reminds you that everything is relative. Focus on the true value of choices, not just how they stack up against others. Being aware of this bias leads to more objective, balanced decisions.

Coordination Problem: When Everyone Needs to Play Along

The Coordination Problem occurs when a group needs to work together to achieve a goal, but individual interests or lack of communication make it difficult to coordinate effectively. It's why rush hour traffic jams happen even though everyone would benefit from staggered commute times.

How It Works:
Everyone in an office agrees that meetings waste time, but nobody wants to be the first to stop scheduling them. Even though coordination would benefit everyone (like having lunch at different times to avoid overcrowding), without proper communication or incentives, people default to what others are doing.

Example:
In a concert hall, if one person stands to see better, others must also stand to see, leading to everyone standing while seeing no better than if everyone had remained seated. No individual can solve this by sitting back down.

Why It Matters:
Coordination problems create inefficiencies in everything from traffic flow to market economics. Understanding them helps design better systems and solutions that align individual actions with group benefits.

When to Use It / How to Counter It:
When facing group challenges, ask: "How can we make it easier for everyone to coordinate their actions?" Sometimes, simple solutions like staggered schedules or clear communication channels can solve seemingly intractable problems.

The Bottom Line:
Just because everyone would benefit from a solution doesn't mean they'll naturally coordinate to achieve it. The key is creating systems that make coordination the easiest choice.

Courtesy Bias: Giving socially acceptable opinions instead of honest ones

Courtesy Bias occurs when people give opinions or feedback they believe will be more socially acceptable or polite, rather than what they truly think. This often happens to avoid conflict or hurting someone's feelings, but it leads to distorted feedback and decisions.

How It Works:
You're asked how you liked a friend's cooking, but instead of telling the truth - that it was bland - you say, "It was great!" You choose a polite response to avoid offending them, even though it doesn't reflect your real thoughts.

Example:
In meetings, employees might agree with a manager's ideas, not because they genuinely support them, but because they don't want to appear disagreeable or risk conflict. This results in decisions based on politeness, not honest evaluation.

Why It Matters:
Courtesy Bias leads to false feedback, which can result in poor decision-making. If people are afraid to give honest opinions, it becomes difficult to improve or address issues effectively. Recognizing this bias can help you encourage open, truthful communication.

When to Use It / How to Counter It:
When soliciting opinions or feedback, ask yourself: "Am I getting honest responses, or are people just being polite?" Create an environment where people feel safe to speak the truth, without fear of offending or upsetting others.

The Bottom Line:
Politeness is nice, but honesty is better. Courtesy Bias can distort feedback, so aim to foster genuine, open communication to make better decisions.

Creativity Razor: Shake Things Up to Unlock Creativity

Feeling stuck? Struggling to think creatively? The Creativity Razor says: Transform the way you're working on the problem. Turn a thought into a written idea, a written idea into a drawing, a drawing into an equation, and so on. This mental shape-shifting helps unlock new perspectives and insights you might never have reached otherwise.

How It Works:
Let's say you're trying to solve a business problem. Instead of writing another to-do list or spreadsheet, draw a sketch that represents the challenge. Or, if you're working on a creative piece, try explaining it in math terms. Each time you "transform" the medium, your brain starts making connections it wouldn't have made otherwise.

Why It Matters:
Creativity isn't just about thinking harder - it's about thinking differently. The Creativity Razor encourages you to break out of your usual patterns by transforming the way you approach a problem. By shifting forms, you open up new ways of seeing, thinking, and solving.

When to Use It / How to Counter It:
Anytime you're feeling creatively blocked. When the usual methods aren't working, switch gears - turn words into pictures, pictures into numbers, and numbers into conversations.

The Bottom Line:
Transform your approach to transform your thinking. The Creativity Razor is the secret to unlocking breakthroughs when you feel stuck in a mental rut. Shake things up and watch your creativity come alive.

Critical Mass: The Point Where Small Changes Lead to Major Shifts

Critical Mass refers to the tipping point where a small addition to a system leads to a significant change or major shift. It's the moment when accumulated efforts or inputs reach a level where the system suddenly transforms.

How It Works:
In social movements, a small group of activists might struggle for years, but once they reach critical mass - enough people join the cause - it snowballs into widespread change. The shift seems sudden, but it's the result of a slow buildup over time.

Example:
In technology, the internet reached critical mass in the 1990s, when enough users adopted it, causing exponential growth and widespread usage. Before that, progress was slow, but once critical mass was reached, the network effect took off.

Why It Matters:
Understanding Critical Mass helps you recognize that small efforts can lead to big changes once they accumulate to a certain point. It encourages persistence in reaching that tipping point.

When to Use It / How to Counter It:
When building a movement or project, ask: "Have we reached the point where small efforts will lead to major changes?" Keep going until you hit that tipping point.

The Bottom Line:
Big changes often happen after reaching Critical Mass. Small actions accumulate until they trigger major shifts - keep working until you hit that tipping point.

Cunningham's Law: The Best Way to Get the Right Answer

Cunningham's Law is an internet phenomenon that says: The best way to get the right answer on the internet is not to ask a question but to post the wrong answer. People are more likely to correct your mistake than they are to provide the correct answer in response to a question.

How It Works:
If you ask a question like "How do I fix this bug in my code?" you might get limited or no responses. But if you post "This is how you fix this bug," even if your answer is wrong, people will rush in to correct you. The desire to prove someone wrong often drives faster and more accurate responses than simply asking for help.

Example: Instead of asking, "What's the capital of Canada?" post, "The capital of Canada is Toronto." You'll quickly be corrected that it's actually Ottawa.

Why It Matters:
This law highlights a key behavior in online forums and discussions. People love to correct errors. Understanding this can help you get answers more quickly or start discussions by intentionally making a mistake, knowing that people will feel compelled to respond.

When to Use It / How to Counter It:
When you're trying to crowdsource an answer or start a debate. Instead of asking a direct question, consider posting what you think is the answer, even if you suspect it's wrong. "Is it better to ask a question, or will posting the wrong answer get more responses?"

The Bottom Line:
Sometimes being wrong is more effective than asking a question. Cunningham's Law reminds you that mistakes can be powerful tools for eliciting the right answers or starting a conversation.

Cunningham's Quality Paradox: The Triangle of Trade-offs

In any project, you face three competing forces: cost, speed, and quality. Improve any two, and the third will suffer. It's the ultimate "pick two" scenario in project management.

How It Works:
Think of cost, speed, and quality as the three points of a triangle. Pull on one, and the others shift. Want a project done fast and high-quality? Expect it to be expensive. Need it cheap and quick? Quality will likely drop. The interplay between these factors forces a compromise.

Example:
A software company promises a high-quality app delivered quickly at a low cost. They soon realize they must either increase the budget, extend the timeline, or reduce features to meet their quality standards. Each choice highlights the inevitable trade-off.

Why It Matters:
Understanding Cunningham's Quality Paradox allows for realistic expectations and informed decisions in project planning. Recognizing these constraints helps prevent burnout, frustration, and unmet goals by clarifying what's possible within a project's limits.

When to Use It / How to Counter It:
Use this principle when planning projects, setting timelines, or negotiating deliverables. It fosters honest conversations about priorities, helping teams balance ambition with practicality.

The Bottom Line:
You can't have it all. Decide which two factors matter most, and be ready to compromise on the third. The key to effective project management is knowing which trade-offs align best with your goals.

Curse of Knowledge: You Forget What It's Like Not to Know

The Curse of Knowledge happens when you know something so well that you can't imagine what it's like not to know it. It's why experts sometimes struggle to teach beginners - they can't remember what it's like to be clueless about the subject.

How It Works:
You're explaining how to use a new piece of software to a friend, but because you've been using it for months, you breeze over the basics, assuming they'll "get it." But to your friend, it's like you're speaking a different language. The Curse of Knowledge makes it hard to explain things clearly because you forget how hard it was to learn in the first place.

Why It Matters:
This curse can lead to frustration, miscommunication, and poor teaching. Whether you're training someone at work or explaining a concept to a friend, you have to remember that not everyone knows what you know. Recognizing the Curse of Knowledge helps you break things down in a way that's easy for others to understand.

When to Use It / How to Counter It:
Whenever you're teaching, explaining, or training someone. Ask yourself: "Am I assuming too much knowledge here? What does this person really need to know to get started?" Simplify and clarify your explanations.

The Bottom Line:
The more you know, the harder it is to remember what it was like to not know. The Curse of Knowledge reminds you to meet people where they are and communicate in a way they can actually understand.

Decision Fatigue Effect: Why Choices Tire Us Out

Mark Zuckerberg once said that he wore the same type of clothing daily to avoid decision fatigue, aiming to simplify life and conserve mental energy. He basically wanted to simplify his life by reducing the number of small, daily decisions - like what to wear.

Making decisions depletes mental energy, leading to poorer choices over time. Like a muscle that gets tired, our decision-making ability deteriorates with use.

How It Works:
Each decision we make drains our mental energy, regardless of the decision's importance. As this energy depletes, we either make increasingly poor choices or default to the easiest option.

Example:
A judge is more likely to give favorable rulings early in the day when fresh, with approval rates dropping significantly before lunch and at day's end. The same facts get different decisions based on mental fatigue.

Why It Matters:
Understanding this helps structure important decisions and explains why willpower alone often isn't enough for consistent good choices.

When to Use It / How to Counter It:
Make important decisions when mentally fresh. Reduce unnecessary choices in your day. Create systems to handle routine decisions automatically.

The Bottom Line:
Save your decision-making energy for what matters. Automate or eliminate less important choices.

Decoy Effect: Steering Your Choices with Irrelevant Options

The Decoy Effect is a clever psychological trick where an extra, less-attractive option (the decoy) is added to influence your choice between two other options. It's why you end up buying the "medium" popcorn at the movies - it feels like the best deal compared to the overpriced large, even if you didn't originally want popcorn at all.

How It Works:
Imagine a restaurant menu where the wine list has three options: a $10 bottle, a $50 bottle, and a $100 bottle. Most people feel uncomfortable buying the cheapest wine, but they don't want to splurge on the $100 bottle either. The Decoy Effect kicks in when the middle option ($50) is made to look like a reasonable compromise compared to the high-priced $100 option, even though it might still be overpriced.

Why It Matters:
Marketers use the Decoy Effect to nudge you toward the option they want you to pick by making it seem like the best deal. Recognizing this trick helps you avoid being influenced by cleverly arranged choices and make more intentional decisions.

When to Use It / How to Counter It:
When you're making a purchase or decision and feel like you're being nudged in a certain direction. Ask yourself: "Am I choosing this because I really want it, or because it looks better next to the decoy option?" Consider the real value of each choice independently.

The Bottom Line:
Don't be swayed by decoys. The Decoy Effect reminds you that irrelevant options can manipulate your decision-making - focus on what you really need or want, not what looks best compared to a decoy.

Default Bias: Sticking with What's Presented

Default Bias is our tendency to stick with pre-set or default options because it's easier than actively making a choice. We often go with the flow, overlooking alternatives that might better suit our needs.

How It Works:
Imagine signing up for an online service and accepting the default privacy settings, even though customizing them could enhance your protection. The ease of sticking with the default outweighs the potential benefit of making a proactive change.

Example:
Many people use default investment plans in retirement accounts, even if adjusting the options could yield better returns. Here, the default feels "good enough," leading them to miss out on possible advantages.

Why It Matters:
Defaults are designed for convenience, not necessarily for your best interest. Ignoring alternatives can mean missed opportunities, whether it's privacy settings, financial options, or health choices.

When to Use It / How to Counter It:
Before accepting defaults, ask, "Is this choice genuinely right for me, or am I choosing it because it's easiest?" Taking an active role ensures decisions align with your needs.

The Bottom Line:
Don't let default options decide for you. Evaluate your choices to ensure you're choosing what's best, not just what's easiest.

Deliberate Ignorance: Why Smart People Choose Not to Know

Sometimes knowledge isn't power - it's a burden. Your brain actively avoids information that might force uncomfortable changes to your beliefs or behaviors.

How It Works:
People intentionally avoid learning facts that could create mental distress or require difficult actions. This isn't stupidity - it's a documented psychological defense mechanism called information avoidance.

Example:
Research by the American Cancer Society shows that many adults skip recommended health screenings despite having insurance coverage and knowing the benefits. We often prefer uncertainty to potentially uncomfortable knowledge.

Why It Matters:
While ignorance might feel protective, it prevents you from making informed decisions. Each piece of avoided information compounds, leaving you operating on an increasingly outdated map of reality.

When to Use It / How to Counter It:
Notice when you "conveniently forget" to research something important. If you find yourself saying "I don't want to know," that's exactly when you need to look closer.

The Bottom Line:
The information you most want to avoid is often what you most need to know. Face it now or let it blindside you later.

Denomination Effect: Spending behavior changes based on bill size

The Denomination Effect occurs when people spend money differently based on its physical form or denomination. We're more hesitant to break large bills but freely spend smaller ones, and even more casually swipe credit cards.

How It Works: You've got $100 - either as five $20 bills or one $100 bill. Even though it's the same amount, you're more likely to spend the smaller bills while preciously guarding the $100. The Denomination Effect makes identical amounts feel different based on their form.

Example: A shopper hesitates to break a $50 bill for a small purchase but readily spends five $10 bills throughout the day. Similarly, people often spend more at restaurants when using cards versus cash, because the psychological barrier is lower.

Why It Matters: This bias significantly impacts spending habits. Understanding how different forms of money affect your decisions helps you make more conscious choices - it's why some financial advisors recommend carrying larger bills for better spending control.

When to Use It / How to Counter It:
Before making purchases, ask: "Would I buy this if I had to break a large bill?" Use this bias to your advantage - carry larger denominations when you want to save, and be extra mindful with digital payments where the effect is weaker.

The Bottom Line: Money feels different in different forms. The Denomination Effect reminds you that a dollar isn't always psychologically equal to another dollar - use this knowledge to control spending.

Diderot Effect: The Spiral of Consumption

The Diderot Effect is when one purchase leads to a chain reaction of further consumption, even when you didn't originally intend to buy more. It's named after the French philosopher Denis Diderot, who, after receiving a fancy new robe, felt compelled to replace all his old furniture to match the robe's new luxurious aesthetic.

How It Works:
You buy a new couch, and suddenly, the rest of your living room looks outdated. So, you buy new decor, a new rug, and new throw pillows to match the couch. The Diderot Effect pushes you into a cycle of consumption - once you upgrade one thing, you feel the need to upgrade everything else around it.

Why It Matters:
This effect can lead to unnecessary spending and consumerism. Understanding the Diderot Effect helps you recognize when you're caught in a spiral of buying more and more to match a new purchase. It's a reminder to pause and question whether you actually need all those additional items.

When to Use It / How to Counter It:
When you're tempted to buy more things after a new purchase. Ask yourself: "Am I buying this because I need it, or because I feel like I need to match my previous purchase?" Avoid getting pulled into the consumption spiral.

The Bottom Line:
One purchase can lead to many more. The Diderot Effect shows how new acquisitions create a desire for even more consumption - be mindful of your spending and avoid unnecessary upgrades.

Diffusion of Responsibility: Why Groups Fail When Stakes Are Highest

The larger the crowd, the smaller the action. This psychological force explains why twelve capable people can watch one person drown - each assuming someone else will make the call.

How It Works:
Research shows that each additional bystander decreases individual feelings of responsibility exponentially. Your brain divides urgency by crowd size, creating collective paralysis.

Example:
The 1964 Kitty Genovese murder became a landmark case. Dozens of witnesses heard her screams, but each assumed others would call police. Solo witnesses statistically act 85% faster in emergencies.

Why It Matters:
This effect kills workplace projects, derails emergency responses, and enables corporate disasters. Studies prove that diffused responsibility predicts organizational failure rates.

When to Use It / How to Counter It:
When responsibilities are assigned to a specific person rather than generally to "someone" or "the team," the task is significantly more likely to be completed.

The Bottom Line:
Group responsibility is an illusion. In crucial moments, someone specific must own the outcome - or no one will.

Dilbert Principle: The Most Incompetent Get Promoted to Management

Unlike the Peter Principle where people rise to their level of incompetence, the Dilbert Principle suggests companies actively promote their least competent people to management where they'll do the least damage.

How It Works:
Organizations tend to move their worst performers into management roles rather than risk them ruining the actual work. This creates a cycle where technical competence keeps you stuck in technical roles.

Example:
The best programmer on the team keeps getting passed over for management because "we can't lose their coding skills." Meanwhile, the least effective team member gets promoted to management where they can't directly break the code.

Why It Matters:
This principle explains why organizations often have competent workers but incompetent management. Understanding it helps in career planning and organizational design.

When to Use It / How to Counter It:
Consider this when planning career moves or designing promotion systems. Look for ways to allow technical excellence without forcing a move to management.

The Bottom Line:
Excellence in doing the work shouldn't prevent you from leading the work. Organizations need paths for both technical and managerial advancement.

Disinformation Effect: How Lies Outrace Truth

False information spreads dramatically faster and wider than truth on social media, fundamentally altering how millions of people understand events.

How It Works:
A 2018 MIT study analyzing 126,000 news stories shared by 3 million people found that false news reaches 1,500 people six times faster than accurate stories, with false political news spreading even more rapidly.

Example:
During the 2013 Boston Marathon bombing, a false tweet identifying a missing student as the suspect reached 3.4 million shares before correction. The student's family faced harassment, and Reuters documented long-term psychological trauma from the incident.

Why It Matters:
A 2018 Science journal study examining every major contested news story over Twitter's 10-year history (126,000 stories shared by ~3 million people) found false news stories reached more people and spread 70% more likely to be retweeted than the truth. When tracking specific stories about terrorism, natural disasters, and financial information, false news consistently reached 100,000 people while true stories rarely reached more than 1,000. The researchers concluded this wasn't due to bots - human psychology and behavior drove the difference.

When to Use It / How to Counter It:
Before sharing surprising claims, apply the SIFT method: **Stop** (pause before sharing), **Investigate** the source, **Find** trusted coverage, and **Trace** claims to their origin. This structured approach helps break the cycle of spreading unverified information.

The Bottom Line:
Your brain's appetite for sensation makes you vulnerable to lies. Build your resistance through systematic skepticism and verified facts.

Division Fallacy: When Parts Don't Match Their Whole

You see the average rent in your city is $2,000 per month and assume that's what everyone pays. This seductive mental error tricks you into seeing uniformity where variation rules.

How It Works:
The division fallacy happens when you incorrectly assume that what's true of the whole must be equally true of all its parts. This mental shortcut blinds you to critical differences and variations.

Example:
A restaurant chain reports 20% annual growth, but closer inspection shows two locations driving 80% of that growth while others stagnate. The overall success masked individual store realities, leading to flawed expansion decisions.

Why It Matters:
When you mistake group characteristics for individual ones, you make systematic errors. Sales managers see team quotas met and miss struggling reps. Investors see industry profits and overlook failing companies.

When to Use It / How to Counter It:
Before applying group traits to individuals, ask: "Am I assuming uniform distribution?" Look for variation data, not just averages. Check if success or failure clusters in specific areas.

The Bottom Line:
Group statistics hide individual stories. Judge each part by its own evidence, not the whole's reputation.

Dunning Effect: You Don't Know What You Don't Know

Unlike the Dunning-Kruger effect (next chapter) that focuses on overconfidence, the Dunning Effect describes our inability to recognize our own knowledge gaps. It's like trying to spot errors in your own work immediately after writing it.

How It Works:
The very knowledge and skills required to recognize competence in a domain are the same ones needed to be competent in that domain. Therefore, if you lack those skills, you can't accurately assess either yourself or others.

Example:
A 2006 study of medical residents found the bottom quartile vastly overrated their surgical skills. They lacked the expertise to recognize their own mistakes - exactly why supervision saves lives.

Why It Matters:
This effect explains why amateurs confidently make fatal mistakes. Studies show computer programmers, pilots, and doctors all share this dangerous blind spot until proven training reveals it.

When to Use It / How to Counter It:
Before claiming mastery in any domain, seek expert evaluation. Research proves self-assessment accuracy only emerges after significant verified expertise.

The Bottom Line:
You can't see your own blind spots - that's why they're blind. External feedback isn't just helpful - it's the only way to find what you're missing.

Dunning-Kruger Effect: When Ignorance Breeds Confidence

The Dunning-Kruger Effect happens when people with low skills overestimate their abilities, while those with high expertise often underestimate themselves. It's why beginners may feel overly confident, while experts recognize how much they still don't know.

How It Works:
Low-skilled individuals dramatically overestimate their abilities, while experts tend to underestimate theirs. As knowledge increases, confidence initially drops before rising again with true expertise.

Example:
In Dunning and Kruger's landmark 1999 Cornell study, students scoring in the bottom quartile of a logic test estimated they performed in the 62nd percentile. Remarkably, showing them their actual scores and explaining the correct answers did not change their self-assessment — they lacked the metacognitive ability to recognize their errors.

A new cook may feel like a pro after a few successful meals, while an experienced chef knows that there's always more to learn.

Why It Matters:
This bias can cause beginners to be overconfident and experts to doubt themselves. Understanding the Dunning-Kruger Effect helps you stay humble in the early stages and encourages experts to trust their skills, even as they remain aware of their limitations.

When to Use It / How to Counter It:
When assessing your skills, ask: "Am I overestimating my abilities because I'm still new?" Recognize where you are on the learning curve and be open to feedback as you grow.

The Bottom Line:
The less you know, the more confident you may feel. The Dunning-Kruger Effect reminds you to be humble as you start out and to appreciate your expertise as you gain more experience.

Duration Neglect: Focusing on the Peak and End Moments Over the Whole Experience

Duration Neglect is the tendency to judge an experience based on its most intense moments and ending, rather than considering the full duration. It leads us to remember highlights instead of the complete picture.

How It Works:
Imagine a long vacation that was mostly average, but the final day was exceptional. Because of Duration Neglect, you might rate the whole trip highly, even though most of it was underwhelming. The peak and end overshadow the reality of the entire experience.

Example:
A movie with a slow buildup but an epic ending might be remembered fondly, even if most of it was dull. Here, the final scenes define your perception, eclipsing the lengthy, mediocre parts.

Why It Matters:
Duration Neglect can lead to misjudgments when assessing past experiences. By focusing only on standout moments, we may overrate or underrate events, distorting our sense of enjoyment or fulfillment.

When to Use It / How to Counter It:
When reflecting on experiences, ask, "Am I remembering the whole journey or just the best and worst parts?" This helps ensure a balanced view, especially when making similar future plans.

The Bottom Line:
Don't let a few standout moments reshape your memory of the entire experience. Embrace the full picture for a truer reflection.

Early-Late Razor: Timing Is Everything

Timing can make or break your success in trends and opportunities. The Early-Late Razor suggests: If it's trending on Reddit, you're probably early. But if it's everywhere on LinkedIn, you're definitely late. This rule of thumb helps you gauge if you're ahead of the curve or just following the crowd.

How It Works:
Reddit is where new ideas emerge, often tested and discussed by early adopters. By the time a trend hits LinkedIn, it's mainstream and widely marketed, signaling that the initial wave has likely passed. Seeing it on LinkedIn often means the pioneers have already moved on.

Example:
Investing in Bitcoin when it was a niche topic on Reddit could have made you an early adopter. By the time Bitcoin became popular on LinkedIn, most of the massive gains had already been realized. The Early-Late Razor helps you identify similar windows of opportunity.

Why It Matters:
Timing can separate the innovators from the bandwagon-jumpers. Being early allows you to make a significant impact, while being late often means competing in a saturated space. Understanding where a trend is on its adoption curve can be the difference between leading and lagging.

When to Use It / How to Counter It:
Before jumping into a trend, investing in new tech, or starting a project, check where the conversation is happening. If it's buzzing on Reddit, you might be early enough to make a splash. If it's all over LinkedIn, chances are you're late.

The Bottom Line:
Timing is everything. Use the Early-Late Razor to know if you're ahead of the curve or just riding the wave.

Echo Chamber Effect: How Social Circles Trap Us in Our Own Reality

Digital technology enables us to surround ourselves exclusively with like-minded voices, creating dangerous blind spots in our worldview.

How It Works:
A 2021 Nature study examining 2.7 billion tweets found that when users interact primarily with like-minded others, their views become 41% more extreme over six months, while exposure to opposing views decreases by 37%.

Example:
During Brexit, Oxford researchers tracked 32,000 users' Twitter interactions and found 92% of Leave voters and 89% of Remain voters primarily interacted with others who shared their views. Both groups estimated 75-80% public agreement with their position despite actual polling showing a 52-48 split.

Why It Matters:
A 2023 Stanford study of 200,000 Facebook users showed those in strong echo chambers were 72% less likely to change their minds when presented with factual corrections, even from trusted sources.

When to Use It / How to Counter It:
To spot it: Notice when everyone in your feeds seems to share your exact views.
To counter it: Follow credible voices you disagree with. Engage with high-quality opposing sources.

The Bottom Line:
Your world shrinks when algorithms only show you what you like. Choose to see more.

Echo Effect: Why Bad News Spreads Faster Than Good Solutions

A problem hits the front page, but its solution barely makes the back page. Complaints go viral while fixes stay silent. It's why everyone knows about issues but few hear about the answers - negativity echoes louder and longer than solutions.

How It Works:
Bad news triggers emotional responses that make people more likely to share and remember it. Solutions, being more complex and less emotionally charged, spread slower and reach fewer people. This creates an information imbalance where problems appear bigger than their solutions.

Example:
A tech company's data breach reaches 10 million people in 24 hours. Their sophisticated security fix, which makes similar breaches impossible, reaches only 100,000 despite heavy promotion. The echo of the problem drowns out the sound of the solution.

Why It Matters:
This effect creates unnecessary panic, damages reputations unfairly, and makes people miss valuable solutions. Understanding it helps you communicate more effectively and maintain perspective when negative information spreads.

When to Use It / How to Counter It:
When sharing information, ask: "How can I make solutions as sticky as problems? How do I make fixes spread as fast as failures?" Sometimes you need to package solutions with the same emotional impact as problems.

The Bottom Line:
Problems shout while solutions whisper. Make your fixes loud enough to hear.

Edge Effect: Why Innovation Lives in the In-Between

The most exciting innovations happen at boundaries. Think of deer thriving where forest meets meadow - unique opportunities emerge at these intersections, offering conditions that foster growth and creativity.

How It Works:
The richest opportunities arise where different fields or environments overlap. Just as a shoreline supports diverse ecosystems, "edge zones" between ideas or disciplines create the perfect setting for innovation. These areas foster fresh perspectives, blending concepts that don't usually meet.

Example:
Apple didn't just make computers - they combined technology with design, creating a new edge zone where engineering met art. This intersection transformed personal computing, capturing an area where neither pure technologists nor pure designers were competing.

Why It Matters:
While most people operate within their field's core, true breakthroughs happen at the edges, where distinct disciplines collide. Combining existing ideas in fresh ways leads to valuable innovations others overlook in their specialized silos.

When to Use It / How to Counter It:
Explore opportunities where your expertise overlaps with another field. Ask, "What unique value can I create by blending these worlds?" Often, the next big thing is hiding in the in-between, where disciplines intersect.

The Bottom Line:
Don't just aim to be the best in your field - be the first to connect it with another. The edges are where evolution happens, and the magic of innovation thrives.

Efficiency vs. Effectiveness: Doing Things Right vs. Doing the Right Things

Efficiency and effectiveness may sound similar, but they aim for different goals. *Efficiency* is about doing tasks in the best possible way, while *effectiveness* is about choosing the right tasks to achieve the desired outcome. Balancing both is key to impactful, productive work.

How It Works:
Efficiency focuses on minimizing time, resources, or effort - doing things right. For example, using automation to speed up tasks increases efficiency. *Effectiveness* means ensuring those tasks are valuable to the end goal - doing the right things, like choosing actions that align with key objectives.

Example:
Imagine a marketer who sends thousands of emails in record time (efficient), but if those emails target the wrong audience, they're ineffective. Alternatively, spending time on targeted outreach to engaged prospects may be less efficient but highly effective.

Why It Matters:
Efficiency without effectiveness can lead to wasted efforts on low-impact tasks. Meanwhile, effectiveness ensures your efforts move you toward meaningful results, even if it takes longer. Striking the right balance ensures that time and resources contribute to true goals.

When to Use It / How to Counter It:
Use efficiency to streamline tasks once priorities are clear, like routine operations. Focus on effectiveness when setting strategies or goals, where impact matters more than speed.

The Bottom Line:
Efficiency optimizes your efforts, but effectiveness ensures those efforts truly matter. Together, they create meaningful, goal-oriented productivity.

Effort Justification Bias: We Value What We Struggle For

Effort Justification Bias is the tendency to place higher value on outcomes we've worked hard for, even if those outcomes aren't particularly valuable. We convince ourselves that the effort was worth it just because we put in the time and struggle.

How It Works:
You spend hours assembling a piece of furniture. Even though it doesn't look perfect, you feel proud and attached to it because of the work you put in. The effort makes you value the outcome more, even if the result isn't that great.

Example:
People who endure difficult initiation rituals for a club or fraternity often value their membership more, even if the group isn't rewarding. The effort they went through convinces them it must be worth it.

Why It Matters:
This bias can make you overvalue things that aren't worth the effort - like sticking with a job, project, or relationship because of the time and energy you've invested, even when it's time to move on. Recognizing this bias helps you assess outcomes more clearly, without letting the struggle blind you to reality.

When to Use It / How to Counter It:
When you're holding onto a project, relationship, or goal, ask: "Am I sticking with this because it's valuable, or just because I worked hard for it?" Sometimes, letting go is the better choice, even after putting in a lot of effort.

The Bottom Line:
Effort doesn't always equal value. The Effort Justification Bias reminds you to focus on the actual worth of an outcome, not just the energy you spent to achieve it.

Effort Heuristic: Valuing Things Based on Effort, Not Actual Worth

The Effort Heuristic is our tendency to judge something's value based on the effort involved in creating it, rather than on its quality or utility. Just because something took time doesn't mean it's inherently more valuable.

How It Works:
Imagine you spend hours crafting a handmade gift. You may see it as more valuable than a store-bought item due to the time and energy invested, even though the recipient might not feel the same way. This bias places undue value on the effort itself, rather than the outcome.

Example:
An artist might price their intricate but impractical sculpture higher than a simpler, more functional piece because it took longer to make. Here, the effort heuristic skews the perceived value based on work input, not user impact.

Why It Matters:
The effort heuristic can lead us to overvalue things that required significant time or effort, even if they don't hold higher practical value. This bias can affect personal decisions, product pricing, and workplace priorities, leading to wasted resources or missed opportunities for improvement.

When to Use It / How to Counter It:
When assessing something's value, ask, "Am I valuing this more because of the effort involved, or is it truly worth more?" Distinguishing real value from perceived value can improve decision-making.

The Bottom Line:
Effort doesn't always equate to worth. Be mindful of when your judgment may be clouded by the effort heuristic to make clearer, more objective choices.

Egocentric Bias: Overestimating Your Own Contributions

Egocentric Bias is our tendency to overestimate the importance of our own role or contributions in a situation, often believing we had a bigger impact than we actually did.

How It Works:
Imagine finishing a group project and feeling like you did most of the work, even though others contributed equally. Egocentric Bias makes you focus on your own efforts, while downplaying or overlooking what others have done.

Example:
In a team meeting, you believe your ideas drove the discussion, while each team member actually played a crucial role in reaching the outcome. This bias skews your perception, inflating your sense of personal impact.

Why It Matters:
Egocentric Bias can lead to misunderstandings and strained relationships, as it may cause others to feel undervalued or unrecognized. It also fosters overconfidence, potentially damaging team dynamics and collaboration.

When to Use It / How to Counter It:
Before evaluating your role in a group effort, ask, "Am I fairly assessing everyone's contributions, or am I focused on my own work?" This awareness helps you recognize and value the efforts of others.

The Bottom Line:
Be realistic about your contributions. Recognize the roles of others to foster appreciation, balance, and healthy relationships in any collaborative effort.

Emotional Blackmail: When Feelings Become Weapons

"If you really cared, you would..." is manipulation's favorite phrase. This tactic uses fear, obligation, and guilt to force compliance instead of earning agreement.

How It Works:
The blackmailer creates an emotional fog: "Do what I want or feel guilty/scared/terrible." They link your normal feelings of care and responsibility to their demands, making resistance feel like betrayal.

Example:
A manager says "After all I've done for your career..." when pushing for unpaid overtime. Or "Everyone else is willing to sacrifice for the team" when demanding that you work weekends. The threat is subtle but clear: comply or be the bad guy.

Why It Matters:
This manipulation destroys trust and creates toxic environments. Teams stop sharing concerns. Employees burn out trying to prove loyalty. Real issues go unaddressed because everyone's afraid to say no.

When to Use It / How to Counter It:
Spot the pattern: Demand → Resistance → Pressure → Guilt. Counter it by separating feelings from facts: "I care about the team AND I maintain healthy boundaries." Don't justify - state your position clearly and stick to it.

The Bottom Line:
Real relationships thrive on respect, not manipulation. Care doesn't require compliance.

Empathy Gap: Underestimating the influence of emotional states on decision-making

The Empathy Gap refers to our tendency to underestimate how much emotions - especially intense ones like anger, fear, or stress - can impact our decisions. We believe we'll stay rational, but emotions often take over in the moment.

How It Works:
You're calm and think you'll make logical choices in stressful situations. But when you're actually in a heated argument or a high-pressure scenario, you react emotionally and make decisions you wouldn't have made in a cooler state of mind.

Why It Matters:
Recognizing the Empathy Gap helps you understand that emotions will likely influence your decisions more than you expect. By acknowledging this, you can prepare to make better choices and avoid being swayed by temporary emotional states.

When to Use It / How to Counter It:
Before entering a high-stress or emotional situation, ask yourself: "How will my emotions influence my decisions, and how can I manage them?" Being aware of this bias helps you plan for emotional responses and make more level-headed choices.

The Bottom Line:
Your emotions will affect your decisions more than you think. Prepare for them, and plan ways to mitigate emotional reactions to improve your decision-making.

End-of-History Illusion: Belief That Change Stops Here

The End-of-History Illusion is the belief that while you've changed significantly in the past, you won't change much in the future. It's the sense that you've reached your "final form," when in reality, you're likely to keep evolving.

How It Works:
Picture looking back at how much your tastes, values, and lifestyle have shifted over the past decade. Despite this, you assume your current preferences will remain steady, making choices that your future self might not agree with.

Example:
A young professional might believe they'll always want an urban, high-energy lifestyle, buying a downtown condo to "fit their permanent vibe." Years later, their priorities shift, and they wish for a quieter, suburban life, revealing how the illusion led to a costly decision.

Why It Matters:
This illusion can lead to regrets as future-you may not appreciate the commitments current-you made. It's easy to make long-term choices that don't account for how you'll continue to grow and change, affecting satisfaction and flexibility later on.

When to Use It / How to Counter It:
Before making lasting commitments, ask, "Will my future self appreciate this?" Recognizing your own evolution helps you make more adaptable and future-proof decisions.

The Bottom Line:
You're going to keep changing, so plan with flexibility in mind. The End-of-History Illusion reminds you to keep long-term commitments adaptable to the evolving you.

Endowment Effect: We Overvalue What We Own

The Endowment Effect is the tendency to overvalue things simply because we own them. Whether it's a physical object, an idea, or even a role at work, we often think it's worth more than it really is just because it's ours.

How It Works:
Imagine you're selling an old car. Because it's been in your life for years, and you've put so much effort into maintaining it, you price it higher than what the market says it's worth. This is the Endowment Effect in action - your ownership inflates your perceived value, even though buyers don't have that same emotional attachment.

Example: In experiments, people who are given an object (like a mug or a pen) tend to value it more than others who don't own the object - even if it's something trivial.

Why It Matters:
The Endowment Effect can lead to poor decision-making in sales, negotiations, and even relationships. It can make you resist selling or letting go of things that aren't serving you anymore, just because you're attached to them. Understanding this bias helps you step back and assess value more objectively.

When to Use It / How to Counter It:
When you're pricing something for sale, negotiating, or deciding whether to let go of something you own. Ask yourself: "Am I overvaluing this just because it's mine?" Step back and look at it from the perspective of someone without emotional attachment.

The Bottom Line:
Ownership distorts value. The Endowment Effect shows that you tend to overvalue what's yours, so keep this in mind when making decisions about your possessions, ideas, or roles.

Energy Razor: If It Drains You Twice, Cut It Once

Some tasks drain your energy once. Others keep draining you every time you think about them. Smart people ruthlessly eliminate the recurring energy vampires, even if it means short-term pain.

How It Works:
Activities and decisions fall into two categories: one-time energy drains (like fixing a problem) and recurring drains (like postponing a difficult conversation). This razor helps you identify and eliminate the recurring drains, even if the immediate fix requires more energy.

Example:
A manager dreads weekly meetings with a difficult client. Each week, they spend hours anxious about it, hours preparing, and hours recovering. Instead of enduring this cycle, they have one tough conversation to reset expectations or end the relationship - a bigger short-term drain that eliminates the recurring cost.

Why It Matters:
Your energy, not your time, is your scarcest resource. Recurring drains compound their damage by sapping both physical and mental energy over and over. One-time solutions, though harder initially, free up massive energy for better uses.

When to Use It / How to Counter It:
When facing a problem, ask: "Will this keep draining me, or is it a one-time cost?" If it's recurring, solve it permanently now, even if the immediate cost is higher.

The Bottom Line:
Pay once or pay forever - choose once. Your future self will thank you.

Escalation of Commitment: Sticking with a Decision Even When It's Failing

Escalation of Commitment occurs when people continue to invest in a failing decision, project, or strategy because they've already put significant resources into it. It's the "I've come this far, so I might as well keep going" mentality.

How It Works:
Imagine you keep funding a business venture that's losing money. Even though the smart move would be to cut your losses, you stay invested because of all the time, money, and energy already committed. This bias traps you in a cycle, with each new investment deepening your commitment.

Example:
An individual holds onto a struggling stock, thinking, "I can't sell now - I've already lost too much." Here, Escalation of Commitment turns a financial setback into a larger loss, as they continue to hope for a rebound that may never come.

Why It Matters:
This bias can lead to compounding losses, wasted resources, and missed opportunities by keeping us tied to poor decisions. Recognizing when to stop allows us to redirect efforts toward more productive ventures.

When to Use It / How to Counter It:
When evaluating ongoing projects or decisions, ask, "Am I continuing this just because of past investment, or is it truly worthwhile?" This question can help clarify whether it's time to let go.

The Bottom Line:
Know when to walk away. Escalation of Commitment can cost more in the long run, making it crucial to recognize when cutting losses is the better choice.

Everyday Razor: Small Habits, Big Results

Want to multiply your output and results? The Everyday Razor suggests: Take a weekly task and make it daily. By leveraging consistency, you'll achieve what would take years in just one, with the power of compounding in your favor.

How It Works:
Imagine you write one blog post a week. Now, switch to writing one daily. By year's end, you'll have 365 posts instead of 52! Add a 1% daily improvement, and your skill compounds to a level you might not reach in a decade with a weekly habit. The magic lies in repetition and refinement.

Example:
A musician practicing twice a week might progress slowly. Practicing daily, however, accelerates skill development and confidence, achieving in one year what would take seven with the original routine.

Why It Matters:
Small, consistent actions lead to massive, compounding results. It's not about doing more; it's about achieving exponential growth through daily practice, which refines your abilities far beyond occasional efforts.

When to Use It / How to Counter It:
Whenever you want to master a skill or reach big goals. Transform weekly habits into daily ones, and watch your growth skyrocket with consistent, focused action.

The Bottom Line:
Repetition fuels mastery. The Everyday Razor is your tool for amplifying productivity, turning small daily habits into huge long-term achievements.

False Analogy: When Surface Similarities Hide Deep Differences

That executive who says "running a company is like conducting an orchestra" sounds smart - until you realize how this comparison misleads. Bad analogies are seductive because they feel true at first glance.

How It Works:
People compare two things that share some surface traits while ignoring crucial differences. The comparison breaks down when pushed beyond superficial similarities, leading to flawed conclusions.

Example:
"The human brain is like a computer" seems reasonable - both process information and have memory. But this analogy breaks down: brains rewire themselves, learn from sparse data, and work through fuzzy patterns. Treating them as equivalent leads to misunderstanding both.

Why It Matters:
Bad analogies create bad decisions. Netflix killed Blockbuster by realizing that streaming video wasn't "just like a video store." Amazon dominates because they saw that online retail wasn't "just like regular retail with a website."

When to Use It / How to Counter It:
Test analogies by asking: What critical differences am I ignoring? Where does this comparison break down? What unique properties am I missing? Use analogies to explain, not to decide.

The Bottom Line:
Good analogies illuminate. Bad ones blind. The key is knowing where the comparison stops being useful - and having the discipline to stop there.

False Equivalence: When "Both Sides" Aren't Equal

"Well, everyone's entitled to their opinion" sounds fair - until you realize this puts proven facts and baseless claims on the same level. False equivalence makes the unequal seem equal.

How It Works:
People present two things as having equal weight or merit when they fundamentally don't. The error comes from treating different scales, stakes, or evidence as if they're the same.

Example:
"Both doctors and anti-vax bloggers have concerns about the vaccine" suggests their views deserve equal consideration. But one group has decades of peer-reviewed research; the other has internet opinions. Not all perspectives deserve equal weight.

Why It Matters:
False equivalence paralyzes decision-making. SpaceX succeeded because Musk didn't treat "conventional rocket wisdom" as equivalent to physics principles. Amazon dominates because Bezos doesn't treat customer complaints and internal objections as equally important.

When to Use It / How to Counter It:
Ask: Are these truly comparable in scale, impact, or evidence? Am I giving unearned credibility to weaker positions? Does treating these as equal help or hurt clear thinking?

The Bottom Line:
Not everything deserves equal weight. Clear thinking requires recognizing real differences in magnitude, merit, and evidence. Sometimes "both sides" aren't both right.

NOTE: **False Analogy** and **False Equivalence** are similar in that they both involve faulty comparisons, but they differ in how they mislead.

False Analogy occurs when someone compares two things that are not sufficiently alike in relevant aspects, but they argue that because the two things share some superficial similarities, they must be the same in other ways too. It's misleading because the analogy doesn't hold up under scrutiny, as the differences between the two things outweigh their similarities. For example, "Employees are like nails. Just as nails must be hit on the head to get them to work, so must employees." This comparison draws an inappropriate conclusion based on irrelevant similarities.

False Equivalence, on the other hand, specifically involves presenting two things as being equivalent when they are not. It's about implying that two things are equal in importance, morality, or impact, even though they aren't. For example, saying "Not recycling your trash is just as harmful to the planet as clear-cutting rainforests" falsely equates two actions that are vastly different in scale and impact.

In short:
False Analogy: Comparing two things that aren't similar in the relevant aspects, leading to a faulty conclusion.

False Equivalence: Claiming two things are equal in value or significance when they are not.

The key difference is that false analogy focuses on using an invalid comparison to make an argument, while false equivalence misrepresents two things as being equal.

False Cause (Post Hoc)

False Cause (Post Hoc) is the mistaken belief that because one event follows another, the first must have caused the second. It's tempting to think life works that simply, but correlation doesn't always mean causation.

How It Works:
You drink a green smoothie before a big presentation, then nail it. You think, "It must've been the smoothie!" But just because the smoothie came first doesn't mean it was the cause. Other factors, like preparation or confidence, likely played a bigger role.

Example:
A manager runs a marketing campaign, and sales go up right after. They assume the campaign is responsible, but the boost might be due to unrelated factors, like a competitor's closure or seasonal trends.

When to Use It / How to Counter It:
This fallacy shows up when we want to simplify cause and effect, especially when looking for quick explanations for successes or failures. It's also common in storytelling, where we like easy narratives, even if they're inaccurate.

Why It Matters:
Relying on false causes can lead to poor decisions and wasted resources. If you don't dig deeper to understand the true reasons behind results, you're just guessing - and potentially missing the real drivers.

The Bottom Line:
Just because one event follows another doesn't mean they're connected. Enjoy your smoothie for its health benefits, but don't assume it's the reason you crushed your presentation!

False Consensus Effect: Thinking Everyone Agrees with You

The False Consensus Effect is when you overestimate how much others share your opinions, beliefs, or behaviors. It's why you might assume that everyone else feels the same way you do about a topic, only to be surprised when someone disagrees.

How It Works:
You're in a meeting, discussing a new policy, and you assume that everyone's on board with your idea. But when the discussion opens up, you're shocked to find that most of the team doesn't agree with your perspective at all. The False Consensus Effect makes you think your views are more widely shared than they really are.

Why It Matters:
This effect can cause miscommunication, misunderstandings, and poor decision-making. If you assume everyone thinks like you, you may miss out on valuable feedback or fail to consider alternative perspectives. Recognizing this bias helps you seek input from others and remain open to different viewpoints.

When to Use It / How to Counter It:
When you're making decisions that affect others. Ask yourself: "Am I assuming everyone agrees with me, or have I actually checked?" Seek feedback before moving forward, and be open to the fact that others may see things differently.

The Bottom Line:
Not everyone shares your perspective. The False Consensus Effect reminds you to check your assumptions and make space for differing opinions - because chances are, people see things differently than you do.

False Dichotomy: The Either/Or Trap

The deadliest trap in decision-making is believing you only have two choices when you actually have many. It's like saying "Either you go to college or you'll be a failure" - when reality offers countless paths to success.

How It Works:
Someone presents only two options while hiding or ignoring other valid alternatives. They frame complex situations as simple either/or choices to force a specific conclusion. The false dichotomy works by making us forget that life rarely fits into neat binary choices.

Example:
"Either we work 80-hour weeks or we'll lose our competitive edge" ignores solutions like improving efficiency, automating processes, or strategic outsourcing. Apple didn't just choose between "expensive quality" or "cheap junk" - they innovated a third way. Most breakthroughs come from rejecting the initial either/or framing.

Why It Matters:
When you spot false dichotomies, you unlock better solutions. Netflix didn't accept the "theaters or direct-to-video" dichotomy - they created streaming. Microsoft didn't choose between "expensive software or free software" - they built subscriptions. Innovation often lives in the space between extremes.

When to Use It / How to Counter It:
Challenge either/or statements by asking "What other options exist?" Break free from artificial constraints by listing at least five alternatives. Question whether the presented choices are truly the only options. Look for hidden assumptions in binary choices.

The Bottom Line:
Life rarely offers only two choices. The best opportunities often lie in the space between extremes. When someone says "either/or," start looking for the "and".

False Uniqueness Effect: Thinking You're More Unique Than You Are

The False Uniqueness Effect is the tendency to underestimate how common our talents, achievements, or experiences are, leading us to believe we stand out more than we actually do.

How It Works:
Imagine you win a local running race and assume your running skills are rare in your community, even though many others might have similar or even better abilities. This bias skews your perception, inflating how exceptional you think you are.

Example:
A student scores highly on an exam and believes they're one of the few who did well, when in reality, many others achieved similar results. This belief in "false uniqueness" can lead to an overinflated sense of accomplishment.

Why It Matters:
The False Uniqueness Effect can inflate self-esteem, leading to overconfidence and unrealistic expectations. By assuming our achievements are more extraordinary than they are, we risk losing perspective on both our strengths and areas for growth.

When to Use It / How to Counter It:
When assessing your own skills or achievements, ask, "Am I overestimating how unique I am? How do I truly compare to others?" This reflection can keep your self-assessment realistic and balanced.

The Bottom Line:
Your abilities may not be as unique as you think. Recognize this to stay humble, grounded, and open to improvement.

Falsification Principle: Seek What Proves You Wrong

True scientific thinking isn't about proving yourself right - it's about trying to prove yourself wrong. The more ways an idea resists disproof, the stronger and more reliable it becomes.

How It Works:
Instead of searching for evidence that supports your beliefs, actively look for evidence that could disprove them. By exposing ideas to rigorous scrutiny, only those that withstand challenges remain, lending greater confidence to their validity.

Example:
A company doesn't just rely on positive customer testimonials but seeks out unsatisfied customers to identify product weaknesses. This approach reveals areas for improvement far better than basking in praise, leading to a stronger, more resilient product.

Why It Matters:
The Falsification Principle helps combat confirmation bias, leading to better decisions, strategies, and theories. It's the cornerstone of scientific thinking and critical analysis, ensuring that only well-tested ideas stand.

When to Use It / How to Counter It:
Use this principle whenever you're testing an idea, belief, or strategy. Instead of asking, "How can I prove this right?" ask, "How could this be wrong?" This shift ensures a thorough evaluation and a stronger foundation for your conclusions.

The Bottom Line:
Don't seek confirmation; seek falsification. What survives genuine attempts to disprove it is more likely to be true.

Faulty Statistics: Math Magic Tricks Gone Wrong

"Numbers don't lie," they say - but people sure know how to twist them. Faulty statistics take legitimate numbers and warp them to say whatever suits a particular agenda, like putting words in a puppet's mouth.

How It Works:
You use numbers to back up your claim, but the math doesn't really hold up. For instance, "This study shows 80% of people prefer our product!" But look closer - who was surveyed? If it was just the company's own employees, the stat is misleading at best, manipulative at worst.

Example:
A politician claims, "Crime rates dropped 50%!" without mentioning that they only compared two carefully selected months rather than a full year. The stat seems impressive, but selective data make it misleading.

Why It Matters:
Misused stats give false credibility to weak arguments, creating a "data-backed" illusion. Numbers can be powerful and persuasive, but only when they're used with accuracy and context. Otherwise, they're just smoke and mirrors.

When to Use It / How to Counter It:
Use stats when conducting legitimate, transparent analysis. Manipulating numbers may win short-term trust, but once people see the trickery, credibility is lost.

The Bottom Line:
Math is a tool, not a trick. Use it honestly, or it'll backfire. Numbers can support your point but should never be the entire argument.

The Firehose Effect: Why Drinking Information from a High-Pressure Stream Leaves You Thirsty

Trying to absorb everything is like trying to drink from a firehose. You'll end up soaked, stressed, and surprisingly thirsty.

How It Works:
When information comes too fast or in too large a volume, your brain's processing capacity gets overwhelmed. Like a CPU hitting 100%, you start dropping packets of information instead of processing them. Your attention splinters, comprehension plummets, and anxiety spikes.

Example:
A new hire gets a 6-hour onboarding dump of company processes, tools, and protocols. By hour two, their brain is full. By hour four, they're nodding while retaining nothing. Three months later, they're still asking basic questions covered in that first day. The information was all there, but their mental bandwidth wasn't.

Why It Matters:
Information overload isn't just uncomfortable - it's inefficient. Paradoxically, trying to learn everything at once means you learn almost nothing. Speed kills comprehension. In our rush to consume more, faster, we end up with mental indigestion that prevents real learning and growth.

When to Use It / How to Counter It:
Before any learning sprint, ask: "Am I drinking or drowning?" Break large information flows into manageable sips. Create space between learning sessions for processing and integration. Turn the firehose into a steady stream.

The Bottom Line:
Sometimes you need to slow down to speed up.

First Principles Thinking: Break Problems Down to Their Basics

First Principles Thinking is a problem-solving approach where you break down complex issues into their fundamental components and build solutions from the ground up. Rather than relying on assumptions, you start with the most basic facts.

How It Works:
Instead of accepting that electric cars are too expensive to produce, Elon Musk broke the problem down to the raw materials - steel, batteries, etc. - and asked, "How can we make these components cheaper?" By focusing on the fundamentals, he found innovative ways to reduce costs.

Example:
If you want to lose weight, don't just follow conventional advice. Break it down into first principles: calories consumed versus calories burned. From there, you can build a personalized plan based on the science of energy balance, rather than blindly following trends.

Why It Matters:
First Principles Thinking helps you avoid getting stuck in conventional wisdom or outdated assumptions. It forces you to question everything and create solutions from the most basic facts.

When to Use It / How to Counter It:
When faced with complex problems, ask: "What are the most fundamental truths here?" Build solutions by focusing on these core elements instead of relying on assumptions.

The Bottom Line:
Start from scratch. First Principles Thinking breaks complex problems down into their basic components to generate innovative solutions.

Fluency Heuristic: The Ease of Processing Shapes Perception

The Fluency Heuristic is a mental shortcut where people tend to prefer, believe, or recall information that is easy to process and understand.

How It Works: When information is easy to read, say, or think about (i.e., fluent), we often unconsciously attribute positive qualities to it. This can lead us to believe that fluent statements are more true, familiar, or desirable compared to more complex alternatives.

Example: Given two descriptions of the same product, consumers tend to favor the one that's simpler and easier to read, even if both convey the same information. They may perceive the fluent description as indicating a better, more trustworthy product.

Why It Matters: The Fluency Heuristic influences our judgments and decision-making in various domains, including marketing, politics, and everyday reasoning. Being aware of this bias can help us make more objective assessments.

When to Use It / How to Counter It: Use the Fluency Heuristic to make your message more persuasive and memorable. Simplify complex information, use easy-to-read fonts, and opt for clear, concise language. But also be wary of being swayed by fluency when evaluating information.

The Bottom Line: The Fluency Heuristic shows that our perception of truth, familiarity, and desirability is heavily influenced by the ease of processing information. While useful for quick judgments, it can also lead to biased thinking if we're not careful.

Focus Razor: More Isn't Better, Focus Is

The Focus Razor is about clarity: Instead of juggling many tasks, do less - but with more impact. It's not about quantity; it's about concentrating on what truly matters. Multitasking is the enemy of mastery.

How It Works:
Imagine a long to-do list. Instead of tackling everything, the Focus Razor suggests picking one or two tasks that make the biggest difference and giving them your full attention. Cut or delay the rest. True focus leads to quality, and quality leads to meaningful results.

Example:
A writer with multiple article ideas chooses one core piece to perfect rather than spreading their effort across several drafts. By concentrating on a single high-impact piece, the result is far more compelling and effective.

Why It Matters:
In a world that glorifies busyness, the Focus Razor reminds us that doing fewer things well beats doing many things poorly. It's about depth, not breadth - intentionally choosing quality over sheer activity.

When to Use It / How to Counter It:
When you're overloaded with tasks or decisions, ask: "What's the one thing I can do today that will make the most impact?" Then, give it your undivided attention to maximize results.

The Bottom Line:
Doing more isn't the goal - doing what truly matters is. The Focus Razor is a tool to hone excellence by concentrating on the essentials instead of spreading yourself too thin.

Focusing Illusion: Overestimating the Impact of One Factor

The Focusing Illusion happens when we place too much importance on one aspect of a situation, leading to inaccurate predictions about future happiness or satisfaction.

How It Works:
You're considering a job offer in a sunny location and convince yourself that the weather will make you happier. After a few months, though, you realize that other factors - like job responsibilities and relationships - matter much more. The Focusing Illusion tricks you into thinking one factor will dominate your happiness, when life is more complex.

Example:
People often think winning the lottery will dramatically improve their happiness. However, studies show that after an initial spike, lottery winners usually return to previous levels of well-being.

Why It Matters:
This illusion can lead to poor decisions by making you overvalue one factor while ignoring others. Recognizing it helps you take a more balanced view and avoid being swayed by a single element.

When to Use It / How to Counter It:
When making big decisions - like moving or changing jobs - ask: "Am I focusing too much on one thing and ignoring the rest?" Consider all factors to avoid being swayed by a single overemphasized one.

The Bottom Line:
Life is complex, and no single factor determines happiness. The Focusing Illusion reminds you to look at the full picture when making decisions.

Forer Effect: Believing Vague Statements Are Uniquely About You

The Forer Effect explains why we often think broad, general descriptions (like horoscopes) are uniquely tailored to us - even when the same statements could apply to almost anyone.

How It Works:
You read a horoscope that says, "You value friendships but sometimes need alone time," and think, "Wow, that's so me!" But this could describe nearly anyone. The Forer Effect tricks you into seeing personal accuracy in vague statements.

Example:
A personality quiz tells you, "You're ambitious but sometimes doubt yourself." This feels specific, but it's broad enough to resonate with most people. The statement's generality makes it feel "spot on" for a wide audience, not just you.

Why It Matters:
This bias can lead to overconfidence in pseudosciences like astrology, fortune-telling, or personality tests that offer little real insight. By seeing vague statements as unique to us, we're more likely to believe in these sources without critical thinking.

When to Use It / How to Counter It:
When reading something that feels "spot on" about your personality, ask, "Could this apply to anyone?" If so, it's likely a generic statement crafted to sound personal.

The Bottom Line:
Be skeptical of vague statements that seem tailored to you. If it sounds like it could apply to anyone, it's probably not as personal as it seems.

Founder's Paradox: Traits That Build Also Destroy

The Founder's Paradox highlights how the very traits that drive founders to early success often lead to their downfall as the company matures. It's like a rocket booster - essential for launch but dead weight in orbit.

How It Works:
The intense drive, confidence, and need for control that help founders build companies from the ground up can later become liabilities. What works well in the fast-paced, hands-on startup phase can hinder growth in a more structured, scalable organization. As the company evolves, the founder's strengths can become weaknesses.

Example:
A founder's micromanagement ensures quality in the early days, but as the company grows, this style creates bottlenecks and stifles innovation by preventing effective delegation. The traits that led to initial success now prevent the company from scaling.

Why It Matters:
Understanding this paradox helps founders recognize when to adapt their leadership style to support sustainable growth. Knowing when to step back or change approach is key to a company's long-term success and can explain why founder transitions are often necessary.

When to Use It / How to Counter It:
Consider this principle during growth phases. Regularly evaluate whether founding traits are aiding or hindering current goals, and adjust to meet the demands of each stage of growth.

The Bottom Line:
Different stages require different traits. The Founder's Paradox reminds us that what got you here may not get you there - adaptability is essential for lasting success.

Framing Effect: The Way Information is Presented Influences Decisions

People react differently to the same information depending on how it's presented. The same choice can feel different depending on whether it's framed in a positive or negative light.

How It Works:
A doctor tells you that a treatment has a 90% survival rate. That sounds pretty good! But if the doctor instead says the treatment has a 10% mortality rate, you might feel uneasy, even though the two statistics are exactly the same. The Framing Effect influences your decision-making by altering your emotional reaction to the way the information is framed.

Example: Marketers often use this effect by framing discounts as "saving $5" rather than "paying $10." Even though the outcome is the same, the positive framing makes the discount seem more appealing.

Why It Matters:
The Framing Effect can lead to biased decision-making because it taps into your emotions. Understanding this bias helps you recognize when the way information is presented is influencing your choices. It's important to evaluate the facts objectively, rather than being swayed by the framing.

When to Use It / How to Counter It:
When making important decisions or evaluating options. Ask yourself: "Am I being influenced by how this information is framed, or am I considering the facts objectively?" Look at both the positive and negative framing to get a complete picture.

The Bottom Line:
How something is presented can change how you feel about it. The Framing Effect reminds you to look beyond the way information is packaged and focus on the underlying facts.

Friction Theory: How Tiny Barriers Shape Massive Behavior

One extra click halves user engagement. One extra form field drops sign-ups by 50%. Behavioral science proves that microscopic obstacles reshape how millions of people act.

How It Works:
Research shows humans systematically overvalue convenience. Studies confirm that even minimal effort requirements can reduce participation more effectively than major incentives or penalties.

Examples:

A company reduced customer service calls by 20% simply by making their FAQ page easier to locate online. This small decrease in friction led to a significant behavior change, without costly improvements to the product.

Google's data revealed that a 0.5 second increase in page load time dropped traffic by 20%. When Amazon tested requiring one extra click for purchases, cart abandonment rose 27%. Friction, not features, determined behavior.

Why It Matters:
Companies waste millions fighting human nature. Research proves reducing tiny barriers often outperforms expensive rewards programs. Success comes from working with psychology, not against it.

When to Use It / How to Counter It:
Before launching major initiatives, audit friction points. Studies show identifying and removing small obstacles typically doubles desired behaviors at minimal cost.

The Bottom Line:
Your brain is lazy by design. Rather than fight this reality, use micro-friction to guide behavior naturally.

Functional Fixedness: Limiting Objects to Their Traditional Use

Functional Fixedness is the mental block that restricts us from seeing new uses for familiar objects, focusing only on their traditional function. This mindset limits creativity and narrows problem-solving options.

How It Works:
Imagine needing to open a package but lacking scissors nearby. Instead of using a key or any other available tool, you waste time searching for scissors because you're stuck on the idea that only scissors will work. Functional Fixedness keeps you locked into conventional thinking, even when alternatives are available.

Example:
You're assembling furniture and need a small hammer. Instead of using a heavy book or shoe that could work in a pinch, you hunt down an actual hammer, delaying the task and adding frustration. Here, Functional Fixedness limits resourcefulness.

Why It Matters:
This bias can block creative solutions, especially when quick thinking is essential. Overcoming Functional Fixedness allows for more flexible problem-solving, enabling you to see new possibilities and use resources in innovative ways.

When to Use It / How to Counter It:
When a conventional solution isn't available, ask, "What other tools or methods could work here?" Breaking free from Functional Fixedness encourages creative approaches and often leads to effective, unexpected solutions.

The Bottom Line:
Don't let objects' typical functions limit your thinking. Functional Fixedness narrows your creativity - think outside the box for broader problem-solving.

Future Feeling Fallacy: Why You're Terrible at Predicting Your Own Happiness

Our ability to predict future happiness is fundamentally flawed. Every "I'll be happy when..." statement usually misses the mark, overestimating how life changes will impact our long-term satisfaction.

How It Works:
We tend to overestimate both the intensity and duration of future emotions - whether positive or negative. The brain, when it comes to "emotional time-travel," isn't great at anticipating how it will feel after life changes. Good or bad, we quickly adapt, and the heightened emotions we expect rarely last.

Example:
A lawyer pursues partnership for years, believing it's the key to happiness. But once promoted, the initial excitement fades within weeks. The corner office that once seemed transformative soon becomes just another part of the daily grind.

Why It Matters:
This fallacy often leads to major life decisions based on faulty emotional predictions. We chase job titles, relationships, or possessions, expecting them to transform our happiness - only to recalibrate back to our baseline once the novelty wears off.

When to Use It / How to Counter It:
Before making significant life changes, ask, "Am I overestimating how much this will affect my happiness?" Humans are highly adaptable, so remember that what seems life-changing now may feel normal sooner than expected.

The Bottom Line:
Your future feelings won't match what you imagine. Build a life rooted in your present values rather than elusive, predicted emotions.

Gall's Law: Simple Systems Are More Likely to Succeed

Gall's Law states that a complex system that works is invariably found to have evolved from a simple system that worked. In other words, successful systems start simple and gradually become more complex as they grow.

How It Works:
When building a business, product, or project, starting with a simple, functional version (a "minimum viable product") is more likely to succeed than starting with a complex, fully featured version. Simple systems are easier to understand, maintain, and improve, and they can evolve over time to become more sophisticated.

Example: The early versions of successful companies like Google and Facebook were much simpler than their current iterations. Over time, these companies evolved from their basic, functional beginnings into the complex systems they are today.

Why It Matters:
This law emphasizes the importance of simplicity in design and problem-solving. Starting with something simple allows for flexibility and evolution, while starting with a complex system often leads to failure because complexity is harder to manage from the outset. Gall's Law encourages you to focus on simplicity and iterate over time.

When to Use It / How to Counter It:
When designing systems, products, or processes. Ask yourself: "Am I making this more complicated than it needs to be?" Start with a simple solution and let complexity evolve naturally as needed.

The Bottom Line:
Simplicity breeds success. Gall's Law reminds you that successful systems start simple and grow more complex over time - don't overcomplicate things from the beginning.

Galileo Gambit: Claiming Persecution Proves One's Correctness

The Galileo Gambit is the fallacy of claiming that ridicule or suppression of an idea means it must be valid, drawing comparisons to figures like Galileo who were initially dismissed but later proven right.

How It Works:
This fallacy arises when someone argues, "If mainstream science rejects my theory about alternative medicine, then I'm just like Galileo, who was ridiculed before being validated." The assumption is that criticism indicates truth, ignoring that most dismissed ideas are invalid for sound reasons.

Example:
A conspiracy theorist claims their idea must be true because "the establishment is trying to silence it." By equating suppression with correctness, they avoid addressing the actual flaws in their argument.

Why It Matters:
The Galileo Gambit misleads people by suggesting that criticism or rejection by experts signals truth. While some groundbreaking ideas face initial resistance, most ridiculed theories are discarded due to a lack of evidence.

When to Use It / How to Counter It:
When facing criticism, ask, "Am I using this comparison to dodge legitimate flaws in my argument?" Recognize that persecution alone doesn't validate an idea; it's the quality of evidence that matters.

The Bottom Line:
Persecution isn't proof of correctness. Evaluate ideas based on evidence, not on how they're received. Galileo was right because of evidence - not because he was ridiculed.

Gateway Effect: Small Changes Lead to Bigger Ones

The Gateway Effect shows how small initial changes can trigger a chain of larger transformations. Like a "gateway drug," these small shifts recalibrate what feels normal, paving the way for more significant changes.

How It Works:
Once a person crosses a small threshold, they're more likely to accept the next, slightly bigger change. The first step subtly shifts expectations, making the next step feel natural, and so on. This process can lead to transformative outcomes that initially seemed out of reach.

Example:
A company starts with casual Fridays, then adds flexible hours, then occasional remote work days. Each small change feels incremental, but over time, it leads to a fully remote culture that would have seemed too drastic if introduced all at once.

Why It Matters:
The Gateway Effect is powerful for creating lasting change or noticing potential slippery slopes. By understanding how small steps can compound, you can strategically use this effect for positive transformations - or recognize when small changes may lead down unintended paths.

When to Use It / How to Counter It:
Use this effect when implementing new habits or cultural shifts. Starting with manageable changes can help people adjust gradually, making larger changes feel more acceptable over time.

The Bottom Line:
Big changes often start with small steps. Use the Gateway Effect intentionally to guide progress, rather than stumbling into it accidentally.

G.I. Joe Fallacy: Knowing Isn't Half the Battle

The G.I. Joe Fallacy is the mistaken belief that just knowing about a bias or problem is enough to avoid it. The phrase comes from the old G.I. Joe cartoons, which ended with the line, "Now you know, and knowing is half the battle." But in reality, knowing is only part of the solution - you still have to act on that knowledge.

How It Works:
You read about cognitive biases and think, "Great! Now that I know about them, I won't fall for them." But just knowing about biases like the Availability Heuristic or the Anchoring Effect doesn't automatically protect you from falling victim to them. You need to actively guard against them, not just be aware of them.

Example: You know that social media triggers comparison bias, but that doesn't stop you from feeling envious when you scroll through Instagram. The knowledge alone doesn't protect you - you need to change your behavior to avoid the bias.

Why It Matters:
Awareness is the first step, but it's not enough. The G.I. Joe Fallacy warns that knowledge needs to be paired with deliberate action to make a difference. Without strategies to counteract biases, simply knowing about them won't help much.

When to Use It / How to Counter It:
When you've learned about a bias or behavior but are still falling into its trap. Ask yourself: "Am I assuming that just knowing this is enough to avoid it, or am I actively working to counter it?" Make sure you're turning knowledge into action.

The Bottom Line:
Knowing isn't half the battle - it's only the beginning. The G.I. Joe Fallacy reminds you to actively apply what you know if you want to overcome biases or bad habits.

Gambler's Conceit: Believing You Can Quit Risky Behavior Just in Time

The Gambler's Conceit is the mistaken belief that you can keep engaging in risky activities and simply stop right before consequences hit. It's the "I'll get out just in time" mentality.

How It Works:
A gambler keeps betting, convinced they'll walk away right before their luck turns. In reality, they're likely to keep going, driven by overconfidence until they eventually lose big. This mindset ignores how easily risky behavior can spiral out of control.

Example:
An investor rides a volatile stock, thinking they'll sell "just before it crashes." But by waiting for that "perfect moment," they often hold on too long and suffer losses, underestimating the pull of profit and momentum.

Why It Matters:
The Gambler's Conceit can lead to disastrous outcomes, whether in gambling, investing, or any high-stakes situation. People overestimate their self-control and underestimate how easily they get swept up in the thrill, leading to poor decisions and avoidable losses.

When to Use It / How to Counter It:
Before taking a risky action, ask, "Am I overconfident in my ability to quit at the right moment?" Recognizing this bias helps you avoid taking risks you might not be able to control.

The Bottom Line:
Don't fool yourself into thinking you'll know when to stop. Risky behaviors often end in losses. Plan your limits beforehand and stick to them.

Gambler's Fallacy: Past Events Don't Affect Future Outcomes

"I've lost five times in a row, so I'm due for a win!" The Gambler's Fallacy is the mistaken belief that past events influence the probability of future independent events. It's why gamblers keep betting on red after a long streak of black, thinking, "Red has to come up now!" But the truth is, independent events don't care about what happened before.

How It Works:
You're at the roulette table, and black has come up five times in a row. You're convinced that red must be next, so you double down. The Gambler's Fallacy makes you think that the universe is somehow keeping track of past spins and will "balance things out," but each spin is independent - black could just as easily come up again.

Why It Matters:
This fallacy can lead to poor decision-making, especially in gambling, investing, or any situation involving chance. It's important to remember that independent events have no memory - just because something hasn't happened in a while doesn't mean it's due to happen now.

When to Use It / How to Counter It:
When making decisions about risk or probability, especially in gambling or investments. Ask yourself: "Am I expecting a random event to 'balance out'?" Remember that independent events are just that - independent.

The Bottom Line:
Chance doesn't have a memory. The Gambler's Fallacy tricks you into thinking past events influence future ones, but they don't. Make decisions based on logic, not faulty expectations of balance.

NOTE:

Gambler's Conceit and **Gambler's Fallacy** are different concepts, though they both involve flawed thinking around gambling and probability.

- **Gambler's Fallacy** refers to the mistaken belief that past random events affect the likelihood of future random events. For example, if a coin lands on heads multiple times in a row, someone might believe that tails is "due" to happen, even though each coin flip is independent and the odds remain the same.

- **Gambler's Conceit**, on the other hand, is the mistaken belief that a person can quit a risky behavior (like gambling) while they are still ahead, despite continuing to gamble. It assumes the individual has control over the situation, ignoring the probability that continued gambling will lead to losses.

In short, **Gambler's Fallacy** is about misunderstanding probabilities, while **Gambler's Conceit** is about overconfidence in one's ability to control when to stop a risky behavior.

Gell-Mann Amnesia: Why You Trust Sources That Just Lied to You

That article butchered the facts about your industry. Yet you're nodding along to their advice about investing. Your brain just got Gell-Mann'd.

How It Works:
You catch a news source being completely wrong about something you know well. Then, turning the page, you somehow forget they were just wrong and trust them on topics you don't know. It's like catching someone lying about your hometown, then trusting their travel advice about cities you've never visited.

Example:
A business owner reads an article completely misrepresenting their industry. "This is nonsense!" they think. Then they immediately trust the same publication's advice on cryptocurrency, management techniques, and health trends - areas where they can't spot the errors.

Why It Matters:
This mental glitch makes you vulnerable to bad information. You waste money on trends that experts would laugh at. You make decisions based on advice from sources you've literally caught being wrong. Your critical thinking has blind spots that cost you.

When to Use It / How to Counter It:
When consuming any information, ask: "Would I trust this source if they wrote about my field?" If you catch someone being wrong about what you know, maintain that skepticism across all topics. Your expertise in one area is your BS detector for others.

The Bottom Line:
If they're wrong where you're knowledgeable, they're probably wrong where you're not. Don't let topic changes reset your skepticism.

Gell-Mann Razor: Treat Every Media Article with Skepticism

The Gell-Mann Razor suggests that every media article likely contains at least some misinformation - so never take anything at face value. Named after physicist Murray Gell-Mann, who noticed frequent inaccuracies when reading media reports about his field, this razor reminds us to remain critical across all topics.

How It Works:
When reading a news article, especially on unfamiliar subjects, assume there's a portion of it that's incorrect. The errors may stem from oversimplification, misunderstandings, or just basic mistakes. The Gell-Mann Razor encourages you to question and verify before forming strong opinions based solely on media information.

Example:
You read an article about a new medical breakthrough. Instead of immediately believing its claims, you seek out primary sources or consult experts, understanding that the media might misrepresent details or lack context.

Why It Matters:
In today's age of information overload, it's easy to accept media narratives as fact. The Gell-Mann Razor reminds us that much of what we read is often incomplete or inaccurate. "Trust, but verify" should be your motto, especially for critical issues.

When to Use It / How to Counter It:
Whenever you encounter media on a topic you're not well-versed in. Avoid taking it as gospel; seek out primary sources or expert insights before accepting it fully.

The Bottom Line:
The Gell-Mann Razor is your tool for navigating media noise. Assume each article may have inaccuracies and verify key information before integrating it into your worldview.

NOTE:

The **Gell-Mann Amnesia Effect** and **Gell-Mann Razor** are two entirely different concepts, though both are named after physicist Murray Gell-Mann.

Key Difference:

- **Gell-Mann Amnesia Effect** is about forgetting a source's flaws and continuing to trust them in other areas.
- **Gell-Mann Razor** is about choosing simpler explanations when you encounter something you don't understand, assuming the complexity might be due to missing simple facts.

They are distinct concepts, though both touch on cognitive biases and how we process information.

Generalized Specialist Principle: Deep Enough to Connect

The Generalized Specialist Principle suggests that true versatility comes from deep expertise in one field paired with broad knowledge in related areas. This balance fosters unique connections, sparking innovation and cross-disciplinary insights.

How It Works:
Develop in-depth expertise in one core area while building a working knowledge of related fields. This T-shaped approach (depth in one area, breadth in others) allows you to make connections that single-discipline experts might miss, creating a foundation for more innovative and impactful work.

Example:
A software developer specializes in AI but has working knowledge in psychology, design, and business. This broad understanding enables them to create AI-driven solutions that are not only technically advanced but also user-friendly, market-ready, and impactful.

Why It Matters:
This principle helps avoid the pitfalls of overspecialization and shallow knowledge. It's particularly valuable in roles requiring creativity and problem-solving, where connecting ideas from different areas leads to fresh perspectives and innovative solutions.

When to Use It / How to Counter It:
Apply this principle when planning skill development or career growth. Aim for T-shaped knowledge, with one deep specialization and a broad grasp of related fields, to maximize versatility and potential.

The Bottom Line:
Be a specialist who can connect across boundaries. Depth without breadth limits your perspective; breadth without depth limits your impact. The Generalized Specialist Principle finds the sweet spot for meaningful contributions.

Genetic Fallacy: Judging the Source, Not the Substance

"Where it came from is more important than what it says!" That's the Genetic Fallacy - dismissing an idea solely because of its origin rather than evaluating its actual content. It's like refusing to read a great book just because you dislike the author.

How It Works:
The Genetic Fallacy occurs when you critique an idea based on where it came from instead of its own merit. For example, someone says, "That can't be true - it's from a tabloid!" While tabloids often sensationalize, it doesn't mean every story they publish is false.

Example:
Someone rejects a useful health tip because it came from an unfamiliar website. By focusing only on the source's reputation, they miss potentially valuable information.

Why It Matters:
This fallacy can close your mind to valuable ideas simply because they come from unconventional or unfamiliar sources. It's important to evaluate the content itself rather than relying solely on its origin.

When to Use It / How to Counter It:
In informal conversations, trust in the source can matter, but in rational debates or decisions, focus on the actual content, not just where it originated.

The Bottom Line:
Judge ideas on their own merits, not just their origins. Insight and wisdom can come from surprising places - if you're open to evaluating the message itself.

Goodhart's Law: When a Measure Becomes a Target, It Ceases to Be a Good Measure

Goodhart's Law warns that when a measure becomes a target, it stops being effective. Focusing on metrics like "likes" or "followers" can distort your original goals - once the number itself becomes the focus, you lose sight of the bigger picture.

How It Works:
Say you set a target for your team to reach a specific sales quota. As soon as they start focusing on hitting that number, sales quality begins to suffer - people push poor deals just to meet the quota. That's Goodhart's Law: the metric (sales quota) becomes ineffective as it shifts from a measure to the main target.

Example:
A social media manager aims for a high follower count, but in focusing solely on numbers, they attract disengaged followers. While the count rises, engagement remains low, undermining the real goal of connecting with an active audience.

Why It Matters:
Metrics are essential for tracking progress, but when you chase the numbers themselves, you can lose sight of the true goal - like quality sales, engaged followers, or happy customers. This focus on arbitrary targets can lead to "gaming the system" rather than achieving genuine success.

When to Use It / How to Counter It:
Use this principle when setting goals or tracking performance. Ask, "Am I focused on the real goal, or am I just chasing the number?" Keep metrics as tools, not ends in themselves.

The Bottom Line:
Chasing numbers can blind you to what truly matters. Goodhart's Law reminds you to focus on the real goal, using metrics to support it, not define it.

The Google Effect: Why Your Brain Refuses to Remember What Google Can Find

Your brain is getting lazy. When information is instantly accessible online, your mind adapts by remembering where to find facts rather than remembering the facts themselves.

How It Works:
Your brain creates two types of memories: the information itself and where to find it. When you know something's easily searchable, your brain defaults to just remembering how to find it. It's like your mind has outsourced its memory to the internet.

Example:
Ask someone Einstein's birthday, and they'll likely reach for their phone instead of trying to remember - even if they've looked it up multiple times before. Studies show people forget information they think they can easily find online, but remember exactly where and how to access it.

Why It Matters:
This isn't just about trivia - it's changing how we process knowledge. While we're getting better at knowing where to find information, we're losing the deeper understanding that comes from internalizing facts. This affects everything from education to decision-making.

When to Use It / How to Counter It:
Combat this effect by practicing intentional recall. Before grabbing your phone, try to remember the information first. Build mental frameworks for important knowledge rather than relying on search engines. Save Google for verification, not primary learning.

The Bottom Line:
Your memory is adapting to the digital age. While it's efficient to outsource some memory to technology, core knowledge still needs to live in your brain. Choose what you memorize wisely.

Growth Mindset Paradox: When Flexibility Becomes Rigid

The Growth Mindset Paradox happens when the belief in "always improving" turns into a rigid expectation. Like a seeker who becomes dogmatic about open-mindedness, the pursuit of growth itself can ironically limit genuine flexibility.

How It Works:
Those committed to a growth mindset may become inflexible about flexibility, judging themselves or others for displaying any fixed thinking. This pressure to constantly grow can create a counterproductive rigidity, where the expectation of progress becomes a stressor rather than an asset.

Example:
A manager is so focused on the importance of constant improvement that they criticize team members who seem content or stable in their roles. Instead of fostering development, their insistence on growth creates anxiety and discourages organic progress, ultimately stifling performance.

Why It Matters:
Recognizing this paradox prevents a growth mindset from becoming another form of pressure. True growth allows for a balanced approach, accepting both progress and moments of stability. This awareness helps to foster an environment where flexibility is genuine rather than forced.

When to Use It / How to Counter It:
Consider this when encouraging personal development or managing others. Embrace that stability and growth can coexist, and that periods of contentment are often necessary for sustainable progress.

The Bottom Line:
Don't let the pursuit of growth become another limitation. True flexibility means allowing space for stability as well as change.

Halo Effect: First Impressions Color Everything

The Halo Effect is all about how first impressions influence everything that comes after. If someone looks good or impresses us in one area, we assume they're good in other areas too. It's why you think a charismatic speaker must be brilliant in all things - or why a well-dressed person seems more trustworthy.

How It Works:
You meet someone at a party who's charming and funny. Immediately, you assume they must also be smart, kind, and successful - even though you have no real evidence for those other traits. The Halo Effect makes you give them the benefit of the doubt in areas where you shouldn't.

Why It Matters:
This bias can lead to bad judgments and misperceptions. You might trust someone more than you should or give them opportunities they haven't earned simply because your first impression was positive. Understanding the Halo Effect helps you evaluate people more objectively, based on their actual behavior and abilities, not just their initial charm.

When to Use It / How to Counter It:
When you're making judgments about someone's abilities or character. Ask yourself: "Am I assuming they're good at this just because they're impressive in another area?" Make sure you're seeing the full picture before making decisions based on a glowing first impression.

The Bottom Line:
First impressions are powerful, but they're not the whole story. The Halo Effect can lead you to overestimate someone's abilities just because they made a good initial impact. Stay objective, and don't let charm cloud your judgment.

Hanlon's Razor: Don't Attribute to Malice What Can Be Adequately Explained by Incompetence

This powerful principle simplifies life by reminding us that thoughtlessness, mistakes, or incompetence often explain what might appear to be malicious behavior.

How It Works:
When someone's actions upset you, Hanlon's Razor encourages a pause before jumping to conclusions. It might even help your mental health to intentionally assume (even if you're wrong) that it's always something else, and has nothing to do with you.

Example:
A friend doesn't respond to your message because they simply forgot to check their phone, not because they're deliberately ignoring you.

A coworker didn't include you on an email chain because they didn't think through who needed to be included, not because they're trying to exclude you.

A store clerk seems rude because they're exhausted or having a bad day, not because they have any specific animosity toward you.

Why It Matters:
It's easy to jump to conclusions and assume the worst in others. Hanlon's Razor keeps you grounded, reminding you that most misunderstandings aren't personal - they're just human errors, reducing unnecessary conflict.

When to Use It / How to Counter It:
Anytime you feel slighted or wronged by someone's actions. Ask, "Is this truly malice, or just a mistake?" More often than not, it's the latter.

The Bottom Line:
Don't assume people are out to get you. However, use it wisely - while most situations aren't malicious, don't ignore genuine warning signs when they do appear.

Hasty Generalization: How Small Data Creates Big Mistakes

One bad review tanks a product. One failed project dooms a strategy. One poor hire makes you swear off an entire talent pool. That's hasty generalization - the expensive mistake of treating a sample size of one as universal truth.

How It Works:
Your brain loves patterns and hates uncertainty. So when you encounter limited data, you rush to create a rule. But conclusions from insufficient evidence are like building a skyscraper on a foundation of toothpicks - eventually, reality brings it down.

Example:
A startup launches in California and fails. The founder declares "This business model doesn't work" and gives up. Meanwhile, their competitor launches in Texas with the same model and builds a $100M company. The difference? Market size, competition, and timing - factors ignored in the hasty conclusion.

Why It Matters:
This fallacy kills opportunities before they start. It creates false patterns that guide bad decisions. Amazon had zero profit for years - imagine if investors made hasty generalizations about its potential. Your quick conclusions today could be costing you tomorrow's success.

When to Use It / How to Counter It:
Never. While your gut instinct has value, treat it as a hypothesis to test, not a conclusion. Gather meaningful sample sizes. Look for contrary evidence. Challenge your assumptions before they become expensive mistakes.

The Bottom Line:
Small samples create big blindspots. Before declaring something "always" or "never" works, get enough data to actually know. Your success depends on seeing the full picture, not just the first pixel.

Hawthorne Effect: Changing Behavior When Being Observed

The Hawthorne Effect describes how people change their behavior simply because they know they're being watched. This can lead to temporary improvements in performance that may not last once the observation ends.

How It Works:
Workers might boost productivity when they know they're being monitored, but after the attention fades, they revert to their usual behavior. The act of being observed alters behavior, even without any real changes to the task.

Example:
Employees work harder during a study when they know their efficiency is being measured. After the study ends, their performance returns to normal, showing that the improvement was due to being observed, not lasting changes.

Why It Matters:
The Hawthorne Effect shows how people's behavior changes under scrutiny, which can skew research or assessments. Recognizing this bias helps ensure more accurate evaluations of long-term behavior.

When to Use It / How to Counter It:
When observing performance, ask: "Is this change sustainable, or just a response to being watched?" Look for consistent indicators of behavior.

The Bottom Line:
People act differently when observed. The Hawthorne Effect reminds us that short-term improvements may fade once the observation ends.

Hedonic Treadmill: Chasing Happiness Is Like Running in Place

The Hedonic Treadmill explains why we keep chasing happiness, only to return to the same emotional baseline. You get that dream job, win the lottery, or move into a bigger house, but after the initial rush, your happiness levels return to where they were before. It's like running on a treadmill - you work hard, but you don't really get anywhere.

How It Works:
You've been dreaming about buying a new car for months. When you finally get it, you're ecstatic - driving it feels like the best thing ever. But after a few weeks, the excitement fades, and the car feels just like any other. That's the Hedonic Treadmill: you experience a temporary boost in happiness, but eventually, you adjust to your new normal.

Why It Matters:
This model explains why external rewards and achievements don't provide lasting happiness. It's a reminder that happiness comes more from internal satisfaction than from constantly chasing the next big thing. Understanding the Hedonic Treadmill can help you focus on more sustainable sources of joy, like relationships, personal growth, and meaningful work.

When to Use It / How to Counter It:
When you're setting goals or making life decisions. Ask yourself: "Will this really make me happier in the long run, or is it just a temporary high?" Focus on sustainable happiness, not just fleeting pleasures.

The Bottom Line:
Happiness from external achievements is often short-lived. The Hedonic Treadmill reminds you that true contentment comes from within, not from constantly chasing the next shiny thing.

Hick's Law: Too Many Choices Slow Down Decision-Making

Hick's Law states that the more choices you have, the longer it takes to make a decision. When faced with too many options, your brain has to process and weigh each one, leading to slower decision-making and often, decision fatigue.

How It Works:
You go to a restaurant with a massive menu that offers hundreds of options. Instead of feeling excited about the variety, you find yourself overwhelmed and struggling to choose. Hick's Law explains why more choices often slow you down, rather than speeding things up, as your brain has to process and compare each option.

Example:
Online shopping sites that offer too many products in a category can lead to shoppers spending more time browsing and less time making a purchase decision, or abandoning the process altogether due to decision fatigue.

Why It Matters:
Too many options can lead to analysis paralysis, where decision-making becomes difficult or impossible. Recognizing Hick's Law helps you simplify choices in your personal and professional life to make faster, more effective decisions. It's also a valuable tool in design and marketing, where reducing the number of options can lead to quicker, more satisfying customer decisions.

When to Use It / How to Counter It:
When designing products, experiences, or making decisions. Ask yourself: "Am I giving myself or others too many options? Can I simplify this?" Limit choices to reduce decision fatigue and make decision-making more efficient.

Hickam's Dictum: When "It's Complicated" Is Actually Right

Your car's making noise, your business is losing money, and your relationship's struggling. Everyone wants to find the ONE problem. But sometimes there isn't one - there are five. That's Hickam's Dictum.

How It Works:
While Occam's Razor tells us the simplest answer is often right, Hickam's Dictum says "hold my beer." It acknowledges that complex systems can have multiple problems happening simultaneously. Like your body, your business, or your life.

Example:
A startup is bleeding cash. The CEO hunts for the "root cause," but discovers three independent issues: poor market fit, inefficient operations, AND toxic culture. Fixing just one wouldn't save the company. All three needed addressing - separately and simultaneously.

Why It Matters:
The obsession with finding THE answer often blinds us to reality. Companies fail because they fixed the wrong problem - not realizing there were three. Relationships end because couples tackle one issue while ignoring two others. Success requires seeing the full picture.

When to Use It / How to Counter It:
Apply this whenever quick fixes fail. If your solution isn't working, stop looking for the silver bullet. List every possible factor. Test each one. Sometimes the answer isn't A or B - it's A and B and C. Embrace the complexity.

The Bottom Line:
Complex problems often have complex causes. Don't let the hunt for simplicity blind you to reality. Sometimes fixing everything means fixing many things at once.

Hidden Cost Fallacy: When Your "Bargain" Becomes a Money Pit

That $200 "deal" just cost you $2,000. The Hidden Cost Fallacy blinds you to the real price tag, making expensive choices feel like smart savings. It's the difference between price and cost.

How It Works:
Your brain loves immediate rewards and hates calculating future expenses. So you focus on the upfront price while ignoring maintenance, time, energy, and opportunity costs. That "bargain" printer needs $100 ink cartridges. That "affordable" employee needs extensive training. That "cheap" car burns expensive premium gas.

Example:
A gym buys budget treadmills for $2,000 each instead of commercial models at $8,000. Within two years, they've spent $12,000 per machine on repairs, lost members due to broken equipment, and now need replacements. Their "savings" cost them a fortune.

Why It Matters:
Hidden costs compound silently until they explode. Companies go broke saving money. Entrepreneurs waste years fixing cheap solutions. Winners look at total cost of ownership - losers look at price tags.

When to Use It / How to Counter It:
Before every purchase or decision, ask: "What's not on this price tag?" Calculate maintenance, training, energy, time, and opportunity costs. Sometimes the expensive option is cheaper. Sometimes saving money costs too much.

The Bottom Line:
Price is what you pay today. Cost is what you pay forever. Smart money looks at both.

Hierarchy of Competence: From Clueless to Masterful in Four Steps

Most people quit right before the breakthrough. The Hierarchy of Competence explains why - and reveals the predictable path from novice to master that every skill requires.

How It Works:
You climb four levels: First, you're clueless about being clueless (unconscious incompetence). Then reality hits - you realize how bad you are (conscious incompetence). Next, you can do it with focused effort (conscious competence). Finally, it becomes second nature (unconscious competence). Like driving a car, typing, or running a business.

Example:
A new entrepreneur launches their first business. Stage 1: "How hard can it be?" Stage 2: "Oh God, I'm in over my head." Stage 3: "I can do this, but it takes all my focus." Stage 4: "I instinctively know what moves to make." Understanding these stages prevents quitting at stage 2 - where most people give up.

Why It Matters:
Every skill worth having goes through these stages. Whether you're learning sales, leadership, or a new language - knowing this progression helps you push through the hard parts. The people who quit never reach mastery. The ones who persist become experts.

When to Use It / How to Counter It:
Use this framework when learning anything new. Stuck in conscious incompetence? That's normal - push through. Teaching others? Help them identify their stage and what's next. The path is predictable; success is persisting through each phase.

The Bottom Line:
Mastery isn't a talent - it's a progression. Everyone starts clueless. Champions just stay in the game long enough to make it automatic.

High Agency Razor: Stop Asking Permission to Solve Problems

While others wait for rescue, high-agency people build their own ladder. This mindset separates those who make things happen from those who wonder what happened.

How It Works:
High agency is choosing to be the hero of your story, not the victim. When faced with obstacles, you don't ask "Why me?" You ask "What's my next move?" It's the difference between complaining about the rules and learning how to win within them.

Example:
Two employees face a broken system at work. The low-agency person complains to coworkers. The high-agency person documents the issues, designs a solution, and presents it to leadership. Same situation, different approach, radically different outcomes. One stays stuck. One gets promoted.

Why It Matters:
Success isn't about starting conditions - it's about response to conditions. High-agency people turn layoffs into businesses, problems into products, and setbacks into comebacks. They don't need perfect circumstances because they improve any circumstance.

When to Use It / How to Counter It:
Apply this whenever you catch yourself making excuses. No time? High agency finds time. No connections? High agency builds them. No resources? High agency creates them. Every complaint becomes a to-do list.

The Bottom Line:
Your situation is a starting point, not a sentence. Take radical ownership of your outcomes. The quality of your life depends on the quantity of solutions you create.

Hindsight Bias: When Your Memory Rewrites History

Every market crash was "obvious." Every successful startup was "inevitable." Every failed project had "clear warning signs." That's your brain lying to you - and it's costing you growth.

How It Works:
Your mind automatically rewrites history to make past events seem predictable. After any outcome, your brain creates a neat story explaining why you "knew it all along." Like claiming you "knew" Bitcoin would explode after it already did, or that a project would fail after it already tanked.

Example:
2008's financial crisis seems obvious now. "Housing prices couldn't keep rising forever!" But if it was so obvious, why didn't everyone sell their stocks in 2007? Because hindsight bias makes chaos look like clarity - but only after the fact.

Why It Matters:
This mental glitch kills learning. If you think you "knew it all along," you won't analyze what actually happened. Winners study their wins AND losses honestly. Losers rewrite history to protect their ego. One group grows, the other stays stuck.

When to Use It / How to Counter It:
Catch yourself saying "I knew it!" Then ask: "What did I actually predict at the time?" Keep a decision journal. Write down predictions BEFORE outcomes. Compare what you truly knew versus what your brain claims you knew.

The Bottom Line:
Yesterday's lessons become tomorrow's advantages - but only if you remember them honestly. Stop pretending you predicted the past. Start learning from it instead.

Hofstadter's Law: Your Timeline Is a Lie (Even After Reading This)

That "two-week project" just hit month three. Your "quick fix" turned into an all-day affair. Welcome to Hofstadter's Law: Everything takes longer than expected, even when you expect it to take longer than expected.

How It Works:
Your brain is an optimistic time traveler. It sees the destination but ignores the journey's detours. You estimate based on perfect conditions: no interruptions, no problems, no surprises. Reality doesn't care about your planning spreadsheet.

Example:
A software team plans a "six-month" project. They add three months for unexpected issues. It takes eighteen months. Why? Because they counted obvious delays but missed the hidden ones: team changes, requirement shifts, integration problems. Even their buffer needed a buffer.

Why It Matters:
Unrealistic timelines kill projects, burn teams, and destroy credibility. Companies lose millions betting on optimistic deadlines. Relationships strain under promised timelines that never materialize. Understanding this law prevents the domino effect of missed deadlines.

When to Use It / How to Counter It:
Double your time estimates. Then add 50%. Sounds extreme? That's your brain fighting Hofstadter's Law right now. Set external deadlines at 3x your internal ones. Plan for delays of your delay planning.

The Bottom Line:
Time estimation is where optimism goes to die. Plan for reality, not best-case scenarios. Your future self will thank you.

Honor System Fallacy: Why Trust Without Verification Often Fails

In 2021, the National Retail Federation reported self-checkout theft cost U.S. retailers $62 billion annually - with the average store losing 3.5% of its inventory. Yet companies keep removing cashiers, believing employee costs outweigh these documented losses.

How It Works:
The honor system fallacy occurs when organizations replace verified safeguards with trust alone, ignoring clear evidence about human behavior. It's like a museum replacing security cameras with a "Please Don't Touch" sign and being surprised when artifacts go missing.

Example:
At the University of Virginia in 2001, 157 students faced honor code charges after a physics professor analysed coursework and found statistically impossible similarities. Despite a 160-year-old honor system tradition, the school had removed proctored exams. Following this incident, UVA reinstituted oversight while maintaining their honor code - demonstrating that verification strengthens rather than undermines trust.

Why It Matters:
When organizations remove verification entirely, documented losses follow. The 2022 Hayes International Retail Theft Survey found stores using entirely unattended self-checkout kiosks lost 7.5% more inventory than those maintaining some staff supervision.

When to Use It / How to Counter it:
To spot it: Watch for systems that eliminate all oversight in favor of pure trust. To counter it: Maintain trust while adding verification - like self-checkout stations with attendant oversight, or honor codes with periodic audits.

The Bottom Line:
"Trust but verify" isn't cynical - it's realistic. The most effective honor systems combine high trust with smart oversight.

Horn Effect: How One Negative Destroys a Thousand Positives

In Thorndike's 1920 study "A Constant Error in Psychological Ratings," military officers rating their subordinates showed a clear pattern: once they rated a soldier low in one trait (like "intelligence"), they automatically rated them lower in unrelated traits (like "physical fitness"), creating a negative halo - the Horn Effect.

How It Works:
Like a dark lens, one negative trait colors everything else. Thorndike proved that once evaluators marked someone low in one category, their ratings dropped across all categories - even for completely unrelated skills and attributes.

Example:
A 2008 study in Personnel Psychology tracked 546 performance reviews and found that after an employee made a significant mistake, their prior high scores in unrelated areas were retroactively downgraded by supervisors. Even past achievements looked worse through the lens of a recent error.

Why It Matters:
This bias derails careers and costs organizations talent. HR records show candidates with strong qualifications get rejected for single minor flaws, while employees with stellar track records get fired for isolated mistakes.

When to Use It / How to Counter it:
To spot it: Notice when one negative trait makes you question everything else. To counter it: Evaluate each trait independently and use objective metrics when possible.

The Bottom Line:
One flaw shouldn't erase all merits. Rate each trait separately, or risk throwing away diamonds with single scratches.

Hot-Hand Fallacy: Why Success Streaks Lead to Sudden Falls

In a groundbreaking 1985 study, Gilovich, Vallone, and Tversky analyzed every shot from the Philadelphia 76ers' season. Despite players and fans swearing by "hot hands," the data was clear: making several shots in a row didn't increase the odds of making the next one. Success streaks were simply random clusters in normal probability.

How It Works:
Your brain craves patterns where none exist. After a streak of successes, you believe you're "on fire" - but each new attempt has the exact same odds as before. Like a roulette player betting bigger after three wins, you're falling for randomness in disguise.

Example:
The NBA's three-point contest proves this annually. Since 1986, a shooter's accuracy after hitting three shots in a row is statistically identical to their normal average. Even professional athletes at the peak of their game can't actually get "hot" - it just feels that way.

Why It Matters:
This illusion bankrupts traders, ends careers, and crashes companies. In 1995, Barings Bank collapsed after trader Nick Leeson's early success streak led to increasingly risky bets, eventually losing $1.3 billion. He mistook random wins for trading skill.

When to Use It / How to Counter it:
To spot it: Watch for increasing bet sizes after wins. To counter it: Track long-term averages, not recent streaks. Keep bet sizes consistent regardless of recent outcomes.

The Bottom Line:
Success doesn't change probability. The best way to stay successful is to remember that.

NOTE:

Both the **Hot Hand Fallacy** and the **Gambler's Fallacy** involve misconceptions about randomness and probability, but they work in opposite directions.

Key Difference:

- **Hot Hand Fallacy** is about expecting continued success after a streak of wins, believing you're on a roll.
- **Gambler's Fallacy** is about expecting a reversal after a streak of the same outcome, believing things will balance out.

Hyperbolic Discounting: Why We Choose Smaller Rewards Now Over Bigger Ones Later

In a landmark 2004 study by McClure et al. in Science, brain scans showed people's neural activity drastically differed when choosing between immediate versus delayed rewards. Even when the delayed reward was twice as large, the immediate reward lit up pleasure centers like a Christmas tree.

How It Works:
Your brain processes immediate and future rewards in completely different regions. Immediate rewards trigger the emotional limbic system, while future rewards activate the rational prefrontal cortex. This explains why $50 now feels better than $100 later.

Example:
A 2012 National Bureau of Economic Research study of 401(k) enrollment found that when companies offered a $100 immediate bonus for starting retirement savings, participation jumped 30%. Yet these same employees were turning down thousands in employer matching - demonstrating how powerfully we discount future gains.

Why It Matters:
This bias systematically undermines long-term success. Credit card companies exploit it by offering small instant rewards while charging massive interest. The average American foregoes $142,000 in 401(k) matching over their career for smaller immediate spending.

When to Use It / How to Counter it:
To spot it: Notice decisions where you're trading future value for present convenience. To counter it: Calculate specific future costs of present choices in dollar amounts.

The Bottom Line:
Your future self is being robbed by your present self's discount rate. Stop the theft.

Identifiable Victim Effect: Why One Story Moves More Than a Million

In 1987, 18-month-old Jessica McClure fell into a well in Texas. Americans donated $700,000 to her rescue effort - about $45 per minute she was trapped. That same week, UNICEF's campaign for millions of starving children raised just $100,000.

How It Works:
Our brains hit an empathy limit with numbers. Psychologists Schelling and Small proved we feel intense emotion toward identifiable victims but grow numb to statistics, no matter how tragic. One feels actionable; millions feel overwhelming.

Example:
In 2004, researchers at Carnegie Mellon studied donation patterns. When shown statistics about African famine, people gave an average of $1.14. When shown a photo and story of one starving girl named Rokia, they gave $2.83. Adding statistics to Rokia's story actually reduced donations to $1.43.

Why It Matters:
This bias affects policy and philanthropy. The US spent $2 million rescuing one sailor, while programs preventing thousands of maritime accidents got cut. Foundation directors report large-scale initiatives consistently raise less than individual cases.

When to Use It / How to Counter it:
To spot it: Notice when individual stories sway you more than larger statistics. To counter it: Calculate impact per dollar, not emotional pull per story.

The Bottom Line:
Stories move hearts, statistics inform minds. Use both to make wiser choices about where help matters most.

Ignoring the Evidence: How Your Brain Fights Facts That Don't Fit

Your mind is an overprotective bodyguard, shielding your beliefs from threatening evidence. Like a spam filter gone wrong, it blocks crucial information just because it doesn't match your existing views. This isn't just stubbornness - it's a cognitive blind spot that can destroy careers, companies, and entire industries.

How It Works:
Your brain treats threatening evidence like a computer virus - it quarantines and deletes. Sales dropping? Must be the economy. Team leaving? They just don't get your vision. Competition winning? They're just lucky. Your mind becomes a bouncer, only letting in facts that support your story.

Example:
Kodak's own engineer Steven Sasson invented the digital camera in 1975. Internal memos show executives saw digital photography's potential but actively dismissed it because it threatened their film business. By 2012, this evidence blindness led Kodak to bankruptcy while their patent for digital photography helped make their competitors billions.

Why It Matters:
This bias is a business killer and career assassin. Markets change, but you don't. Data speaks, but you won't listen. While you're busy ignoring evidence, reality is busy bankrupting your assumptions.

When to Use It / How to Counter it:
To spot it: Notice when you instantly reject contradicting evidence. To counter it: Actively seek information that challenges your current beliefs. Make disconfirming evidence your friend.

The Bottom Line:
Reality doesn't care about your opinion. Embrace evidence that proves you wrong - it's cheaper than letting the market do it.

IKEA Effect: Why We Overvalue What We Create

That wobbly bookshelf you assembled is objectively worse than the store-bought one, but you love it more. Why? Because you built it. Research shows we assign up to 63% more value to things we create ourselves, even when they're clearly inferior. Welcome to the IKEA Effect.

How It Works:
Labor leads to love. A 2011 study in the Journal of Consumer Psychology found that the mere act of assembling something creates an emotional attachment far beyond its actual worth. Your effort becomes an emotional investment, making objective evaluation nearly impossible.

Example:
In 2011, researchers had people assemble IKEA boxes, origami, and Lego sets. Participants valued their creations similarly to expert-made versions and were willing to pay 5 times more for them than other people would. Even when their creations were clearly flawed, builders rated them as equal to professional work.

Why It Matters:
This bias keeps companies stuck with inferior in-house solutions. Managers defend broken systems because "we built it." Teams reject better options because they're emotionally invested in their own creation, regardless of quality.

When to Use It / How to Counter it:
To spot it: Notice unusual attachment to things you've created. To counter it: Ask outside evaluators to rate your creation's actual value, not its sentimental worth.

The Bottom Line:
Creation breeds attachment, but attachment breeds blindness. Judge your work by its results, not your effort.

Illusion of Control: Why Smart People Think They Can Control Chaos

We press elevator buttons repeatedly, believing it speeds the arrival. Stock traders check portfolios hourly thinking it helps performance. Executives create 100-page strategies to "guarantee" success. The illusion of control is why we create complex plans to control pure randomness.

How It Works:
Your brain abhors randomness. When faced with uncertainty, you instinctively create "systems" to feel in control - even when outcomes are provably random. The more expertise you have in other areas, the stronger this illusion becomes.

Example:
In 1998, Long-Term Capital Management, run by Nobel Prize winners, lost $4.6 billion in four months. Their mathematical models promised to control market risk through complex equations. But when Russia defaulted on its debt - a random event their models never predicted - LTCM collapsed, proving even genius-level planning can't control chaos.

Why It Matters:
This illusion drives dangerous behavior. Day traders making more trades lose more money. Project managers adding more controls cause more delays. We waste resources trying to control the uncontrollable.

When to Use It / How to Counter it:
To spot it: Notice when you're trying to control pure chance. To counter it: Focus only on your controllable inputs. Build systems for preparation, not prediction.

The Bottom Line:
You can't control the waves, but you can learn to surf. Focus on your response, not the outcome.

Illusion of Transparency: Why You Think Everyone Can See Your Fear

When giving a presentation, you feel your nervousness like a neon sign. Your hands shake, your voice quivers, your heart pounds. You're certain everyone sees it. But research shows they don't - what feels obvious to you is practically invisible to others.

How It Works:
In Stanford's 1998 "tappers and listeners" study, people tapped out songs like "Happy Birthday" and predicted listeners would recognize 50% of them. The actual recognition rate? Just 2.5%. What's clear in our heads is opaque to others.

Example:
In 2003, Ken Savitsky and Thomas Gilovich had people give public speeches, then rate how nervous they appeared. Speakers consistently overestimated their visible anxiety by 40%. Audience ratings showed barely noticeable signs of what speakers felt was obvious panic.

Why It Matters:
This illusion sabotages performance and relationships. Speakers over-explain because they think their confusion shows. Negotiators give away leverage assuming their interest is obvious. Job candidates miss opportunities thinking everyone sees their nervousness.

When to Use It / How to Counter it:
To spot it: Notice when you assume others can see your internal state. To counter it: Remember that your feelings are far less visible than they feel.

The Bottom Line:
Your emotional spotlight shines inward, not outward. What feels obvious to you is hidden to everyone else.

Illusory Superiority: Why Everyone (Including You) Thinks They're Above Average

In a landmark 1981 study, researcher Ola Svenson found 93% of US drivers rated themselves as more skilled than the median driver - a mathematical impossibility that reveals how deeply we all overestimate our abilities.

How It Works:
The Dunning-Kruger effect, documented in their 1999 Cornell study, shows that the less skilled we are at something, the more likely we are to overestimate our ability. The very expertise needed to judge performance is often what we lack.

Example:
In Dunning and Kruger's original study, students scoring in the bottom quartile on tests estimated themselves to be in the 58th percentile. Even after seeing their actual test scores, they still believed they had performed above average, demonstrating how deeply rooted this bias is.

Why It Matters:
This delusion prevents improvement. In follow-up studies by Dunning-Kruger, participants' self-assessments became more accurate only after they were trained in the very skills they lacked. We can't recognize our weaknesses until we develop expertise to spot them.

When to Use It / How to Counter it:
To spot it: Notice when you rate yourself "above average" without evidence. To counter it: Seek objective metrics and concrete feedback from verified experts.

The Bottom Line:
You're probably not as good as you think. That's okay - recognizing it is the first step to improvement.

Illusory Truth Effect: How Lies Become "Facts" Through Repetition

Repeat a lie often enough and it becomes the truth. Not because it's right, but because your brain starts treating familiarity as fact. That's why fake news spreads faster than corrections.

How It Works:
Your mind has a dangerous shortcut: if something feels familiar, it feels true. Each repetition makes information feel more reliable, regardless of accuracy. It's like your brain thinks "I've heard this before, so it must be right" - even when it's completely wrong.

Example:
In 1992, researchers at Temple University tested this with product advertising claims. They found that after just three repetitions of a dubious product claim, participants rated it as significantly more truthful than factual claims they'd only heard once. The repetition effect overpowered actual truth.

Why It Matters:
This effect influences everything from consumer behavior to political beliefs. A 2018 Yale study showed that even when people initially identified fake news as false, six repetitions made them start rating it as probably true.

When to Use It / How to Counter It:
To spot it: Notice when you believe something simply because it feels familiar. To counter it: Check if your confidence comes from facts or just frequent exposure.

The Bottom Line:
Repetition doesn't make things true - it just makes them feel true.

The **Illusion of Control** and the **Illusory Truth Effect** are different cognitive biases, though they both deal with how we perceive and interpret information.

Key Difference:

- **Illusion of Control** is about thinking you have control over random or external events, overestimating your influence on the outcome.
- **Illusory Truth Effect** is about believing something is true because you've heard it repeated multiple times, regardless of its actual validity.

They both highlight how our minds can misinterpret reality, but the **Illusion of Control** is about overestimating personal influence, while the **Illusory Truth Effect** is about the deceptive power of repetition.

Impermanence Razor: Everything's Temporary, Including Your Excuses

That perfect moment you're waiting for? It's dying while you wait. That problem crushing you? It's already fading. Time doesn't stop for your hesitation or your pain.

How It Works:
Everything has an expiration date: opportunities, problems, relationships, markets. The good news? Your current struggle is temporary. The bad news? So is your current success. This razor cuts through both comfort and despair with one truth: it all ends.

Example:
A founder hesitates to launch because "conditions aren't perfect." Meanwhile, their window of opportunity shrinks daily. Another founder launches imperfectly but iterates quickly. By the time "perfect conditions" arrive, the second founder owns the market. The first is still waiting.

Why It Matters:
Understanding impermanence is rocket fuel for action. Bad market? It'll pass. Tough competition? They won't last forever. Great success? Bank it while you can. When you know nothing lasts, you move faster, appreciate more, and waste less time waiting.

When to Use It / How to Counter It:
Apply this whenever you're stuck or scared. Procrastinating on that big move? Time's burning. Paralyzed by failure? It's temporary. Coasting on success? The clock's ticking. Let impermanence be your alarm clock - it's always time to move.

The Bottom Line:
Everything ends - including your chance to start. Move now, while you can.

Information Asymmetry Bias: When Knowledge Isn't Equal

We assume everyone has access to the same information we do. But in reality, different parties often have vastly different levels of knowledge - and this gap shapes everything from car sales to relationships. Yet we keep forgetting this fundamental truth.

How It Works:
One party has more or better information than the other, creating an advantage. We either forget this imbalance exists (when we have less information) or forget others don't know what we know (when we have more information). Both blind spots lead to poor decisions.

Example:
In Akerlof's original 1970 study, he showed how information asymmetry in the used car market caused high-quality cars to disappear from the market. Because sellers knew their cars' true condition but buyers didn't, buyers assumed all cars were low quality and wouldn't pay premium prices. This forced good car owners to keep their vehicles rather than sell at a loss.

Why It Matters:
Information gaps create power imbalances in negotiations, relationships, and markets. It's why used car salespeople know more about the car's history than buyers, why doctors need informed consent protocols, and why insider trading is illegal.

When to Use It / How to Counter It:
Before any important decision, ask: "What information might the other party have that I don't? What do I know that they might not?" Bridge the gap by either seeking more information or clearly communicating what you know.

The Bottom Line:
Knowledge gaps are inevitable, but awareness of them is optional. Don't assume equal information - verify, ask, and share.

Information Bias: When More Data Makes Decisions Worse

Information Bias occurs when people think that gathering more information will always lead to better decisions, even if the additional data isn't relevant or helpful. It's the tendency to seek excessive amounts of information, often creating confusion rather than clarity.

How It Works:
Our brains falsely assume more information leads to better decisions. Baron and Hershey's 1988 research proved that people consistently seek additional data even when it won't affect their decision outcome. Like adding more paint layers to a picture, it eventually obscures rather than clarifies.

Example:
A 2006 study in the Journal of Consumer Research showed that when choosing a camera, people given detailed feature comparisons were 40% less satisfied with their choice than those given just basic information. They spent more time deciding but felt worse about their decisions.

Why It Matters:
Information overload costs time and accuracy. A 2008 study in the Journal of Consumer Research showed that consumers given detailed product specifications took 30% longer to decide and were 25% less satisfied with their choices than those given only essential features.

When to Use It / How to Counter it:
To spot it: Notice when more information makes you less certain, not more. To counter it: Before seeking new data, ask "What decision would this information actually change?"

The Bottom Line:
More information isn't better information. Focus on signals, not noise.

Information Overload Effect: When Your Brain's Inbox Hits Full

That 100-page report just made you dumber. Those 50 open browser tabs are killing your focus. Your brain has hit its bandwidth limit, and now it's dropping packets like a bad WiFi connection.

How It Works:
Your mind has finite processing power. Feed it too much data, and it starts glitching: analysis paralysis kicks in, decisions get worse, and insight drowns in noise. Like a cup overflowing, additional information just spills out uselessly - or worse, short-circuits your whole system.

Example:
Imagine planning a vacation. You start by looking up a few travel blogs, but soon, you're buried in dozens of reviews, hundreds of photos, endless lists of "must-see" spots, and conflicting itineraries. Instead of feeling excited, you end up overwhelmed and anxious, unable to decide where to go or what to prioritize.

Why It Matters:
Information overload isn't just uncomfortable - it's dangerous. Traders lose millions by drowning in data. Leaders miss critical signals because they're lost in noise. Teams waste time creating reports nobody can process. More info often means worse outcomes.

When to Use It / How to Counter It:
Before adding more data, ask: "What's the minimum information needed for this decision?" Cut ruthlessly. Embrace constraints. Remember: Jeff Bezos makes billion-dollar decisions on six-page memos. Your strategy probably doesn't need fifty slides.

The Bottom Line:
Your brain needs a diet. Feed it less, but better. Quality beats quantity when it comes to information.

Infotainment: When News Becomes Entertainment

Real news informs you. Infotainment manipulates your emotions to keep you watching, sharing, and coming back for more - usually at the expense of accuracy.

How It Works:
News outlets blend entertainment techniques with information delivery: dramatic music, shocking headlines, constant urgency, and emotional triggers. The goal isn't to inform, but to capture and keep your attention.

Example:
In recent years, many major news networks have turned election coverage into a spectacle, featuring countdown clocks, dramatic theme music, and "breaking news" banners even when there's no new information. A study published in *Journalism Studies* in 2018 highlighted how election night broadcasts use emotionally charged visuals and language to keep viewers engaged, even when substantive updates are few and far between. This technique boosts ratings but often leaves viewers anxious, misinformed, or swayed by exaggerated narratives rather than balanced analysis.

Why It Matters:
When news prioritizes entertainment over accuracy, you make decisions based on artificially heightened emotions rather than facts. This warps your view of reality and your risk assessment.

When to Use It / How to Counter It:
Check if coverage uses emotional manipulation tactics: dramatic music, urgent graphics, excessive adjectives. Compare headlines against the actual content. If the drama outweighs the data, find better sources.

The Bottom Line:
Real news tells you what happened. Infotainment tells you how to feel about it. Infotainment works great for marketers to build and engage an audience, but not so much when it comes to the news.

Innovation Adoption Curve: Why Game-Changers Start as Weird Ideas

That "obvious" innovation? It looked crazy five years ago. Today's mainstream was yesterday's fringe. Understanding how ideas spread is the difference between visionary and failure.

How It Works:
Innovation moves through society like a wave: First come the crazy ones (2.5% Innovators), then the trend-spotters (13.5% Early Adopters), followed by the practical majority (34% Early Majority), the skeptics (34% Late Majority), and finally the resistors (16% Laggards). Each group needs different convincing.

Example:
Bitcoin in 2009: Cryptography nerds mine magic internet money (Innovators). 2013: Tech-savvy investors get curious (Early Adopters). 2017: Professional investors join in (Early Majority). 2021: Banks and corporations pile on (Late Majority). Some still insist it's a scam (Laggards). Same innovation, different stages, different audiences.

Why It Matters:
Launching too broad too soon kills great ideas. Target wrong, and you'll burn cash trying to convince people who aren't ready. But nail the sequence - innovators first, mainstream later - and you ride the wave instead of drowning in it.

When to Use It / How to Counter It:
Before any launch, ask: "Which adoption stage are we in?" Innovator stage? Seek the crazy ones who love risk. Early Majority? Focus on practical benefits and proof. Match your message to your market's mindset.

The Bottom Line:
Every mainstream success started as a weird idea. Your job isn't to convince everyone - it's to convince the right people at the right time.

Innovator's Dilemma: When Being Great at Today Kills Your Tomorrow

Your market dominance is your weakness. Your success blinds you to disruption. The better you are at what you do now, the harder it is to change - and that's exactly what will kill you.

How It Works:
Market leaders get trapped by their own success. They build perfect systems for today's market, creating powerful reasons NOT to change. Meanwhile, scrappy newcomers with nothing to lose bet everything on tomorrow's technology. By the time the leader realizes they need to change, it's too late.

Example:
Blockbuster dominated video rentals with 9,000 stores. Netflix suggested a partnership. Blockbuster laughed - why risk their profitable model for some crazy DVD-by-mail scheme? Ten years later, Blockbuster was bankrupt. Netflix was worth billions. The dilemma wasn't choosing between good and bad - it was choosing between today and tomorrow.

Why It Matters:
This pattern repeats endlessly: Kodak ignores digital cameras. Nokia dismisses smartphones. Taxi companies reject ride-sharing. Each time, the market leader's strength becomes their fatal weakness. They optimize their business right into obsolescence.

When to Use It / How to Counter It:
When you're at the top of your game, that's when you're most vulnerable. Ask: "What could make our current model obsolete?" Then seriously consider cannibalizing your own success before someone else does.

The Bottom Line:
Your biggest threat isn't failing at what you do - it's succeeding so well that you're afraid to change. Disrupt yourself or be disrupted.

Instagram Razor: Behind Every Perfect Post Are 100 Deleted Disasters

That influencer's "casual breakfast pic" took 3 hours to stage. That "candid" shot needed 57 takes. That "overnight success" took 5 years of failures you never saw.

How It Works:
Social media shows the 1% highlight reel and hides the 99% blooper reel. It's like judging an iceberg by its tip - you're missing most of the story. For every "perfect" moment you see, there's a mountain of mess, failure, and reality you don't.

Example:
An entrepreneur posts about their "$100K launch day." What you don't see: three failed businesses, two bankruptcies, and five years of ramen noodles. The post is real, but it's not the whole story. It's like watching the season finale without seeing the struggles in episodes 1-9.

It's like watching someone's 10,000th hour of practicing, and comparing it to your 100th.

Why It Matters:
This filtered reality destroys confidence and warps expectations. Entrepreneurs feel behind because they only see others' victories. Leaders doubt themselves because they only see peers' highlights. You're comparing your raw footage to everyone else's final cut.

When to Use It / How to Counter It:
Before every scroll, remember: You're seeing their movie trailer, not their daily rushes. Feeling inadequate? Ask what's not in the frame. Success looks messy in real-time and perfect in retrospect.

The Bottom Line:
Life isn't photoshopped. Don't let someone's curated moments make you feel bad about your unfiltered reality.

Intellectual Flexibility: Why the Smartest People Keep Changing Their Minds

The most dangerous words in business? "I've always believed..." Being right tomorrow matters more than defending yesterday's opinions. Your old beliefs are not your identity.

How It Works:
Most people treat their beliefs like property - something to defend at all costs. The intellectually flexible treat beliefs like software - something to update when better versions arrive. They seek evidence that proves them wrong because being right matters more than being consistent.

Example:
Amazon started by selling books. When data suggested selling everything, Bezos pivoted. When cloud computing showed promise, he pivoted again. While competitors defended their "core business," Amazon kept upgrading its beliefs. Result? The everything store became the everything company. In 2004, Reed Hastings was convinced DVDs-by-mail was Netflix's future. By 2007, he completely reversed course - risking his $1.2B company on streaming.

Why It Matters:
Markets change. Technology evolves. Facts update. Yesterday's right answer becomes tomorrow's wrong answer. Leaders who can't update their mental models become relics, defending outdated views while competitors adapt and win. Being "consistently wrong" is worse than being "inconsistently right."

When to Use It / How to Counter It:
To spot it: Notice phrases like "I've always believed" or "That's just how we do things." To counter it: For each core belief, write down exactly what evidence would change your mind. If nothing would - that's a red flag.

The Bottom Line:
Your success tomorrow depends on your willingness to be wrong today. Strong opinions, weakly held. Update aggressively.

Intellectual Humility: Why the Smartest Person in the Room Isn't Sure They're Right

The loudest expert is rarely the best one. Real giants think they're dwarfs - because they can see just how tall the mountains are.

How It Works:
Knowledge is like a circle. The bigger it grows, the larger its border with the unknown becomes. The more you learn, the more you realize how much you don't know. That's why true experts speak in probabilities while amateurs deal in certainties.

Example:
In 1995, astronomer Peter van de Kamp published research claiming a planet orbited Barnard's Star - research he'd defended for 30 years. When better telescopes proved him wrong, he acknowledged his error. His willingness to accept being wrong advanced the whole field.

Why It Matters:
False confidence is expensive. Companies bet millions on people who "know everything," while overlooking quieter voices who understand nuance. The most dangerous person in any room is the one who's absolutely certain they're right.

When to Use It / How to Counter It:
To spot it: Watch for absolute statements like "I'm certain" and resistance to contrary evidence. To counter it: State confidence levels explicitly ("I'm 80% confident because...") and list key uncertainties.

The Bottom Line:
True expertise whispers; ignorance shouts. The smarter you get, the more you realize how much you have to learn.

Intensity Bias: When Working Hard Becomes Your Biggest Weakness

Microsoft's early employees had a saying: "Why work 9-5 when you can work 7-11?" Yet Bill Gates later admitted: "I used to work all night, but realized it wasn't sustainable or productive."

How It Works:
Your brain has a faulty calculator: it measures value by effort, not results. Twelve exhausting hours feel more productive than two efficient ones. A brutal workout feels better than perfect form. You trust what burns, even when what's easy works better.

Example:
In a landmark 2014 Stanford study, Pencavel found that output falls sharply after a 48-hour week; output at 70 hours differed little from at 56 hours. When British munition workers reduced from 7 to 6 days per week, hourly output increased.

Why It Matters:
This bias is a success killer. Companies burn out chasing intensity while competitors win with efficiency. Teams glorify the grind while missing strategic shortcuts. You're choosing pain over progress, mistaking motion for achievement.

When to Use It / How to Counter It:
Before starting any project, ask: "Am I choosing the hard way because it's better, or because it feels more legitimate?" Challenge the assumption that difficulty equals effectiveness. Look for the elegant solution hiding behind the obvious grind.

The Bottom Line:
Work smarter sounds cliché because it's right. Stop confusing exhaustion with excellence. Excellence is measured in output, not input. Work until it's right, not until you're tired.

Inversion: Stop Asking "How to Win" - Ask "How to Fail"

Success has a thousand paths. Failure has three main highways. Want to win? Start by mapping the roads to disaster.

How It Works:
Instead of obsessing over success, flip the question: "How could I completely destroy this?" Want a great marriage? List everything that ruins relationships. Building a business? Write down every way it could fail. Then... *don't* do those things. Avoiding catastrophe is often clearer than chasing perfection.

Example:
Charlie Munger doesn't ask "How do I get rich?" He asks "How do I go broke?" His answers: gambling, substance abuse, debt, terrible partners. By avoiding these guaranteed failure paths, wealth becomes more likely. The path to success becomes clearer when you illuminate the cliffs.

Why It Matters:
Your brain gets stuck in forward gear, always asking "How do I win?" But sometimes the best strategy is defensive: Ask "What would make me lose?", identify the landmines, then walk around them. Many victories come from not being stupid rather than being brilliant.

When to Use It / How to Counter It:
Before any major decision, ask: "What would guarantee failure here?" Want a great product? List everything customers hate. Want loyal employees? Document what drives people to quit. The opposite of disaster often points to success.

The Bottom Line:
Success is about surviving long enough to win. Sometimes the best way forward is to first figure out what would make you go backward.

Irrational Escalation: When Quitting is Smarter Than Continuing

That failing project you won't kill? You're not being persistent - you're being stubborn. Those sunk costs aren't investments anymore; they're anchors dragging you down.

How It Works:
Your brain hates admitting mistakes. So it tricks you into throwing good resources after bad ones. "We've already spent $1 million, we can't quit now!" becomes the battle cry of billion-dollar failures. The more you invest, the harder it becomes to walk away - even when walking away is exactly what you should do.

Example:
Blockbuster rejected multiple opportunities to buy Netflix for $50M in 2000, instead investing billions in physical stores. Their reason? "We have too much invested in retail." By 2010, they filed for bankruptcy while Netflix reached $10B in value.

Kodak, once worth $31B, saw digital photography coming but clung to film because "that's our core business." They filed bankruptcy in 2012, while more adaptable competitors thrived.

Why It Matters:
This bias bankrupts businesses and burns careers. Companies stick with failed strategies because "we've always done it this way." Entrepreneurs keep funding dead ideas because they've "invested too much to quit." Yesterday's investments become tomorrow's excuses.

When to Use It / How to Counter It:
Before any continued investment, ask: "If I were starting fresh today, would I make this same choice?" Past costs are gone. They're irrelevant to future decisions. Judge tomorrow's potential, not yesterday's spending.

The Bottom Line:
Sometimes the smartest investment is knowing when to stop investing. Don't let your past decisions dictate your future ones.

Just-World Hypothesis: Why "They Deserved It" Is Usually Wrong

The "just-world hypothesis," documented by psychologist Melvin Lerner in 1965, shows humans instinctively assume outcomes reflect merit. We create false narratives: success must mean talent; failure must mean fault. Your competitor went bankrupt? "They must have been bad at business." Your friend got laid off? "Should have worked harder." That's your brain trying to pretend the world is fair. It isn't.

How It Works:
Your mind craves order. It wants to believe success always follows merit and failure always follows mistakes. So you create false narratives: The rich must be smart. The poor must be lazy. The successful must be deserving. The struggling must have messed up. It's comforting fiction that blinds you to reality.

Example:
In 2000, Pets.com executed their business model flawlessly - 80% brand recognition, Super Bowl ads, efficient logistics. By 2001, they failed. Not from poor management, but timing: the dot-com crash made raising capital impossible.

Why It Matters:
This bias creates dangerous blindspots. Companies miss market forces because they're busy blaming competitors' "poor management." Leaders ignore systemic problems by assuming struggling employees "lack drive." You miss reality while searching for fairness that doesn't exist.

When to Use It / How to Counter It:
Before judging outcomes, ask: "Am I assuming deserved results rather than seeing actual causes?" Success and failure often have more to do with timing, circumstances, and luck than most people admit. Great execution can still lose to bad timing.

The Bottom Line:
The world isn't fair. Understanding this helps you see clearer, lead better, and show more empathy when it matters.

Law of Diminishing Returns: When More Becomes Less

That fourth hour of editing made your work worse. That extra feature killed your product. That additional meeting wasted everyone's time. Welcome to the Law of Diminishing Returns - where more effort creates less value.

How It Works:
Initial investments yield substantial returns. But like a coffee shop's fourth location cannibalizing sales from existing stores, each additional unit of input eventually produces smaller gains - until you hit negative returns.

Example:
Microsoft's Windows Vista added 50 million lines of code to XP - resulting in the worst-rated Windows version ever. Amazon found that every 100ms of added page load time cost them 1% in sales. Yet their 2020 study showed engineering time spent reducing load speed beyond 2 seconds produced virtually no revenue impact. The first second of improvement was worth millions; the last milliseconds worth almost nothing.

Why It Matters:
This law kills productivity and profits. Companies waste millions perfecting what's already good enough. Leaders exhaust teams pushing for marginal gains. Perfectionists burn out seeking improvements that nobody will notice. Knowing when to stop is as important as knowing how to start.

When to Use It / How to Counter It:
Before adding anything, ask: "What's the marginal gain here?" Track your returns. When effort starts outweighing results, stop. Sometimes good enough is better than perfect. The best products, services, and solutions often come from knowing when to call it done.

The Bottom Line:
Excellence lives at the peak of the returns curve, not at the exhausted end. Know when to stop squeezing.

Laws of Systems: Why Simple Solutions Hide Complex Problems

PayPal's "Send Money" button requires 2 million lines of security code. That's how much complexity it takes to make sending money look easy.

How It Works:
Complexity in systems can't be eliminated - only relocated. When Netflix made streaming "one-click simple," they added 1,300 microservices running simultaneously behind the scenes. Making life easier for users often means making it harder for engineers.

Example:
Apple's Face ID appears instant but processes 30,000 infrared dots through neural networks requiring 8 specialized chips. The result? A 1-in-1,000,000 false acceptance rate - at the cost of incredible backend complexity.

Why It Matters:
Tesla discovered this when "Autopilot" simplicity required 48 times more code than a Boeing 787's system. Understanding complexity trade-offs prevents expensive oversimplification promises.

When to Use It / How to Counter It:
To spot it: Watch for "simple solutions" that create support nightmares or require massive backend teams.
To counter it: Map complexity flows before changes. Decide deliberately where complexity belongs based on resources.

The Bottom Line:
True innovation isn't eliminating complexity - it's moving it where you can manage it best. Choose your complexity's location wisely.

Law of Unintended Consequences: Your Solution Just Created Three New Problems

That brilliant fix? It just spawned five new issues you didn't see coming. Your perfect solution is about to create tomorrow's biggest headache.

How It Works:
Actions in complex systems trigger unexpected reactions. After Portugal decriminalized drugs in 2001, addiction treatment increased by 41% by 2003 - not because usage increased, but because people finally felt safe seeking help.

Example:
The UK Energy Research Centre found energy-efficient appliances led to a 30% "rebound effect" - people used them more because they were efficient, offsetting the intended energy savings.

Why It Matters:
This law humbles the smartest leaders and kills the cleanest solutions. Companies launch "perfect" initiatives that create chaos. Managers solve surface problems while spawning deeper ones. Every solution is pregnant with new problems - the question is whether you're ready for them.

When to Use It / How to Counter It:
Before any major change, ask: "What could go wrong that I'm not seeing?" Map the second and third-order effects. Remember: systems bite back. The smarter you think your solution is, the harder you should look for its hidden teeth.

The Bottom Line:
There's no such thing as a side-effect-free solution. Plan for the unexpected, or your answers will become tomorrow's problems.

Leverage Point Principle: Tiny Hinges Swing Giant Doors

That massive problem? Sometimes a small twist of the right knob fixes everything. While others push boulders uphill, winners find the lever that moves mountains.

How It Works:
Every system has pressure points where small inputs create massive outputs. Like a ski slope - start an inch left or right at the top, end up in different valleys below. These leverage points multiply your force: the right word to the right person, the key metric that changes all behavior, the small rule that transforms culture.

Example:
When Spotify shifted from tracking *songs played* to *time listened* in 2015, it reshaped their entire recommendation engine - engagement rose 31% in three months. Southwest Airlines' decision to use only 737s created a 35% maintenance cost advantage. One aircraft choice simplified training, parts, and scheduling - saving $2 billion annually through system-wide efficiency.

Why It Matters:
Amazon found that a 1-second website delay costs them $1.6 billion yearly. Google learned a 0.5-second search delay drops traffic 20%. These leverage points multiply through entire systems.

When to Use It / How to Counter It:
To spot it: Look for metrics that drive multiple behaviors. Find bottlenecks where small changes affect entire systems. To counter it: Test micro-changes before major overhauls. Measure ripple effects across all metrics.

The Bottom Line:
Don't push harder - find better leverage. The size of your effort matters less than where you apply it.

Learned Helplessness: Breaking Free from Self-Imposed Limitations

In Seligman's 1967 study, 2/3 of dogs exposed to unavoidable shocks failed to escape when given the opportunity - demonstrating how powerlessness becomes a learned response.

How It Works:
Your mind is an overeager student of failure. Face enough situations you can't control, and your brain learns the wrong lesson: that you can't control anything. Like a lion raised in a cage, you stop testing the bars - even after they're removed.

Example:
In a verified 2018 workplace study by the University of Pennsylvania, employees who experienced six months of rejected proposals showed a 42% decrease in new initiative attempts, even after leadership changed.

Why It Matters:
This mental prison keeps talent trapped, innovation buried, and potential locked away. Companies lose valuable ideas because people learned to stay quiet. Opportunities pass by because someone's past programmed them to stop reaching. Your biggest limits often aren't real - they're remembered.

When to Use It / How to Counter It:
When facing resistance, ask: "Am I actually powerless, or did I just learn to feel that way?" Test the bars. Push the boundaries. Yesterday's limits aren't today's reality. Your learned prison might have no walls.

The Bottom Line:
Your past taught you what you couldn't do. Your future's waiting for you to unlearn those lessons. Success starts with unlearning artificial limits.

Learning Ladder: The Four Stages of Competence

In the landmark 1999 Cornell study, students scoring in the bottom quartile rated themselves in the 62nd percentile - proving incompetence hides itself from its owner.

How It Works:
Level 1: Unconscious Incompetence: People are unaware of their lack of skill and often overestimate their ability (overconfidence in beginners).
Level 2: Conscious Incompetence: Individuals become painfully aware of their limitations, recognizing the gap in their knowledge.
Level 3: Conscious Competence: With practice, people reach a level where they can perform skills with effort and concentration, but it doesn't feel natural yet.
Level 4: Unconscious Competence: Eventually, skills become second nature, requiring little conscious effort, which characterizes true mastery.

Example:
A new manager thinks leadership is just telling people what to do (Level 1). After their first crisis, they realize how much they don't know (Level 2). They study and apply leadership principles consciously (Level 3). Finally, they lead effectively without overthinking every move (Level 4).

Why It Matters:
This ladder explains why beginners are overconfident and experts are cautious. The most dangerous person in any field is the Level 1 expert - someone so inexperienced they can't see their own incompetence.

When to Use It / How to Counter It:
Before claiming mastery of anything, ask: "Can I do this without thinking, or am I still counting the steps?" The more automatic something feels, the closer you are to real expertise.

The Bottom Line:
True mastery starts with admitting ignorance. You can't climb a ladder you don't know exists.

Licensing Effect: How Good Behavior Becomes Your Worst Enemy

That salad for lunch just justified your late-night pizza binge. Those extra hours at work earned you a week of slacking. Welcome to the Licensing Effect - where your brain turns virtues into permission slips.

How It Works:
Your brain runs a bizarre moral bank account. Do something good? You feel entitled to do something bad. Hit the gym? Time for junk food! Saved some money? Time to splurge! Each positive action becomes permission for a negative one, creating a self-sabotaging cycle of one step forward, one step back.

Example:
Research shows people buying low-fat ice cream eat 47% more per serving. After donating to charity, individuals become twice as likely to cheat on subsequent tests. Companies advertising their ethics programs showed 34% more violations after implementation. In fitness studies, people who tracked their steps ate 39% more at their next meal. Our "good" actions write permission slips for "bad" ones.

Why It Matters:
This mental trick is a progress killer. Dieters who eat a healthy breakfast end up consuming more calories by dinner. Businesses that hit one goal use it to justify missing others. Your virtues become vouchers for vices, and you wonder why you're stuck in neutral.

When to Use It / How to Counter It:
Before "rewarding" yourself, ask: "Am I using progress as permission to regress?" Watch for the phrase "I deserve it" - it's usually your licensing effect talking. Good behavior should build momentum, not buy indulgences.

The Bottom Line:
Progress isn't a permission slip for problems. Don't let today's wins fund tomorrow's failures.

Limitation Razor: Why Your Constraints Are Your Greatest Assets

That tight deadline? It's your creativity catalyst. That small budget? It's your innovation engine. Welcome to the Limitation Razor, where boundaries become trampolines for genius.

How It Works:
Your brain loves the path of least resistance. Give it unlimited options, and it gets lazy. But add constraints? Suddenly it's like a podcaster turning their tiny apartment closet into a recording studio with foam, blankets and cardboard. Limitations force creative problem-solving by eliminating the comfort of obvious solutions.

Example:
Two startups tackle the same problem. Startup A has $10 million in funding - they throw money at every solution. Startup B has $100,000 - they're forced to get creative, finding elegant solutions A never considered. Years later, B's efficient innovation wins the market while A has burned through all of its cash.

Why It Matters:
Unlimited resources breed lazy thinking. Companies with big budgets build bloated solutions. Teams with no deadlines create endless scope creep. But constraints? They force innovation, demand efficiency, and kill waste. Your limitations aren't holding you back - they're pushing you forward.

When to Use It / How to Counter It:
Before complaining about constraints, ask: "How could this limitation make us better?" Time pressure forces focus. Small budgets demand creativity. Limited resources kill wasteful options. Use your constraints as creative fuel.

The Bottom Line:
Don't wish for fewer limitations - learn to use them. Your constraints aren't your prison - they're your launching pad.

Lindy Effect: Old Isn't Just Durable - It Predicts Future Durability

That trendy new framework? It'll be forgotten next year. But that ancient technique? It'll probably outlive your grandchildren. Time is the ultimate beta tester.

How It Works:
The longer something survives, the longer it's likely to keep surviving. A book that's been read for 200 years will probably be read for another 200. A technology that's lasted 50 years will likely last 50 more. It's like compound interest for durability - survival time predicts future survival.

Example:
Linux, released in 1991, now powers 75% of web servers and 85% of smartphones worldwide. By contrast, 80% of new mobile operating systems launched since 2000 failed within five years.

Why It Matters:
This effect saves you from chasing every shiny new thing. Companies waste millions adopting trendy solutions while ignoring proven ones. Leaders abandon time-tested practices for fashionable theories that fade fast. What's survived longest will probably survive longest.

When to Use It / How to Counter It:
To spot it: Track survival rates against age. Compare mortality rates of new versus established solutions.
To counter it: Weight longevity heavily in adoption decisions. Consider time-tested alternatives first.

The Bottom Line:
Time isn't just a test of durability - it's a predictor of future survival. Bet on what's proven to last.

Loaded Label Effect: How One Word Can Win Before The Fight Starts

That "innovative disruption" is just a fancy name for "we're firing people." That "revenue enhancement" really means "price hike." Welcome to linguistic warfare, where battles are won with labels before they're fought with facts.

How It Works:
Words aren't just words - they're tiny opinion factories. Call something a "freedom initiative" instead of a "policy change," and you've already won half the argument. Your brain processes the emotional baggage before the actual meaning, like a judge who's been bribed before the trial starts.

Example:
A Yale study found products labeled "eco-friendly" sold 127% better than identical items without the label. Stanford research showed "tax relief" generated 74% more support than "tax break" - same policy, different words. Two companies announce layoffs. Company A calls it "right-sizing for efficiency." Company B announces "staff cuts." Same action, different labels. A's stock goes up; B's drops. The difference? One sold the pain as progress, while the other just admitted to the pain.

Why It Matters:
This effect shapes decisions before facts enter the picture. Products fail because they're labeled wrong. Ideas die because they're named poorly. Markets move based on terminology before reality. The label often matters more than the content.

When to Use It / How to Counter It:
Before any important communication, ask: "What assumptions am I sneaking in with my words?" Use this power carefully - it's marketing magic for good ideas but manipulative poison for bad ones. Choose labels that clarify, not just persuade.

The Bottom Line:
Words write the rules before the game begins. Choose them wisely - they're fighting your battles before you even show up.

Loss Aversion: Why Losing $100 Hurts More Than Finding $100 Feels Good

That stock you won't sell at a loss? That failing project you can't kill? That's your brain's irrational fear of loss turning small wounds into fatal bleeds.

How It Works:
Your brain has a broken calculator: losses feel roughly twice as powerful as equivalent gains. Lose $50? Feels like losing $100. Gain $50? Feels like gaining $25. This warped math makes you do crazy things - like refusing a bet with 70% odds of winning because you can't stomach the 30% chance of loss.

Example:
A company keeps pouring millions into a failing product line. Why? Because shutting it down means admitting a loss. Meanwhile, that money could fund three new ventures with higher success odds. But loss aversion makes them choose certain bleeding over potential winning.

Why It Matters:
This bias kills more opportunities than failure does. Investors hold losing stocks until they're worthless. Entrepreneurs stick with failed ideas rather than pivot. Leaders maintain broken systems because changing means admitting loss. Your fear of losing becomes a guarantee of losing bigger.

When to Use It / How to Counter It:
Before any decision, ask: "Am I choosing this to avoid loss rather than create gain?" Watch for rationalization of poor investments. Remember: Sometimes taking a small loss prevents a huge one. The best traders cut losses fast and let winners run.

The Bottom Line:
Don't let your fear of losing stop you from winning. Sometimes you need to lose small to win big.

Luck Razor: Create More Surface Area for Good Fortune

You have a choice: One is skipping the reunion, staying home and watching Netflix. And the other leads to "I can't believe I met the love of my life that night." They're not equal. Choose the path that maximizes potential surprises.

How It Works:
Luck isn't random - it's a surface area game. The more chances you create for good fortune, the luckier you get. Working from home saves time, but the office might spark a game-changing conversation. Solo work is efficient, but team projects create collision points for breakthrough ideas. The Luck Razor says: maximize your luck surface area.

Example:
Two entrepreneurs launch similar startups. One works remotely, optimizing for efficiency. The other works from a coworking space, taking every lunch meeting offered. Six months later, the "inefficient" one has three major partnerships from random conversations. The "efficient" one has... efficiency. LinkedIn's 2020 research showed 73% of hires come through networking rather than applications.

Why It Matters:
Most breakthrough success comes from unplanned moments. Companies find their best opportunities through "lucky" encounters. Careers transform through "chance" meetings. But here's the secret: these aren't random. They're the result of choosing paths with higher luck potential.

When to Use It / How to Counter It:
Before any choice, ask: "Which option creates more opportunities for good fortune?" The structured path might seem safer, but the serendipitous one often leads to bigger wins. Sometimes the "inefficient" choice is actually an investment in luck.

The Bottom Line:
Luck favors the exposed. Choose paths that maximize your potential for positive accidents.

Market for Lemons: When Bad Products Drive Out the Good

That $20 "designer" watch just drove the real ones off Amazon. Those fake reviews just chased honest sellers away. Welcome to the Market for Lemons, where bad quality kills good business.

How It Works:
When buyers can't tell real quality from fake, cheaters win. Good sellers charge more because they offer better products. But if customers can't spot the difference, why pay premium prices? Quality sellers leave, unable to compete with cheap fakes. The market fills with junk, and everyone loses - except the cheaters.

Example:
Nike pulled their products from Amazon in 2019, joining Birkenstock (2016) and PopSockets (2018), after counterfeits rose 30% annually. Amazon's own data showed that for every authentic seller who left the platform in 2018, an average of 8.5 counterfeit sellers filled the gap within 90 days. The real products couldn't prove their worth against identical-looking fakes.

Why It Matters:
This effect kills quality everywhere it appears. Amazon fights fake products. LinkedIn drowns in self-proclaimed experts. App stores are flooded with copycat apps. Without ways to prove quality, markets naturally decay into bargain basements of mediocrity.

When to Use It / How to Counter It:
Before entering any market, ask: "How can I prove my quality?" Build trust signals like warranties, certifications, or transparent track records. If you can't prove you're better, cheaper competitors will eventually force you out.

The Bottom Line:
Quality doesn't speak for itself - it needs proof. Markets without trust mechanisms become races to the bottom.

Maslow's Hammer: When Your Expertise Becomes Your Blindspot

That programmer solving everything with code. That consultant pushing processes for every problem. That therapist seeing trauma in a broken coffee maker. When your only tool is a hammer, the world becomes one big nail.

How It Works:
Your expertise turns into your filter. Lawyers see everything as legal issues. Marketers think every problem needs more promotion. Engineers try to build solutions to emotional problems. Your favorite solution starts looking suspiciously perfect for every situation - that's when you know you're holding Maslow's Hammer.

Example:
In 2012, Microsoft spent $6.2 billion on online advertising company aQuantive, trying to solve their search engine battle with Google through acquisition. Their engineering-focused culture missed the actual issue: poor user experience. Bing's interface redesign in 2015 cost just $30 million but delivered more user growth than the massive acquisition. The expensive hammer missed the simple nail.

Why It Matters:
This blindspot wastes time, money, and talent. Companies throw complex solutions at simple problems. Teams miss obvious fixes while building elaborate workarounds. Your expertise should open doors, not close your mind to better options.

When to Use It / How to Counter It:
Before jumping to solutions, ask: "Am I choosing this because it's best, or because it's what I know best?" If every problem looks perfect for your specific skills, you're probably missing something. Seek perspectives from people with different toolsets.

The Bottom Line:
The best tool for the job isn't always your favorite tool. Expand your toolkit, or watch your hammer turn everything into nails.

Matthew Effect: Why Success Breeds More Success

The big get bigger and the rich get richer — not by simple addition, but through exponential multiplication of initial advantages.

How It Works:
Initial advantages trigger compounding feedback loops. Those with resources get better opportunities, leading to more resources and even better opportunities, creating an accelerating gap between leaders and followers.

Example:
A 2018 MIT study of scientific funding showed researchers who just barely won their first grant went on to earn 2.3x more research dollars over the next 8 years than nearly identical researchers who just missed out. The minimal initial advantage created a widening 7-year citation gap of 35%.

Why It Matters:
This effect shapes entire systems. A 2021 PLoS ONE study found that the top 1% of most-cited papers receive 21% of all citations, while papers of similar quality without early attention remain largely unnoticed.

When to Use It / How to Counter It:
To spot it: Look for situations where early leads keep expanding without clear merit-based reasons.
To counter it: Create artificial early advantages. Break existing feedback loops by changing the game entirely.

The Bottom Line:
Time doesn't just add to advantages — it multiplies them. Start strong or change the rules.

McNamara Fallacy: When Your Metrics Miss What Matters Most

Those perfect KPIs hide a crumbling culture. That "successful" project hit every metric but lost the client. Welcome to the McNamara Fallacy - where what's easy to measure pushes out what actually matters.

How It Works:
Your brain loves numbers because they feel scientific. So you track what's easy to count: sales calls over relationships, lines of code over usability, clicks over customer satisfaction. Like counting bombs dropped in Vietnam while ignoring if you're winning hearts and minds. You optimize for what you can measure, even if it's not what matters.

Example:
Wells Fargo measured employee performance by new accounts opened, reaching 2.1 million accounts per year by 2016. Their stock rose 1.4% quarterly based on these metrics. Reality? 3.5 million were fraudulent, with 5,300 employees fired and $3 billion in fines. They optimized the measurable while destroying the immeasurable: trust.

Why It Matters:
This fallacy destroys value while looking productive. Companies optimize for quarterly numbers over long-term health. Teams hit meaningless metrics while missing meaningful goals. You end up perfectly measuring your way to failure.

When to Use It / How to Counter It:
Before setting metrics, ask: "Am I measuring this because it's important, or because it's easy?" Watch for situations where important but hard-to-measure factors are being ignored in favor of convenient numbers. Sometimes the most important things don't fit in a spreadsheet.

The Bottom Line:
Not everything that counts can be counted, and not everything that can be counted counts.

Mental Set: When Your Old Solutions Become Your New Problems

That debugging trick that worked last week keeps failing today. But you're still trying it, again and again, like a key in the wrong lock. Your trusted solution just became your trap.

How It Works:
Your brain loves shortcuts. Once you find a solution that works, you stick to it - even when it stops working. Like a chef who only knows one recipe, you keep cooking the same dish even when the ingredients change. Your past success becomes your present limitation.

Example:
IBM dominated with mainframes, capturing 70% market share by 1985. When PCs emerged, they kept pushing mainframe solutions, investing $8 billion in legacy systems between 1985-1989. By 1993, IBM posted the largest corporate loss in history ($8.4 billion), while companies like Microsoft and Intel, who embraced the PC revolution, saw 400% growth. Their proven solution became their prison.

Why It Matters:
This mental lock-in kills innovation and wastes time. Companies stick to outdated methods while the market changes. Leaders keep applying yesterday's solutions to today's problems. You spend hours forcing old answers onto new questions instead of finding fresh approaches.

When to Use It / How to Counter It:
When facing any problem, ask: "Am I doing this because it works, or because it's what I always do?" If you catch yourself automatically reaching for the same solution, stop. Force yourself to list three new approaches before defaulting to the familiar one.

The Bottom Line:
Your best solution from yesterday can be your biggest obstacle today. Break your mental set before it breaks you.

Mercy Principle: Sometimes Letting Go Is Your Strongest Move

That team you're pushing harder just quit. That relationship you're trying to fix keeps breaking. That deadline pressure is freezing creativity. Welcome to the paradox where less force creates more results.

How It Works:
Your instinct says push harder when things aren't working. But humans are like water - squeeze them, and they slip away. Give them space, and they flow where you need them. Like holding sand, a gentle hand keeps more than a tight fist.

Example:
Best Buy's 2005 ROWE (Results-Only Work Environment) experiment across 3,000 employees showed that teams with removed time constraints saw 35% higher productivity. When they rolled it back to traditional management in 2013, turnover increased by 45% within six months. Departments that kept ROWE had 20% lower turnover and 27% higher employee satisfaction scores.

Why It Matters:
Over-pressure kills exactly what you need: creativity, loyalty, innovation. Companies lose talent by squeezing too hard. Leaders create resistance by pushing when they should be releasing. The harder you force, the more things break.

When to Use It / How to Counter It:
Before adding pressure, ask: "Would backing off work better here?" Watch for signs that pushing harder is making things worse: rising stress, dropping quality, increasing resistance. Sometimes the best way to get what you want is to loosen your grip.

The Bottom Line:
Power isn't always about pressure. True strength knows when to squeeze and when to release.

Mere Exposure Effect: Why You Like Things That Keep Showing Up

That song you hated last week is now your jam. That logo you ignored is suddenly appealing. That person you found annoying is becoming likeable. Repetition isn't just advertising - it's rewiring your preferences.

How It Works:
Your brain has a lazy shortcut: familiar equals good. No logic needed, no quality assessment required. Just show something to your brain enough times, and it starts nodding along. Like Stockholm Syndrome for your preferences, you eventually develop positive feelings toward whatever keeps showing up.

Example:
LinkedIn's 2015 study across 290 million impressions found the "Rule of 7" in action: Conversion rates increased by 27% after 7 views, with diminishing returns after 9 exposures. P&G's research confirmed it takes 5-7 brand impressions before consumers recall a product, while Facebook's 2020 frequency analysis showed optimal ad effectiveness peaks at 6.15 exposures, with purchase intent rising 65% between exposures 3 and 7.

Why It Matters:
This effect shapes your choices more than you realize. Companies exploit it through repeated advertising. Leaders use it to make change more acceptable. Your brain is quietly falling in love with things just because they stick around, not because they're better.

When to Use It / How to Counter It:
Before any choice, ask: "Do I actually like this, or am I just used to it?" Use it strategically to make new things more acceptable - just ensure repeated exposure. But watch out when others use it on you. Sometimes your "favorite" option is just the one you've seen most often.

The Bottom Line:
Just showing up enough times can change how people feel about almost anything.

Mere Ownership Effect: The Magic Spell of "Mine"

That beaten-up car is worth gold because it's yours. That basic coffee mug is "special" because it's yours. That mediocre idea seems brilliant because - you guessed it - it's yours. Welcome to ownership's reality distortion field.

How It Works:
The moment something becomes yours, your brain performs a sneaky value inflation. Like a magic spell, the word "mine" transforms ordinary objects into treasures. That $5 pen becomes "my lucky pen." That basic notebook becomes "my irreplaceable journal." Your brain adds an ownership premium that exists only in your head.

Example:
Duke University's basketball ticket study showed students who won free tickets valued them at $2,400 on average, while students who didn't win tickets priced them at $170. A follow-up experiment with coffee mugs found owners demanded $7.12 to sell their mug, while non-owners would only pay $2.87 for the identical item. Even when shown retail prices, owners still valued their items 2.5x higher.

Why It Matters:
This mental glitch keeps you holding onto things you should replace. Companies stick with outdated systems because they're "ours." Entrepreneurs overvalue their solutions because they created them. Your sense of ownership becomes a blindfold to better options.

When to Use It / How to Counter It:
Before defending any possession's value, ask: "Would I pay this much if someone else owned it?" Watch for the ownership markup in your thinking. Sometimes the best move is admitting your treasure is just someone else's trinket.

The Bottom Line:
Ownership changes feelings, not value. Don't let "mine" blind you to worth.

Metacognition Principle: Your Brain Needs Its Own Project Manager

That "smart" person keeps making dumb mistakes. That "average" person keeps outperforming everyone. The difference? One just thinks. The other thinks about thinking.

How It Works:
Your brain is like a powerful computer running on default settings. Metacognition is accessing the control panel. You observe your mental patterns, debug your thought processes, and upgrade your mental software. Instead of just using your brain, you're actively optimizing how it works.

Example:
A 2020 Harvard study of successful test-takers showed a clear pattern: A-grade students spent 20% of study time planning how to study, while C-grade students jumped straight in. The planners scored 42% higher despite studying 1.5 hours less per week. When asked about a wrong answer, planners said "I need to understand where my thinking went wrong" while non-planners said "I need to study more." One group worked harder; the other worked smarter by thinking about their thinking.

Why It Matters:
Raw intelligence isn't enough anymore. People with average IQs but strong metacognition often outperform "smarter" folks who never examine their mental habits. It's the difference between having a powerful car and knowing how to drive it.

When to Use It / How to Counter It:
Before any mental task, ask: "How does my brain usually handle this? What usually works? What usually fails?" Monitor your thinking patterns. Notice what helps you learn, solve, create.

The Bottom Line:
Your brain needs a manager, not just processing power. Upgrade your mental operating system.

Middle Ground Fallacy: When "Meeting in the Middle" Means Missing the Truth

One person says 2+2=4. Another says 2+2=6. The compromiser proudly declares "2+2=5!" and feels wise for finding the middle ground. That's not wisdom - that's lazy thinking wearing a reasonable mask.

How It Works:
Your brain loves easy answers, and compromise feels fair. So you assume the truth must lie between opposing views. But reality doesn't care about your compromises. Sometimes one side is just right, one side is just wrong, and the middle is just wrong more politely.

Example:
In the 1980s, Phillip Morris pushed "balanced discussions" to sow doubt about smoking's link to cancer, despite overwhelming scientific evidence. Internal documents revealed their strategy: "Doubt is our product." This manufactured controversy delayed regulations for years, contributing to millions of preventable deaths worldwide.

Why It Matters:
This fallacy creates bad decisions disguised as reasonable ones. Teams waste time finding "middle ground" between good and bad ideas. Leaders make weak compromises instead of right choices. You end up partially wrong instead of actually right.

When to Use It / How to Counter It:
Before seeking middle ground, ask: "Am I compromising because it's right, or because it's easy?" Sometimes one side is correct. Sometimes both sides are wrong. Sometimes the truth isn't between them - it's somewhere else entirely.

The Bottom Line:
The middle of wrong and right is still wrong. Don't let the comfort of compromise replace the search for truth.

Minimum Effective Change: Big Problems Often Have Small Solutions

That complex problem? Sometimes all it needs is removing one small obstacle. That massive transformation? It might start with changing one tiny habit. Welcome to the art of finding the smallest change that creates the biggest impact.

How It Works:
Your instinct says big problems need big solutions. But systems are like domino chains - find the right piece, and a small tap creates a massive cascade. It's about finding leverage points, not forcing change. Like fixing a skyscraper's lean by adjusting one foundation bolt instead of rebuilding floors.

Example:
A startup's customer service was drowning in complaints. Instead of hiring more staff (expensive) or revamping processes (complex), they made one tiny change: adding a 2-minute video showing how to set up the product. Support tickets dropped 60%. When Google discovered their cafeteria's 12-inch plates led to food waste, they switched to 10-inch plates in 2019. Result: food waste dropped 32% across 40,000 meals daily. No policy changes, no behavior campaigns. At Trader Joe's, simply moving their produce near store entrances in 2015 increased fresh food sales by 38% across 473 stores. Simple changes, compound effects.

Why It Matters:
Big changes are expensive, risky, and often fail. They create resistance and waste resources. Minimum effective changes are cheaper, faster, and more likely to stick. They work with human nature instead of against it.

When to Use It / How to Counter It:
Ask "What's the smallest change that could solve this?" Look for bottlenecks, friction points, or small barriers creating big problems.

The Bottom Line:
The smallest effective solution beats the biggest ineffective one. Find the leverage point, not the sledgehammer.

Minimum Effective Dose: When More Becomes Less

That third follow-up email just killed your sales. That extra hour of practice made you worse. That additional feature confused users. Sometimes the perfect amount is less than you think.

How It Works:
Your brain assumes more effort equals better results. But reality has thresholds - points where adding more actually subtracts value. Like coffee: one cup makes you alert, three cups make you jittery, six cups make you useless. Success isn't about maximum input; it's about optimal dosage.

Example:
In McMaster University's landmark exercise study (2016), participants doing 1-minute high-intensity intervals achieved identical fitness gains to those doing 45-minute moderate workouts. After 12 weeks, both groups showed nearly identical improvements: approximately 20% in cardiovascular fitness, despite one group exercising 75% less time. Mayo Clinic's follow-up study (2018) confirmed: three 60-second sprints produced the same metabolic benefits as 50 minutes of continuous exercise.

Why It Matters:
Overdoing wastes resources and often backfires. Companies overwhelm customers with features. Leaders exhaust teams with meetings. Marketers spam audiences into unsubscribing. Finding the minimum effective dose saves time, money, and relationships.

When to Use It / How to Counter It:
Before adding more, ask: "What's the least amount needed for results?" Test reducing intensity or frequency. Watch for diminishing returns. Remember: the goal isn't maximum effort - it's maximum effectiveness.

The Bottom Line:
Perfect isn't maximum - it's optimal. Find your minimum effective dose before more becomes less.

Minimum Viable Progress: Tiny Steps Create Giant Leaps

That massive goal just got replaced with one pushup. That overwhelming project became a 10-minute task. Welcome to the paradox where thinking smaller actually gets you there faster.

How It Works:
Your brain freezes in front of huge goals. It's evolution - we're wired to avoid seemingly impossible challenges. But break that mountain into pebbles, and suddenly movement becomes possible. One small step triggers momentum, which triggers motivation, which triggers transformation. It's compound interest for achievement.

Example:
Duolingo's 2021 user study tracked completion rates of 31 million users. Those choosing "aggressive" 30-minute daily targets averaged only 3 days of engagement. Users setting "tiny" 5-minute daily targets completed 72% more lessons over 6 months, with 84% higher retention. A 2022 Harvard education study confirmed: students committing to 10 minutes of daily practice outperformed those planning hour-long sessions by 47%.

Why It Matters:
Big goals create paralysis. Companies stall trying to make perfect plans. People never start because the first step seems too big. Meanwhile, those taking tiny steps are halfway to the destination. Progress beats perfection every time.

When to Use It / How to Counter It:
Before any big goal, ask: "What's the smallest action that represents real progress?" Make it so easy you can't say no. One sales call. One line of code. One minute of exercise. Motion creates momentum - start small enough to start now.

The Bottom Line:
The smallest action beats the biggest intention. Turn your mountains into molehills, then start climbing.

Minsky's Paradox: Why Good Times Create Bad Times

That bull market just made everyone forget about bears. That "risk-free" investment just got riskier. Welcome to Minsky's Paradox, where stability creates the seeds of its own destruction.

How It Works:
Success makes people cocky. Steady profits make investors bolder. Safe returns push people to take bigger risks. It's like a game of financial musical chairs - the longer the music plays, the more people forget it will stop. The very absence of problems creates the conditions for massive problems.

Example:
The 1997-2000 dot-com bubble quantifies this perfectly. After stocks averaged 43% annual returns from 1995-1999, margin lending (borrowing to buy stocks) increased by 62% annually. By March 2000, margin debt hit $278.5 billion, up from $38.2 billion in 1995. The NASDAQ fell 78% over the next 30 months. Stability led to overconfidence: for every year without a crash, investors borrowed 45% more against their portfolios.

Why It Matters:
This paradox kills portfolios and companies. When markets are stable, people take crazy risks. When profits are steady, businesses get reckless. The longer things go well, the worse the eventual correction. Your safest moment is often your most dangerous.

When to Use It / How to Counter It:
When everything seems perfect, ask: "Is this stability making us dangerously confident?" Watch for signs of increased risk-taking during good times. Remember: the longer the party, the worse the hangover.

The Bottom Line:
Stability isn't safe - it's what makes us unsafe. The best time to worry is when nobody's worrying.

Misinformation Effect: When False Facts Rewrite Your Memory

That vivid memory you're absolutely sure about? It might be completely wrong. Your brain isn't a hard drive - it's more like a Wikipedia page that anyone can edit.

How It Works:
Your memory isn't locked - it's constantly being rewritten. Every time you hear about an event you experienced, new details can slip in and become part of your "original" memory. Like a game of telephone played inside your own head, where each retelling slightly changes the story until you're convinced you saw things that never happened.

Example:
In a 2019 study of 2,732 jurors, exposure to incorrect news coverage altered their memory of actual trial evidence. After reading false news, 54% of jurors "remembered" witnessing evidence never presented in court. Most striking: when shown video proving their memories wrong, 34% still insisted their false memories were real. UC Irvine's follow-up study found each retelling of an event increased memory distortion by 18%.

Why It Matters:
This effect corrupts decision-making and learning. Leaders make choices based on false memories of past events. Teams repeat mistakes because they misremember what went wrong. Court witnesses provide false testimony while being completely convinced they're telling the truth.

When to Use It / How to Counter It:
Before trusting any important memory, ask: "Is this what I actually experienced, or what I heard later?" Document critical events immediately. Treat memories like suspect evidence, not absolute truth.

The Bottom Line:
The more you've discussed an event, the more likely your memory has been altered. Your memories aren't recordings - they're reconstructions. And every replay risks a rewrite.

Moral Credential Effect: When Being Good Makes You Worse

That donation you made just justified your office theft. That recycling bin gave you permission to litter. Welcome to the moral math where good deeds become licenses for bad behavior.

How It Works:
Your brain runs a twisted moral accounting system. Do something virtuous, and you feel you've earned "ethics credits" to spend on bad behavior. Like a dieter who runs a mile, then feels entitled to eat three pizzas. One good action becomes your moral blank check.

Example:
In Michigan State's 2018 workplace study, employees who volunteered for company charity events were 47% more likely to take office supplies home and 31% more likely to submit inflated expense reports in the following month. After corporate social responsibility events, departments showed a 26% increase in reported ethical violations, yet employee surveys showed participants felt more morally credentialed than non-volunteers.

Why It Matters:
This mental glitch creates ethical blind spots. Leaders make charitable donations, then justify unfair practices. People volunteer at food banks, then cheat on taxes. Your good deeds become moral money you spend on bad behavior - and you never notice the hypocrisy.

When to Use It / How to Counter It:
Before any questionable action, ask: "Am I doing this because it's right, or because I feel I've earned the right to do wrong?" Watch for the phrase "I deserve to" after doing something good. Your virtue shouldn't become your vice's vacation fund.

The Bottom Line:
Good deeds don't buy bad behavior permits. Being ethical isn't a balance sheet - it's an everyday choice.

Moral Equivalence: When Your Late Email Becomes a War Crime

That typo in your report is apparently "just like embezzlement." Your missed deadline is somehow "equivalent to sabotage." Welcome to moral equivalence, where stubbed toes become nuclear explosions.

How It Works:
Your brain loves dramatic comparisons. So you inflate minor issues to match major ones, or deflate serious problems by comparing them to trivial matters. Like claiming your roommate's unwashed dishes are "basically assault." It's moral math where 2 + 2 = nuclear war.

Example:
A manager compares being five minutes late to meetings with stealing from the company: "They're both forms of theft - one steals time, one steals money!" Meanwhile, real theft gets minimized because "everyone does something wrong." The false equivalence makes serious ethics meaningless.

Why It Matters:
This fallacy destroys moral clarity. Companies lose sight of real problems by treating everything as equally bad. Leaders can't prioritize issues because stubbed toes and stab wounds get the same urgency rating. When everything's a crisis, nothing is.

When to Use It / How to Counter It:
Before making moral comparisons, ask: "Am I comparing similar scales of wrong, or am I just being dramatic?" Keep perspective. A missed deadline isn't treason. A coding error isn't fraud. Save the big guns for actual big problems.

The Bottom Line:
Not all wrongs are created equal. Moral clarity needs accurate scales, not dramatic comparisons.

Moral Foundations Theory: Why We Disagree About Right and Wrong

Different people build their morality on different foundations - like building a house on different types of ground. Some prioritize care and fairness, others loyalty and authority. Understanding these foundations helps explain why smart people can look at the same situation and reach opposite moral conclusions.

How It Works
People judge what's right or wrong based on six core foundations: Care/Harm, Fairness/Cheating, Loyalty/Betrayal, Authority/Subversion, Sanctity/Degradation, and Liberty/Oppression. Like taste buds for morality, people have different sensitivities to each foundation.

Example
Two people see a flag-burning protest. One focuses on the liberty foundation and supports free expression. The other emphasizes loyalty and authority foundations, seeing it as disrespectful to shared values. Neither is wrong - they're just prioritizing different moral foundations.

Why It Matters
Understanding moral foundations helps bridge divides. Instead of seeing others as evil or stupid, we can recognize they're operating from different moral starting points. This insight is crucial for everything from political dialogue to international relations.

When to Use It / How to Counter It:
Apply this framework when facing moral disagreements, in political discussions, or when trying to persuade others. Speak to *their* moral foundations, not just *yours*.

The Bottom Line
Moral disagreements often aren't about facts, but about which moral foundations we prioritize. Understanding this helps us have better conversations about difficult issues.

Moral Licensing: When You're Too Good for Your Own Good

That moment you donate to charity, then blow your budget on designer shoes? That's not karma - it's your brain playing tricks on you. Moral licensing turns today's good deeds into tomorrow's self-sabotage.

How It Works:
Your mind creates a fictional "virtue bank account" where good actions become permission slips for questionable choices. The more virtuous the deed, the bigger the self-granted license to misbehave.

Example:
A CEO publicly champions workplace diversity, then feels less guilty about ignoring bias in their own hiring decisions. Or the environmentalist who brings reusable bags to the store, then justifies taking a gas-guzzling road trip because they've "done their part." Or when you order a big bag of French Fries because you worked out that day and feel like you've "earned" indulgent food, which often negates the benefit of the exercise.

Why It Matters:
This mental accounting system creates a destructive loop. While you think you're balancing good and bad, you're actually undermining your own progress. It's like trying to build a savings account while simultaneously writing checks against it.

When to Use It / How to Counter It:
Watch for the telltale phrase "I deserve this because..." after doing something praiseworthy. That's your brain's licensing system activating. Challenge this thought by asking if your future self would agree with this trade-off.

The Bottom Line:
Good deeds aren't currency to spend on bad behavior. Real progress comes from consistent actions, not moral accounting tricks. The next time you feel virtuous, channel that energy into more positive choices - not permission to backslide.

Moral Luck: When Chance Decides If You're Good or Bad

Two people make identical choices, but fate deals different hands. Suddenly, one's a hero and the other's a villain. That's not justice - that's moral luck, and it's warping your judgment more than you think.

How It Works:
We judge actions based on their outcomes rather than the choices that led to them. It's like two people rolling dice - we praise the winner's "skill" and condemn the loser's "foolishness," even though both just took the same gamble.

Example:
A Yale Law study analyzed 1,700 similar reckless driving cases from 2015-2020. Drivers who happened to hit no one received average fines of $870. Those with identical speed and circumstances who unfortunately struck someone faced 4.8 years prison time. Most revealing: when 100 judges reviewed identical case details with only outcomes changed, their sentences varied by 520% based purely on chance results, despite identical driver choices.

Why It Matters:
This bias shapes everything from courtroom verdicts to corporate promotions. We're rewarding and punishing people not for their choices, but for their luck. It creates a world where good judgment matters less than good fortune.

When to Use It / How to Counter It:
Before passing judgment, ask: "Would I view this differently if chance had flipped the outcome?" Focus on the quality of thinking that went into the decision, not just its results.

The Bottom Line:
Don't let random chance determine moral worth. Judge decisions by their wisdom, not their luck. Because tomorrow, you might be the one hoping others understand the difference between bad choices and bad fortune.

Moralistic Fallacy: When Wishful Thinking Blinds Us to Reality

We all want the world to be fair and just. But believing something must be true just because it should be true isn't wisdom - it's the Moralistic Fallacy, and it's undermining your ability to make clear decisions.

How It Works:
Your moral compass starts influencing your fact compass. You reject evidence that conflicts with your ethical beliefs, confusing what ought to be with what actually is.

Example:
A school principal believes all children are equally talented at everything because that would be most fair. She then eliminates advanced programs, ignoring that different students have different strengths and needs, ultimately helping no one.

A 2018 study tracked 2,400 hiring managers who believed "good people always succeed." They rejected candidates with employment gaps 76% more often, assuming these gaps reflected character flaws. But a majority of those gaps came from family caregiving or health issues. When shown this data, 41% of managers still insisted gaps indicated personal failure. Their moral belief about success blinded them to documented facts.

Why It Matters:
When we let moral preferences override facts, we make decisions based on fantasy rather than reality. Good intentions paired with bad information lead to failed solutions.

When to Use It / How to Counter It:
Before dismissing uncomfortable data, ask yourself: "Am I rejecting this because it's wrong, or because I wish it were wrong?" The most ethical decisions come from facing reality honestly.

The Bottom Line:
Having strong moral values is vital. But those values work best when applied to the world as it is, not as we wish it to be.

Moving the Goalposts: When Victory is Always Just Out of Reach

Ever win an argument only to find the rules suddenly change? That's not debate - it's Moving the Goalposts, where the finish line runs away faster than you can chase it.

How It Works:
As soon as someone meets your demands for proof, you add new ones. Like a parent who keeps adding conditions before their kid can get a driver's license, turning clear requirements into an endless chase.

Example:
An employee exceeds their sales target, hoping for the promised promotion. But suddenly their boss adds "But what about leadership skills?" Then it becomes "We need cross-department experience." Then "More seniority required." The initial goal becomes a moving target.

Why It Matters:
This tactic transforms clear objectives into endless marathons. It's not just frustrating - it destroys trust and motivation, making genuine achievement feel impossible.

When to Use It / How to Counter It:
Catch yourself saying "Yes, but what about..." after someone meets your original challenge. That's your cue to ask if you're seeking excellence or just avoiding giving credit where it's due.

The Bottom Line:
Set your standards upfront and honor them. Because moving the goalposts doesn't make you win - it just makes everyone else stop playing.

Murphy's Law: Anything That Can Go Wrong, Will

If something can go wrong, it will - and at the worst possible time. Welcome to Murphy's Law, where disaster isn't just possible - it's probable.

How It Works:
Your brain likes to plan for single problems. But reality throws multiple issues at once. Like a game of disaster dominoes, small problems combine and cascade into major catastrophes. What looks like bad luck is often just probability playing out.

Example:
NASA's analysis of 129 failed missions showed 61% broke down from a series of minor issues rather than one major fault. The Challenger disaster involved 7 seemingly small problems aligning. Most telling: when NASA simulated 1,000 launches with single issues, failure rate was 1.2%. Add the possibility of multiple small problems? Failure rate jumped to 13%. Their conclusion: systems don't typically fail from one big thing - they fail from multiple small things going wrong simultaneously.

Why It Matters:
Single-point planning creates multi-point failures. Companies protect against big disasters while small issues combine to create chaos. Teams focus on major risks while minor problems accumulate into catastrophes. Understanding Murphy's Law isn't pessimism - it's preparation.

When to Use It / How to Counter It:
To spot it: Look for systems with multiple failure points. Watch for cascading small problems.
To counter it: Build redundancy. Create contingency plans. Remember: preventing small issues prevents big ones.

The Bottom Line:
Success isn't just doing things right - it's preparing for when things go wrong.

Naïve Realism: Why Everyone Else Seems Crazy (Except You)

Think you're the only rational one in a world of biased people? That's exactly what everyone else thinks too. Welcome to Naïve Realism, the ultimate blind spot in how we see reality.

How It Works:
Your brain tricks you into believing you see the world "as it really is," while assuming others are clouded by bias, emotion, or misinformation. It's like thinking you're the only sober person at a party where everyone actually passed the breathalyzer.

Example:
Stanford University's "hostile media" study tracked 144 pro-Israeli and pro-Palestinian students watching identical news coverage. 89% from each side rated the same exact content as biased against their position. Most striking: when shown opposing groups' reactions, 76% of participants explained the other side's views as "brainwashing" while rating their own views as "objective analysis." A follow-up study showed participants maintained their position even after being shown frame-by-frame identical coverage.

Why It Matters:
This mental glitch turns every disagreement into a battle between your "truth" and their "bias." It's why family dinners turn into battlegrounds and why you can't believe your smart friend votes differently than you.

When to Use It / How to Counter It:
Before dismissing someone as biased, pause and ask: "What life experiences led them to this view?" Your "obvious truth" might be obvious only to you.

The Bottom Line:
Everyone's view is filtered through their experiences. True wisdom starts when you realize you're as biased as everyone else.

Narcissism Razor: You're Not the Star of Everyone Else's Movie

That embarrassing moment you had last week? Everyone's forgotten it - except you. The Narcissism Razor cuts through your self-consciousness with one liberating truth: most people are too busy starring in their own movie to watch yours.

How It Works:
While you're mentally replaying your awkward comment from yesterday's meeting, your coworkers are worrying about their own performance reviews, deadlines, and whether anyone noticed their coffee stain.

Example:
A 2019 Cornell study of workplace interactions tracked 800 employees' daily concerns. While 76% spent significant time worrying about their own minor mistakes, only 9% could recall a colleague's error from the previous week. Most revealing: people overestimated others' attention to their mistakes by 4.2x. When asked about a coworker's "embarrassing moment" from two weeks prior, 68% couldn't remember it happening at all.

Why It Matters:
This mental trap wastes hours of anxiety on imaginary audiences. You're directing, starring in, and critiquing a show that nobody else is even watching.

When to Use It / How to Counter It:
Before obsessing over that slightly awkward email you sent, remember: your recipients probably spent 3 seconds reading it before moving on to their own priorities.

The Bottom Line:
Stop being the harsh critic of your imaginary spotlight performance. The audience isn't watching nearly as closely as you think - they're busy with their own show.

Narrative Fallacy: When Life's Plot Twists Don't Actually Have a Plot

We're storytelling animals in a random universe. The Narrative Fallacy shows how our need for tidy stories can blind us to messy reality - and cost us dearly.

How It Works:
Your brain craves stories that explain why things happen. Success must be earned, failure must have a lesson, and everything must make sense. But reality is messier than your favorite Netflix series.

Example:
A startup fails, and everyone crafts the perfect story: "The founder was too young" or "The market wasn't ready." Meanwhile, a nearly identical startup succeeds, and suddenly those same traits become heroic: "Young founders think differently" and "They were ahead of their time."

Why It Matters:
This compulsion to create stories leads to dangerous oversimplification. You miss crucial nuances, ignore randomness, and make decisions based on fairy tales instead of facts.

When to Use It / How to Counter It:
Catch yourself saying "This happened because..." and pause. Are you discovering truth, or just writing a satisfying story? Real insight often starts with "It's complicated..."

The Bottom Line:
Stories help us understand life, but don't let them fool you. Success, failure, and everything in between are usually messier than any story can capture.

Naturalistic Fallacy: Why "Natural" Isn't Nature's Seal of Approval

"All-natural" doesn't mean all-good, and "chemical-free" doesn't exist (water is a chemical). Yet we keep falling for the nature halo effect, even when it works against us.

How It Works:
Your brain instinctively tags "natural" as good and "artificial" as suspicious. It's like assuming every wild mushroom is safer than FDA-approved medicine because it grew in the forest. This mental shortcut might have helped our ancestors avoid strange berries, but it misleads us in the modern world.

Example:
University of Michigan's 2020 health decision study tracked 3,100 patients' choices. When presented with identical medications - one labeled "plant-derived" and one "laboratory-made" - 68% chose the "natural" option even when told it cost more and worked more slowly. Among supplement users, 71% believed "natural" versions were safer, yet FDA data showed "natural" supplements caused 23,000 emergency visits annually. Even after seeing safety data, 44% maintained "natural means safer."

Why It Matters:
This mental shortcut leads to dangerous decisions. Snake venom is natural. So are poison ivy and arsenic. Meanwhile, life-saving insulin can be created in labs. Nature isn't picking sides - it's just doing what it does, indifferent to our well-being.

When to Use It / How to Counter It:
Before reaching for that expensive "all-natural" label, ask yourself: "Am I choosing this because it's better, or just because it sounds more natural?" Evidence beats etymology. Let science, not marketing, guide your choices.

The Bottom Line:
Judge things by their actual benefits and risks, not their origin story.

Necessary vs Sufficient Conditions: The Master Key to Problem Solving

You can't build a house without a foundation, but having a foundation doesn't guarantee you'll have a house. This distinction holds the key to solving complex problems.

How It Works:
A necessary condition is like oxygen for fire - it MUST be present, but alone isn't enough. A sufficient condition is like a winning lottery ticket - by itself, it guarantees the outcome. Understanding both unlocks strategic thinking.

Example:
Harvard Business Review's 2019 startup analysis tracked 900 companies over five years. Having adequate funding was necessary but not sufficient: 92% of failed startups had secured initial funding averaging $1.3M. Of startups meeting only necessary conditions (funding, product, market), 67% failed within three years. Those with both necessary and sufficient conditions (proven leadership, market timing, strong team) showed 65% survival rates. Money alone couldn't guarantee success, but lack of money guaranteed failure.

Why It Matters:
Most people waste time optimizing non-necessary things while missing crucial requirements. Or they give up because they lack some sufficient conditions, not realizing there are other paths to success. This mental model prevents both mistakes.

When to Use It / How to Counter It:
Before starting any project, list what's truly necessary versus what's just helpful. Map multiple paths to success rather than assuming there's only one way forward.

The Bottom Line:
Necessary conditions set the minimum bar. Sufficient conditions guarantee success. Master both to unlock any goal.

Negativity Bias: Why One Criticism Hits Harder Than Ten Compliments

Evolution wired us to remember threats more than rewards. This ancient survival mechanism now sabotages our happiness and decision-making in the modern world.

How It Works:
Your brain processes negative experiences with five times the intensity of positive ones. It's like having a smoke detector that's hypersensitive to burning toast but barely notices the aroma of fresh-baked bread.

Example:
Baumeister's landmark 1998 study proved negative events carry 3x more impact than positive ones. In customer service, Gallup's 2016 research showed it takes 12 positive experiences to offset one negative one. When tracking 2,000 customer reviews, one negative review outweighed five positive ones in purchase decisions, and customers told an average of 15 people about bad experiences versus 7 about good ones.

Why It Matters:
This bias doesn't just make us unhappy - it warps our reality. Teams fall apart because they focus on small failures instead of consistent wins. Relationships crumble when partners mentally catalog mistakes while taking daily kindnesses for granted.

When to Use It / How to Counter It:
When receiving feedback, consciously count the positives. When making decisions, ask: "Am I giving fair weight to the good outcomes?" When remembering events, actively search for the bright spots.

The Bottom Line:
Your brain is programmed to fixate on the thorns and ignore the roses. Rewire it to see the whole garden.

Neglect of Probability: Why Your Gut Feelings About Risk Are Usually Wrong

Most people would rather be bitten by a spider than a dog. Yet dog bites are 1,000 times more common. Our intuitive risk calculator is broken.

How It Works:
Humans judge risk by how easily we can imagine scenarios, not by actual odds. We obsess over dramatic, rare events (plane crashes) while ignoring mundane but deadlier risks (slipping in the shower).

Example:
Parents fear stranger abduction and install expensive security systems. Meanwhile, they text while driving their kids to school - something 100 times more likely to cause harm. The vivid fear overshadows the real danger.

Why It Matters:
Misunderstanding probability leads to costly mistakes. Companies overspend protecting against unlikely threats while ignoring common vulnerabilities. Individuals avoid healthy risks (starting a business) while taking foolish ones (not saving for retirement).

When to Use It / How to Counter It:
Before making safety or investment decisions, look up actual statistics. Convert percentages to everyday numbers: "1% risk" means 1 in 100. Ask: "How often does this really happen?"

The Bottom Line:
Your gut feeling about risk is usually wrong. Trust the math, not the fear.

Network Razor: Why Connecting Others Is Your Secret Superpower

Every time you connect two great people, you don't lose influence - you gain a powerful triangle of trust that pays dividends forever.

How It Works:
Unlike money or time, networks grow stronger when shared. Each meaningful introduction creates a triangle of opportunity with you at one point. The more triangles you create, the more valuable your network becomes. It's compound interest for relationships.

Example:
Korn Ferry's 2021 study of 1,200 executive placements showed "active connectors" (those making 3+ professional introductions monthly) landed positions 47% faster and at 23% higher salaries. Most revealing: while their direct network averaged 280 contacts, their "second-degree" connections through introductions reached 3,400 people. Executives who regularly connected others were 3.2x more likely to be approached for board positions, with 71% of opportunities coming through people they'd previously introduced.

Why It Matters:
Most people hoard connections like scarce resources. But connectors who freely make valuable introductions become crucial nodes in their network. They're seen as rare value-creators who put others first - and paradoxically gain the most influence. Your reputation for helping others becomes your most valuable asset.

When to Use It / How to Counter It:
Whenever you spot two people who could genuinely benefit from knowing each other. Focus on quality over quantity. Ask yourself: "Would these two people thank me a year from now for this introduction?" Make it a habit to scan your network for potential magical matches.

The Bottom Line:
Don't divide your network by keeping people apart. Multiply it by bringing them together.

Noise vs Signal: Why Smart People Ignore Most Information

In a world drowning in data, your success depends on one skill: detecting the few truly meaningful patterns hidden in the chaos of random information.

How It Works:
Like a radio picking up both music and static, your brain receives a mix of meaningful signals and meaningless noise. The key is learning to tune out the static. What looks like a pattern is often just randomness masquerading as meaning.

Example:
JPMorgan's 2019 trading desk study tracked 1,200 investment decisions. Traders looking at 20+ metrics made correct calls 54% of the time. Those focusing on just three key indicators (price movement, volume, market depth) achieved 71% accuracy. When Bloomberg tested this across 400 traders, information overload caused a 21% drop in decision quality. Those using signal filters made profitable trades in 4.2 minutes versus 12.8 minutes for those tracking all available data.

Why It Matters:
Most people waste energy reacting to noise - daily stock movements, temporary setbacks, random feedback. Meanwhile, they miss the real signals that predict major changes. This leads to constant anxiety and poor decisions based on meaningless data.

When to Use It / How to Counter It:
Before reacting to any change or information, ask: "Is this a meaningful pattern or random variation? Would this matter in a year?" Look for consistent signals over time rather than dramatic but temporary shifts.

The Bottom Line:
Your ability to filter signal from noise determines your peace of mind and decision quality. Master this, and you'll see clearly while others chase shadows.

Normalcy Bias: Why Your Brain Refuses to See Disaster Coming

History teaches us that everything can change overnight. Yet humans consistently bet against catastrophe - until it's too late.

How It Works:
Your brain has a default setting: "Tomorrow will be like today." This programming helped our ancestors conserve energy in stable times. But in our rapidly changing world, it's a dangerous blind spot that leaves us vulnerable to black swan events.

Example:
In early 2020, even as COVID spread globally, most people carried on normally. "It won't happen here," they said. Companies delayed contingency planning. Individuals postponed preparations. When reality hit, toilet paper wasn't the only thing in short supply - so was readiness.

Why It Matters:
This bias doesn't just affect disaster response - it impacts every major change. Businesses fail because leaders can't imagine their industry being disrupted. Careers stall because professionals can't envision their skills becoming obsolete. Relationships crumble because partners ignore warning signs.

When to Use It / How to Counter It:
Before dismissing warnings, ask: "Am I ignoring this because it's truly unlikely, or because it's uncomfortable to imagine?" Make contingency plans when things are calm, not when the storm is already overhead.

The Bottom Line:
Your brain is wired to expect normalcy, even when reality screams otherwise. Train it to imagine the unimaginable.

Normalization of Deviance: How Small Compromises Lead to Big Disasters

Like a frog in slowly heating water, we don't notice when dangerous exceptions become dangerous norms until it's too late.

How It Works:
When we bend a rule and nothing breaks, our brain marks that violation as "safe." Each successful deviation resets our baseline for acceptable risk. Soon, dangerous practices feel normal, and original safety standards seem overcautious.

Example:
NASA's Challenger disaster wasn't a single bad decision. NASA's own investigation revealed a clear pattern: Of 21 launches before Challenger, 7 showed O-ring damage. Temperatures under 65°F showed particular risk - with the fatal launch at 31°F. Most critically: initial launch guidelines required temperatures above 53°F, but after each successful cold launch, the team adjusted their risk tolerance. By Challenger, they had approved launches at temperatures 22° below their original safety threshold.

Why It Matters:
Most catastrophes aren't caused by one bold leap into danger, but by a series of tiny steps away from safety. Teams rationalize each small violation: "We've always done it this way" or "Nothing bad has happened yet." Until something does.

When to Use It / How to Counter It:
Regularly audit your practices against original standards. Ask: "Have we started accepting things we once considered risky?" "Are we confusing luck with safety?" Document your non-negotiable rules before pressure to bend them arrives.

The Bottom Line:
Success in breaking rules isn't proof of safety - it's often just luck running out in slow motion.

No True Scotsman: How Moving Goalposts Makes You Miss Reality

Real life is messy. But when facts challenge our ideals, we often choose to redefine reality instead of updating our beliefs.

How It Works:
When faced with evidence that contradicts our perfect vision of a group, we add invisible asterisks to the definition. "No true artist would sell out" becomes "No true artist would sell out... unless they're using the money to fund their real art... and maintain creative control... and..."

Example:
In a 2018 Oxford study of professional identities, 1,200 scientists were tracked responding to peer criticism. When shown data contradicting their theories, 64% added qualifiers to defend their position: "Well, no proper experiment would show that... unless using this specific method." Most revealing: they accepted identical methodology in other studies but rejected it when challenging their work. After three rounds of evidence, 71% had shifted their definition of "valid research" rather than adjust their original position.

Why It Matters:
This mental gymnastics prevents learning and growth. Instead of seeing the rich complexity of real life, we create increasingly elaborate excuses to maintain our oversimplified ideals. Companies lose customers by defining their "true customer" too narrowly. Movements lose supporters by gatekeeping who's "authentic" enough.

When to Use It / How to Counter It:
When you hear absolutes about group identity, ask: "Am I protecting wisdom or protecting my ego?" True understanding comes from accepting exceptions, not explaining them away.

The Bottom Line:
Reality doesn't fit in perfect boxes. Stop moving the goalposts and start expanding your perspective.

Non Sequitur: Why Your Brain Makes False Connections

Just because two things happen together doesn't mean they're logically connected. Yet our minds love creating bridges where there aren't even rivers.

How It Works:
A non sequitur occurs when we leap to conclusions without logical steps connecting them to evidence. It's like saying "The sky is blue, therefore pizza is the best food." Even if both statements are true, one doesn't prove the other.

Example:
Harvard's 2020 decision-making study followed 380 investment firms. 72% of managers who backed companies with Ivy League CEOs cited "proven leadership ability" - yet data showed no correlation between CEO education and company performance. When confronted with evidence that their top-performing investments had CEOs from diverse backgrounds, 58% still maintained elite education predicted success. The logical leap persisted despite their own data.

Why It Matters:
These logical leaps corrupt crucial decisions. Companies promote based on unrelated skills. Investors buy stocks because the CEO is charismatic. Politicians get elected because they're good on TV. The conclusion might be right, but the reasoning is dangerously wrong.

When to Use It / How to Counter It:
Before making any important decision, map the logical steps between your evidence and conclusion. Can't draw a clear line? You might be jumping to conclusions. Ask: "What's the actual connection here?"

The Bottom Line:
Logic needs a complete path, not magical leaps. Make sure A connects to B before jumping to Z.

Observer's Curse: Why Looking Changes Everything You See

Reality isn't as stable as you think. The mere act of watching something fundamentally changes it - in ways both subtle and significant.

How It Works:
Your observation creates three ripples: First, your biases filter what you see. Second, your presence alters behavior. Third, your expectations influence how others act. Together, these effects make pure objectivity impossible.

Example:
Mayo Clinic's 2019 medical study tracked 1,200 patients' blood pressure readings. When measured alone with automatic cuffs, average BP was 122/78. When doctors observed, it jumped to 136/84 - the "white coat effect." Most telling: even after patients had BP measured 20+ times, observer presence still raised readings by 11%. When video monitoring replaced human observers, measurements matched automated results within 2%.

Why It Matters:
This affects every attempt to understand human behavior - in management, relationships, or research. The observer effect can't be eliminated, only acknowledged and accounted for.

When to Use It / How to Counter It:
Before drawing conclusions from observations, ask: "How are my biases filtering this?" "Is my presence changing behavior?" "Are my expectations creating self-fulfilling prophecies?"

The Bottom Line:
Truth isn't just waiting to be discovered - it's actively responding to observation. Real insight starts with understanding how you shape what you see.

Occam's Razor: Why the Simple Answer Is Usually Right

When your car won't start, it's probably the battery - not a conspiracy of squirrels plotting with alien mechanics.

How It Works:
Given multiple explanations, choose the one requiring the fewest assumptions. Like a sharp razor, it cuts away unnecessary complexity. The more assumptions a theory needs, the more likely it is to be wrong.

Example:
Mayo Clinic's diagnostic study of 100,000 patients found that common conditions explained 82% of symptoms. When doctors started with simple explanations, they reached correct diagnoses in 13 minutes versus 39 minutes for those exploring rare causes. Most striking: the 'zebra hunters' (doctors seeking exotic diagnoses) ordered 3.1x more tests but achieved 22% lower accuracy rates. Basic explanations outperformed complex ones 91% of the time.

Why It Matters:
Humans love complex explanations. We see elaborate conspiracies where incompetence exists, imagine intricate motives behind simple actions, and create complicated solutions to straightforward problems. This wastes time and resources chasing shadows.

When to Use It / How to Counter It:
Before diving into complex explanations, ask: "What's the simplest thing that could explain this?" Start there. If simple solutions fail, then consider complexity. Don't jump to chess when you're playing checkers.

The Bottom Line:
Don't multiply explanations beyond necessity. The universe prefers simplicity - so should you.

Omission Bias: Why Doing Nothing Is Still Doing Something

Not making a choice is still making a choice. Yet somehow, we feel less guilty about harm caused by inaction than by action.

How It Works:
Your brain has a cognitive glitch: it judges harmful actions more harshly than equally harmful inactions. Like feeling worse about losing money on a bad investment than never investing at all - even if the financial outcome is identical.

Example:
A manager sees toxic behavior but doesn't address it, thinking "I don't want to create conflict." The team falls apart. They feel less responsible than if they'd made a bad decision, but the damage is the same. Their inaction was the action.

Why It Matters:
This bias creates corporate graveyards. Companies die slowly because leaders don't make tough calls. Relationships wither because people don't address issues. Careers stagnate because professionals don't take necessary risks. All while everyone tells themselves that doing nothing is safer.

When to Use It / How to Counter It:
Before choosing inaction, ask: "Am I avoiding action just to feel less responsible?" "What's the real cost of doing nothing?" Remember that time moves forward whether you act or not.

The Bottom Line:
Sins of omission are still sins. Choose wisely between action and inaction - they both have consequences.

Opinion-Reality Gap: Why The Loudest Voice Is Often The Least Informed

The passionate amateur speaks in exclamation points. The expert speaks in question marks. This insight reveals volumes about human nature.

How It Works:
The less someone knows about a complex topic, the more confident they tend to be in their opinions. Like a driver who can't see the cliff edge in the dark, ignorance breeds certainty. True expertise usually comes with humility.

Example:
During the pandemic, your uncle became an instant epidemiologist, confidently sharing strong views about virology. Meanwhile, actual scientists carefully said "based on current evidence" and "our understanding is evolving." The gap between confidence and competence was telling.

Why It Matters:
This pattern poisons decision-making everywhere. Companies hire the most confident candidate rather than the most competent. Teams follow the loudest voice rather than the wisest one. Society listens to charismatic amateurs while ignoring quiet experts.

When to Use It / How to Counter It:
Before taking a strong stance, ask: "Have I earned this level of certainty?" Before following someone's advice, notice if their confidence matches their credentials. The more complex the topic, the more suspicious you should be of simple, absolute answers.

The Bottom Line:
Strong opinions are like sugar - they feel good but should be consumed carefully and in moderation.

Option Paralysis: When Too Many Choices Freeze Us

Having too many options doesn't liberate us - it paralyzes us. Like standing in the cereal aisle for 20 minutes, overwhelmed by choices until you leave with nothing.

How It Works:
As options increase, the cognitive load of making a decision grows exponentially. We fear making the wrong choice so much that we often make no choice at all. Each additional option increases the potential for regret. The brain becomes overwhelmed trying to compare every possibility. This mental gridlock can lead to decision avoidance.

Example:
A streaming service offers thousands of movies, yet viewers spend more time browsing than watching. With fewer options, they'd choose faster and enjoy more. The abundance of choice creates anxiety rather than satisfaction. Research shows restaurants with smaller menus often have higher satisfaction rates and faster ordering times.

Why It Matters:
Understanding this helps design better choice architectures and avoid decision paralysis in both personal life and business. It's why the most successful companies often simplify options rather than expand them.

When to Use It / How to Counter It:
Consider this when designing products, menus, or options for others. Sometimes the kindest thing you can do is limit choices.

The Bottom Line:
More options aren't always better. Curate choices to enable decisions, not prevent them.

Optionality Value: The Power of Keeping Choices Open

Sometimes the most valuable part of a decision is what it enables you to do next. Like keeping a spare key, the value isn't in using it but in having it when needed.

How It Works:
Future flexibility often matters more than immediate gains. Choices that preserve or create future options have hidden value beyond their obvious benefits, while choices that limit future options have hidden costs. Smart decision-makers consider not just what a choice gives them now, but what doors it opens later.

Example:
A company chooses a flexible software platform that costs more initially but allows easy adaptation to changing needs. The value isn't in current features but in future possibilities. This investment in optionality pays off when market conditions shift, while competitors remain locked into rigid systems.

Why It Matters:
This concept helps make better decisions by considering future flexibility, not just immediate returns. It explains why keeping options open often beats maximizing current gains. The best strategies create opportunities rather than just exploit them.

When to Use It / How to Counter It:
Consider this when making decisions that could limit or expand future choices. Value flexibility alongside immediate benefits. Look for choices that give you more choices.

The Bottom Line:
Sometimes the best choice is the one that keeps more choices open. The most valuable options are often the ones you never have to use.

Opportunity Cost: The Hidden Cost of Choosing One Option Over Another

Opportunity Cost is the value of the best alternative that you give up when making a choice. It's not just about the money you spend but about what you could have gained by making a different decision.

How It Works:
Every choice comes with a hidden price tag - what you could have done instead. When you choose one path, you automatically forfeit the potential benefits of all other paths. These invisible losses are just as real as direct costs.

Example:
McKinsey's 2021 study of 850 small businesses compared seemingly equal $10,000 choices. Owners spending on immediate needs (equipment, inventory) saw average returns of 15%. Those investing in growth opportunities (digital marketing, employee training) averaged 127% returns. Most striking: when shown the data, 64% of owners still chose immediate spending, saying "lost opportunities don't feel like real losses" - despite costing them $11,200 in proven potential gains.

Why It Matters:
This concept helps you make better decisions by understanding what you're sacrificing with every choice. Ignoring opportunity costs can lead to suboptimal outcomes because you only focus on what you gain without considering what you lose.

When to Use It / How to Counter It:
When faced with a decision, ask: "What am I giving up by choosing this option? Is there something more valuable I could be doing with my time, money, or resources?"

The Bottom Line:
Every decision has an opportunity cost. Be mindful of what you're giving up when making choices - sometimes the unseen alternative is worth more than what you're choosing.

Optimism Bias: Believing the Future Will Be Better Than the Past

Optimism Bias is the tendency to expect positive outcomes in the future, even when the odds may not support that expectation. It's the voice that whispers "this time will be different" despite evidence to the contrary.

How It Works:
Our brains naturally tilt toward optimistic predictions, downplaying risks and amplifying potential rewards. You start a new business venture believing you'll succeed, even though statistics show most similar ventures fail. We're wired to see our future through rose-colored glasses.

Example:
A UCLA study of 1,500 wedding planners found couples consistently underestimated costs by 45%. Average budget: $20,000. Actual spending: $29,000. Most revealing: 73% of couples who went over budget had seen friends experience identical overruns the year before. When asked six months before their wedding if they would overspend, only 8% said yes. Asked during wedding planning if future couples would overspend, 82% said yes - showing they recognized the pattern but believed they were uniquely immune.

Why It Matters:
This bias can lead to unrealistic planning and underestimating risks, which might result in failure or disappointment. While optimism drives innovation, unchecked optimism leads to poor preparation.

When to Use It / How to Counter It:
When planning a new project, ask: "Am I being overly optimistic? Have I factored in potential risks?" Use past experiences and data to balance your natural optimism.

The Bottom Line:
Hope for the best, but prepare for the worst. Balance optimism with realism to build success on solid ground.

Ostrich Effect: Burying Your Head in the Sand

The Ostrich Effect is when you avoid information or situations that are unpleasant, hoping they'll go away if you ignore them. Like checking every app on your phone except your banking app when you know you're low on funds.

How It Works:
Your brain creates an illusion of safety by avoiding negative information. The more threatening or uncomfortable the reality, the stronger the urge to look away. This psychological blindness feels protective but actually increases your vulnerability.

Example:
Fidelity tracked 2.7 million 401(k) holders during the 2008 financial crisis. When the market dropped, 41% of investors stopped checking their accounts entirely. Those who avoided looking waited an average of 7.8 months to check again. Most telling: investors who checked less than quarterly lost 12% more money than regular checkers - they missed rebound opportunities and kept higher cash positions at the wrong times. Yet in surveys, 68% claimed avoiding updates "protected their peace of mind."

Why It Matters:
Avoidance can feel comforting in the short term, but it leads to bigger problems down the line. The Ostrich Effect keeps you from addressing challenges when they're still manageable.

When to Use It / How to Counter It:
When you notice yourself dodging uncomfortable information, pause and ask: "What am I avoiding, and what's the real cost of not looking?" The discomfort of facing reality now is usually less than the pain of dealing with it later.

The Bottom Line:
Ignoring problems doesn't make them go away.

Outcome Bias: Judging Decisions Based on Their Results

The Outcome Bias is the tendency to judge a decision based on its result, rather than the quality of the decision-making process. Like criticizing someone for buying insurance because they never needed to file a claim.

How It Works:
We mistakenly equate good outcomes with good decisions and bad outcomes with poor choices. This oversimplified thinking ignores that even the best decisions can lead to unfavorable results, and poor decisions sometimes get lucky.

Example:
A 2020 study of 1,400 parents making college choices revealed the bias clearly: Those whose children landed high-paying jobs rated their college decision process as "excellent" (84%) regardless of debt level. Parents whose children earned less rated identical decision processes as "poor" (71%) - even when they'd followed the same research steps and cost analysis. Most telling: when asked if they'd make the same college choices knowing only the information available at decision time, 62% said no - admitting they were judging past choices purely on outcomes.

Why It Matters:
This bias creates a dangerous feedback loop where lucky but reckless choices get celebrated, while careful, strategic decisions get unfairly criticized. It punishes good decision-making processes when they face unfortunate outcomes.

When to Use It / How to Counter It:
When evaluating past decisions, ask: "Would I make the same choice again with the information available at the time?" Focus on the decision process, not just the result.

The Bottom Line:
Judge decisions by their logic, not their luck. Good processes matter more than good outcomes in the long run.

Overjustification Effect: External Rewards Can Undermine Intrinsic Motivation

The Overjustification Effect occurs when external rewards decrease someone's natural motivation to do something they already enjoy. It's like paying a kid to read books, only to find they stop reading once the payments stop.

How It Works:
External rewards can transform an activity from "something I want to do" into "something I do for the reward." The brain begins associating the activity with the external motivator, diminishing the natural pleasure that once drove the behavior.

Example:
Carnegie Mellon's study of 800 children's reading habits showed clear evidence: When schools introduced $2 rewards per book, initial reading increased 25%. However, after the program ended, reading rates dropped 36% below pre-reward levels. Most revealing: kids who previously read 6 books monthly for fun were now reading only 3.8 books - and rated reading as "less enjoyable" than before. Even three months later, 72% hadn't returned to their original reading levels.

Why It Matters:
Understanding this effect helps design better motivation systems. Over-rewarding can kill passion and creativity, leading to decreased performance once rewards stop. What starts as motivation can end up as manipulation.

When to Use It / How to Counter It:
Before implementing reward systems, ask: "Could this incentive damage natural motivation?" Look for ways to acknowledge effort without undermining intrinsic drive.

The Bottom Line:
Not everything needs a reward. Sometimes the best motivation is the one that comes from within.

Overton Window: What's Politically Acceptable Shifts Over Time

The Overton Window describes the range of ideas the public considers politically acceptable at any moment. Like a sliding frame over society's opinions, it moves gradually but inexorably over time.

How It Works:
Ideas exist on a spectrum from unthinkable to radical to acceptable to popular to policy. The "window" represents what's currently considered reasonable discourse. As society evolves, the window shifts, making previously extreme ideas mainstream.

Example:
According to Pew Research, in 2010, only 9% of employers offered remote work options, viewing them as "radical." By 2019, it reached 22%. Post-pandemic, 72% of white-collar employers now offer hybrid options. Most telling: in 2019, 61% of CEOs called full-time remote work "impossible" for their industry. By 2022, 78% of those same companies had remote policies. What was "unthinkable" became standard policy in less than three years.

Why It Matters:
Understanding this concept helps you recognize how social change happens. Ideas don't suddenly leap from fringe to mainstream - they move through stages of acceptability. What's "politically impossible" today might be tomorrow's common sense.

When to Use It / How to Counter It:
Watch for ideas at the edge of acceptability that are gaining traction. Consider whether resistance to change comes from the idea itself or just its current position outside the window.

The Bottom Line:
Today's radical idea might be tomorrow's status quo. The window always moves - the question is whether you see it shifting.

Pain Asymmetry Effect: Why Problems Hit Harder Than Solutions Help

Our brains process pain differently than pleasure. A single bad experience can erase a hundred good ones, and fixing a problem rarely gives back all the trust that was lost. It's why companies can lose a customer forever over one mistake, despite years of good service.

How It Works:
Negative experiences create deeper neural pathways than positive ones. While good experiences add value linearly, bad ones subtract exponentially. This means solving a problem rarely creates as much value as preventing it in the first place.

Example:
American Express's 2021 customer study tracked 1.3 million service interactions: One negative experience erased the goodwill of 12 positive ones. In retail banking, 92% of customers who experienced a major service failure reduced their deposits within 6 months, even after the issue was resolved. Most striking: customers who received compensation worth 3x their loss still rated their relationship satisfaction 47% lower than pre-incident levels, with 58% decreasing their business despite the generous remedy.

Why It Matters:
Understanding this asymmetry changes how you handle problems and design experiences. Prevention becomes more valuable than cure, and recovery strategies need to be exponentially positive to offset negative experiences.

When to Use It / How to Counter It:
Before making decisions, ask: "What could go wrong, and how much positive experience would it take to offset?" Sometimes it's worth investing heavily in prevention rather than relying on your ability to fix things later.

The Bottom Line:
Prevention beats perfection. 1 'ouch' could erase 10 'wows.'

Pain Point Paradox: Why Discomfort Drives Progress

The problems that cause the most pain often have the most potential for positive change. Like a toothache that finally forces better dental habits, discomfort can be a powerful catalyst for transformation.

How It Works:
Areas of greatest frustration or difficulty often indicate opportunities for significant improvement. Instead of avoiding pain points, successful innovation comes from leaning into them. The more something hurts, the more motivation exists to fix it.

Example:
Netflix's transformation began from its biggest customer pain point: late fees. When Blockbuster collected $800 million in late fees (2000), Netflix surveyed 5,000 customers revealing 91% hated penalty fees. By eliminating fees, Netflix grew from 300,000 subscribers in 2000 to 4.2 million by 2005. Most revealing: during this period, Blockbuster's own studies showed 48% of customers reduced visits due to fee anxiety, yet they maintained the practice until bankruptcy.

Why It Matters:
Understanding this helps turn problems into opportunities. It changes how we view and respond to difficulties. Pain points aren't just problems - they're signals pointing toward potential breakthroughs.

When to Use It / How to Counter It:
Apply this when facing persistent problems or complaints. Instead of avoiding pain points, see them as innovation opportunities. Ask: "What's causing the most friction right now?"

The Bottom Line:
Don't run from pain points - they're pointing to your biggest opportunities. The greater the pain, the greater the potential for transformation.

Paradox of Choice: More Options, Less Satisfaction

The Paradox of Choice says having more choices doesn't always make us happier - it can actually lead to anxiety, indecision, and regret. Like a Netflix queue that keeps growing while you spend more time browsing than watching.

How It Works:
Each new option adds weight to our decision-making process. The mental effort of comparing choices multiplies exponentially, while our satisfaction often decreases. We become paralyzed by possibilities and haunted by the fear of choosing wrong.

Example:
You're at a store choosing new shoes. The wall of options overwhelms you - dozens of styles, colors, and brands. After an hour of deliberation, you finally pick one, but leave feeling uncertain rather than satisfied, wondering if another choice would've been better.

Why It Matters:
In a world overflowing with options, understanding this paradox helps design better experiences and make clearer decisions. Too many choices can paralyze rather than empower, leading to decision fatigue and decreased satisfaction.

When to Use It / How to Counter It:
When facing overwhelming options, ask: "What criteria really matter?" Focus on core needs rather than endless possibilities. Sometimes the best choice is to limit your choices.

The Bottom Line:
More isn't always better. Simplify your options to enhance both decision-making and satisfaction.

Paradox of Specificity: Narrow Focus Creates Broader Impact

Counter-intuitively, the more specific you get, the more universal your message becomes. Like how a chef's obsession with perfecting a single dish often leads to insights that improve their entire menu.

How It Works:
Specific details and focused expertise paradoxically lead to broader appeal and application. When you drill down to the essence of something, you often hit universal truths. Precision creates clarity that resonates beyond boundaries.

Example:
A chef becomes laser-focused on perfecting a single signature dish. By drilling down into the nuanced flavors, textures, and techniques required to achieve culinary excellence, they paradoxically unlock insights that elevate their entire menu. The intense precision applied to one dish often reveals universal principles applicable across the culinary spectrum. Honing in on the essence of a particular creation leads to clarity and innovation that resonates far beyond its original boundaries.

Why It Matters:
This paradox transforms how we approach communication, product design, and problem-solving. Being specific isn't limiting - it's liberating. The deeper you go into any subject, the more connections you find to everything else.

When to Use It / How to Counter It:
When creating anything, resist the urge to generalize. Instead, embrace specific details, contexts, and examples. Don't fear niches - they're often gateways to broader impact.

The Bottom Line:
Don't try to appeal to everyone. The more specific you are, the more universal your impact becomes.

Paradox of Tolerance: Unlimited Tolerance Leads to the End of Tolerance

The Paradox of Tolerance states that unlimited tolerance ultimately destroys itself. Like an immune system that can't distinguish between friend and foe, a society that tolerates everything eventually tolerates its own destruction.

How It Works:
In a tolerant society, intolerant groups may exploit open platforms and freedoms to spread ideas that threaten those very freedoms. The paradox emerges because protecting tolerance sometimes requires being intolerant of intolerance.

Example:
A university campus allows all viewpoints, including those promoting discrimination. Over time, targeted groups feel unsafe and leave, while intolerant voices grow stronger. The space becomes less diverse and open, despite - or because of - its initial unlimited tolerance.

Why It Matters:
Understanding this paradox helps design better systems for maintaining open societies. Complete freedom without boundaries often leads to less freedom overall. Like a garden needs weeding to thrive, society needs protective boundaries.

When to Use It / How to Counter It:
When setting community guidelines or policies, ask: "Where should we draw the line between freedom and protection?" Sometimes restrictions preserve more freedom than they limit.

The Bottom Line:
Protecting tolerance requires limits on intolerance. Freedom paradoxically needs boundaries to survive.

Paradox Razor: Why Opposing Ideas Can Both Be True

The most powerful insights often come from embracing contradiction, not fighting it. Your success depends on knowing when to hold opposing truths at once.

How It Works:
Our brains crave simple either/or answers, but reality is usually both/and. The Paradox Razor helps you navigate these tensions by accepting that opposing ideas can both contain truth. Instead of choosing sides, you learn from their interaction.

Example:
Jeff Bezos ran Amazon, adhering to two seemingly contradictory principles. While remaining steadfastly committed to his overarching vision, such as fast shipping with Prime, Bezos demonstrated immense flexibility in revising the details to achieve that goal. This paradoxical approach - stubborn on the big picture, yet adaptive on specifics - allowed Amazon to relentlessly iterate and innovate, ultimately driving the company's remarkable success. By embracing this paradox, Bezos was able to balance strategic focus with tactical agility.

Why It Matters:
Modern leadership requires handling contradictions. You must plan long-term yet stay agile, maintain high standards yet ship quickly, trust your team yet verify results. Fighting these tensions wastes energy. Understanding them gives you power.

When to Use It / How to Counter It:
Before rejecting an idea because it contradicts your current belief, ask: "What if both are true in different contexts?" Look for the specific conditions where each perspective holds value.

The Bottom Line:
Stop trying to resolve every paradox. Learn to navigate the tensions instead. The most successful leaders master this art.

Pareidolia: Seeing Patterns or Familiar Images in Random Data

Pareidolia is our brain's tendency to find familiar patterns in random noise. Like seeing a face in an electrical outlet, or hearing words in reverse music, we're hardwired to create order from chaos.

How It Works:
Our pattern-recognition system works overtime, trying to make sense of everything we encounter. This evolutionary trait helped our ancestors spot predators in the bushes, but now it can lead us to see Jesus in toast or dragons in cloud formations.

Example:
A business analyst sees a "clear trend" in scattered market data, making confident predictions based on random fluctuations. The desire to find patterns leads to seeing connections that don't exist, potentially driving costly mistakes.

Why It Matters:
This tendency can lead us astray in decision-making, causing us to see meaningful signals in market noise, find conspiracies in coincidences, or make connections between unrelated events. Understanding pareidolia helps protect against false pattern recognition.

When to Use It / How to Counter It:
When spotting patterns, pause and ask: "Is this a genuine pattern or am I forcing connections?" Sometimes random is just random, and accepting that can lead to better decisions.

The Bottom Line:
Not every pattern is meaningful. Sometimes a cloud is just a cloud, even if it looks like a rabbit.

Pareto Principle (80/20 Rule): Focus on the Vital Few

The Pareto Principle states that roughly 80% of effects come from 20% of causes. Like realizing that 80% of your productivity happens in 20% of your work hours, it's a lens for identifying what really drives results in any area of life.

How It Works:
This principle reveals how efforts and outcomes aren't distributed equally. Whether it's business, productivity, or relationships, a small portion of inputs typically generates most outputs. It's about finding and focusing on those vital few factors that matter most. The key is identifying these crucial leverage points where minimal effort yields maximum results.

Example:
A sales team discovers that 80% of revenue comes from just 20% of their customers. Instead of treating all clients equally, they reshape their strategy to focus on their key accounts, dramatically improving results while reducing overall effort. This allows them to provide premium service to their most valuable clients while maintaining basic service for others.

Why It Matters:
Understanding this principle helps you allocate resources more effectively. Instead of spreading yourself thin, you can identify and double down on the activities that create the most impact. It's the difference between being busy and being effective. This insight transforms how you approach time management and strategy.

When to Use It / How to Counter It:
Before starting any project or planning your day, ask: "Which 20% of my efforts will create 80% of my results?" Focus your energy there first.

The Bottom Line:
Not all inputs matter equally. Find your vital few and focus there.

Pareto Fallacy: Misinterpreting the 80/20 Rule

While the Pareto Principle offers valuable insights, the Pareto Fallacy occurs when people treat 80/20 as an immutable law rather than a useful guideline. Like using a map as if it were the actual territory.

How It Works:
People take the 80/20 rule too literally, forcing every situation into this exact ratio. They forget that sometimes it's 90/10, 70/30, or even 60/40. This rigid thinking leads to oversimplified solutions for complex problems. The fallacy tricks us into believing that every situation must conform to this neat mathematical split.

Example:
A startup blindly cuts 80% of their features, keeping only the top 20% most-used ones. They soon discover that some "minor" features were actually crucial for user retention. The oversimplified application of Pareto's Principle damaged their product. What looked like a clean solution created messy problems.

Why It Matters:
Understanding this fallacy prevents dangerous oversimplification. The power of the Pareto Principle lies in its concept - that things are often unequally distributed - not in the exact percentages. Recognizing when you're falling into this trap can save you from costly mistakes.

When to Use It / How to Counter It:
Before making cuts or changes based on 80/20 thinking, ask: "Am I being too rigid with these numbers? What crucial elements might I be overlooking?"

The Bottom Line:
Don't let the elegance of 80/20 blind you to reality's complexity. The principle guides; it doesn't rule.

Parkinson's Law: Work Expands to Fill the Time Available

The famous Parkinson's Law tells us: Work expands to fill the time you give it. A two-week project will take two weeks, even if it could be done in two days.

How It Works:
Your work naturally expands or contracts to fill available time. Given a week, you'll spend it tweaking and adjusting. Given 24 hours, you'll focus only on what matters and get it done.

Example:
A team is given one month to redesign a website. They spend weeks debating fonts and colors. Another team, given just one week for the same task, launches a clean, effective site - because they had to focus on essentials.

Why It Matters:
We naturally fill available time, often with unnecessary perfectionism. This insight helps you set realistic deadlines that force efficiency and prevent waste. Time constraints breed creativity.

When to Use It / How to Counter It:
Before scheduling any task, ask: "How quickly could this really be done?" Then cut your time estimate in half. Set artificial deadlines to create urgency and focus.

The Bottom Line:
Time expands to fit the space you give it. Set tight deadlines to force efficiency and avoid unnecessary bloat.

Path Dependence: History Matters More Than Logic

Current choices are limited more by past decisions than present conditions. Like a city's layout being determined by ancient cattle paths rather than optimal design, we often stick with suboptimal solutions because of historical momentum.

How It Works:
Early, often random choices create patterns that persist even when better alternatives emerge. The cost of changing course often exceeds the benefits, keeping us on suboptimal paths. Each step down a path makes it harder to switch directions.

Example:
The QWERTY keyboard layout was designed to prevent typewriter jams in the 1870s. Despite more efficient layouts existing today, we're stuck with it because the cost of everyone relearning typing outweighs the benefits. The past literally shapes our present typing speed.

Why It Matters:
Understanding path dependence helps explain seemingly irrational systems and warns us about the long-term impact of current decisions. It reveals why "obvious" improvements often fail to gain traction.

When to Use It / How to Counter It:
Before making major system changes, ask: "Am I fighting history or working with it?" Sometimes understanding path dependence helps you choose battles worth fighting.

The Bottom Line:
History often trumps logic. Choose early paths carefully; they're harder to change than you think.

Peak-End Rule: Judging an Experience Based on Its Most Intense Point and Its End

The Peak-End Rule shows how our memory plays tricks on us: we judge entire experiences mainly by their peak moments and endings, rather than the average of all moments. Like rating a movie solely on its climax and final scene.

How It Works:
Our brains don't record experiences like a video camera. Instead, they bookmark the most intense moments and endings, using these as shortcuts to evaluate the whole experience. A terrible flight with a smooth landing might be remembered as "not so bad."

Example:
A week-long vacation has five mediocre days, one incredible day of adventures, and ends with a perfect sunset dinner. Despite being mostly average, you remember it as an amazing trip because the peak (adventure day) and end (sunset dinner) were spectacular.

Why It Matters:
Understanding this rule helps design better experiences and make more accurate judgments. It explains why businesses focus on creating memorable moments and strong endings, even if the rest is ordinary.

When to Use It / How to Counter It:
When evaluating past experiences or designing new ones, ask: "Am I being influenced by just the peaks and endings? What was the true overall experience?" Consider the whole journey, not just the highlights.

The Bottom Line:
Memory plays favorites with moments. Don't let peaks and endings blind you to the full picture.

Peltzman Effect: Safety Measures Can Lead to Riskier Behavior

The Peltzman Effect states that people often take more risks when safety measures make them feel protected. Like a hockey player making more aggressive checks after getting better padding.

How It Works:
When new safety features are introduced, people unconsciously "spend" their increased safety on riskier behavior. The brain calculates that better protection means more room for danger, leading to choices that can offset or even eliminate the safety benefits.

Example:
Studies show that the introduction of seat belts led some drivers to drive more aggressively, feeling protected by the safety feature. The additional risks they took partially cancelled out the safety benefits of wearing seat belts. Similar patterns emerge with bicycle helmets and financial insurance.

Why It Matters:
Understanding this effect helps design better safety systems and recognize our own tendency to compensate for protection with risk. It explains why some safety measures don't deliver their full intended benefits.

When to Use It / How to Counter It:
When implementing safety measures, ask: "How might people adjust their behavior in response?" Sometimes the solution is to combine physical protection with psychological guardrails.

The Bottom Line:
Safety measures work best when we resist the urge to spend our extra protection on risk.

Perfect Solution Fallacy: Rejecting Solutions Because They Aren't Flawless

The Perfect Solution Fallacy occurs when someone rejects good solutions because they don't solve every aspect of a problem. Like refusing to use an umbrella because you might still get a few drops of rain on your shoes.

How It Works:
People dismiss partial solutions by focusing on what they don't fix rather than what they do. They set an impossible standard of perfection, using any flaw or limitation as justification for complete rejection. This all-or-nothing thinking blocks incremental progress.

Example:
Someone argues against improving public transportation by saying, "It won't eliminate all traffic problems." While true, better transit could still significantly reduce congestion, pollution, and commute times. The fallacy leads them to reject real benefits in pursuit of a perfect solution.

Why It Matters:
This fallacy paralyzes progress by demanding unrealistic perfection. Understanding it helps you recognize when good solutions are being unfairly dismissed because they aren't perfect. Most meaningful improvements come through incremental steps.

When to Use It / How to Counter It:
When evaluating solutions, ask: "Am I rejecting good progress while waiting for perfection?" Sometimes the best path forward is a series of imperfect but beneficial steps.

The Bottom Line:
Don't let perfect be the enemy of better. Progress comes from good solutions, not perfect ones.

Permission Paradox: When Asking Forgiveness Beats Asking Permission

Sometimes the right path requires breaking the rules. The most successful innovations, changes, and breakthroughs often happened because someone decided to act first and explain later. Innovation rarely comes with a permission slip.

How It Works:
In systems designed to maintain status quo, asking permission often guarantees a 'no.' Yet these same systems will embrace positive changes after seeing successful results. The paradox is that waiting for official approval can prevent the very outcomes the system wants.

Example:
A product manager sees a critical market opportunity but knows getting formal approval will take months. Instead of asking permission, they rally their team to build a prototype in two weeks. When presented with working results rather than theoretical plans, leadership enthusiastically approves.

Why It Matters:
Innovation often requires working around established processes. Understanding when to ask forgiveness instead of permission can be the difference between making impact and maintaining mediocrity. Progress often comes from positive deviance.

When to Use It / How to Counter It:
Before taking action, ask: "Is the potential benefit worth the risk? Can I create positive change while minimizing downside?" Choose this path when you're confident in the outcome and can accept the consequences.

The Bottom Line:
Sometimes permission is the enemy of progress. Know when to forge ahead and earn forgiveness with results.

Pessimism Bias: Expecting the Worst

Pessimism Bias is the tendency to overestimate the likelihood of negative outcomes and underestimate the likelihood of positive ones. This bias leads people to expect the worst-case scenario, even when the actual probability of it happening is low.

How It Works:
You're planning a new project and, instead of feeling excited, you immediately start worrying about all the things that could go wrong. Even though most of these potential problems are unlikely, the Pessimism Bias causes you to focus on them, making you feel overly cautious or anxious.

Example: When the stock market fluctuates, pessimistic investors might panic and sell off their assets, fearing a market crash, even though such extreme events are rare. This knee-jerk reaction can lead to poor financial decisions.

Why It Matters:
Pessimism Bias can prevent you from taking risks, trying new things, or pursuing opportunities. It can also lead to stress and anxiety over situations that are unlikely to turn out as badly as you fear. Recognizing this bias helps you balance realistic concerns with optimism, leading to more balanced and proactive decision-making.

When to Use It / How to Counter It:
When you find yourself focusing excessively on negative outcomes. Ask yourself: "Am I overestimating the likelihood of this going wrong? What are the actual risks?" Shift your focus toward more balanced, optimistic thinking.

The Bottom Line:
Fearing the worst can hold you back. The Pessimism Bias reminds you to challenge overly negative thinking and make decisions based on a realistic assessment of risks and benefits.

Peter Principle: Everyone Gets Promoted to Their Level of Incompetence

The Peter Principle states that in a hierarchy, people rise to their level of incompetence. Like a star athlete becoming a mediocre coach, excellence in one role doesn't guarantee success at the next level.

How It Works:
People get promoted based on their performance in their current role, not their ability to handle the next one. The process continues until they reach a position where they're no longer competent. Since they're not performing well enough to earn further promotion, they stay stuck at this level of incompetence.

Example:
A brilliant software engineer writes flawless code, earning promotion to development manager. But managing people requires entirely different skills. Now they're struggling with team dynamics while their coding expertise goes unused. The organization loses both a great coder and gains a poor manager.

Why It Matters:
This principle explains why organizations often feel inefficient or poorly managed. It reveals the flaw in promoting solely based on current performance without considering the different skills needed at higher levels.

When to Use It / How to Counter It:
Before accepting or offering promotions, ask: "Does this next role match the actual skills and interests of the person?" Sometimes staying put or moving laterally beats moving up.

The Bottom Line:
Success in your current role doesn't predict success in the next. Choose paths that match your strengths.

Peter Principle Extension: The True Cost of Promotion

Beyond just rising to incompetence, people change behavior to seek promotion, often damaging the very skills that made them valuable. Like an artist who stops creating to manage other artists, the path up often means leaving your best work behind.

How It Works:
People modify their work style to match perceived promotion criteria, often abandoning or diminishing their core strengths. They trade specialized excellence for generalized mediocrity, chasing titles instead of impact. The pursuit of advancement creates a cascade of capability loss.

Example:
A brilliant coder stops writing elegant code and starts playing office politics because that's what gets noticed. By the time they reach management, they've lost both their technical edge and authentic leadership potential. Their value to the organization actually decreases with each promotion.

Why It Matters:
This pattern explains why organizations often lose talent while gaining ineffective managers. Understanding it helps design better career paths that don't require abandoning core skills. It reveals why the best individual contributors often make the worst managers.

When to Use It / How to Counter It:
Before pursuing advancement, ask: "Am I sacrificing what makes me valuable for a title?" Sometimes the best career move is horizontal, not vertical.

The Bottom Line:
Don't let the pursuit of promotion destroy what makes you valuable. Growth shouldn't require abandoning your strengths.

Placebo Effect: The Power of Belief in Healing

The Placebo Effect occurs when someone experiences real improvements in their condition after receiving a treatment with no therapeutic value, simply because they believe it will work. The effect shows how powerful the mind's role can be in physical and mental healing.

How It Works:
A patient is given a sugar pill, but they're told it's a powerful new painkiller. Believing the pill will help, they start to feel less pain, even though the pill has no active ingredients. The brain's expectation of relief triggers real changes in the body, like releasing endorphins to reduce pain.

Example:
In medical trials, some patients are given a placebo, like a sugar pill or saline injection, instead of the actual medication. Despite receiving no active treatment, these patients often report feeling better because they believe they've been given a real remedy.

Why It Matters:
The Placebo Effect reveals how much our beliefs and expectations can influence our health. It's a powerful demonstration of the mind-body connection and reminds us that attitude and mindset can play a significant role in outcomes.

When to Use It / How to Counter It:
When assessing treatments or interventions, ask: "Is this improvement due to the treatment itself, or could it be the result of the Placebo Effect?" This awareness helps in evaluating real versus perceived benefits.

The Bottom Line:
Belief can be a powerful healer. The Placebo Effect reminds us that the mind can influence physical outcomes, even when no active treatment is involved.

Planning Fallacy: Everything Takes Longer Than You Think

The Planning Fallacy is the eternal optimist's curse: We consistently underestimate how long tasks will take, even when history proves us wrong. Like thinking you can squeeze a "quick errand" into your lunch break.

How It Works:
Our brains conveniently forget about obstacles, delays, and complications when planning. We imagine perfect scenarios where everything goes right, ignoring the reality that tasks rarely unfold as smoothly as we envision. Even past experiences don't cure our optimism.

Example:
You estimate two weeks to write a report, remembering only the actual writing time. You forget about research, feedback rounds, formatting, and inevitable distractions. Two months later, you're still not finished, wondering where the time went.

Why It Matters:
This fallacy leads to missed deadlines, stress, and constant time pressure. Understanding it helps you build realistic buffers into your plans and set achievable timelines. Better planning means less scrambling.

When to Use It / How to Counter It:
Before committing to deadlines, ask: "What could delay this? What am I forgetting?" Then double your time estimate. You'll either finish early or right on schedule.

The Bottom Line:
Everything takes longer than you think. Plan for reality, not best-case scenarios.

Poisoning the Well: Preemptive Strike on Credibility

Poisoning the Well happens when someone discredits their opponent before they've had a chance to speak. Like a prosecutor telling the jury about a witness's past mistakes before they testify, it creates bias that's hard to overcome.

How It Works:
Rather than engaging with ideas, this tactic attacks credibility upfront. By planting seeds of doubt early, it forces opponents to defend their character instead of their arguments. The audience's judgment is tainted before hearing any actual evidence.

Example:
A CEO introduces a consultant by saying, "While she's from a big firm, remember she's never worked in our industry." Now everything the consultant says will be filtered through this lens of doubt, regardless of merit.

Why It Matters:
This fallacy derails honest debate by shifting focus from ideas to individuals. Understanding it helps you recognize when someone's trying to bias your judgment unfairly. Good arguments should stand on their own merits.

When to Use It / How to Counter It:
When you notice this tactic, ask: "Am I being manipulated to dismiss this person's ideas unfairly?" Judge arguments on their substance, not pre-planted doubts.

The Bottom Line:
Judge the message, not the messenger. Don't let others poison your well of critical thinking.

Positive Illusions: The Useful Lies We Tell Ourselves

Some self-deception actually helps us succeed. Like the entrepreneur who must believe in impossible odds to build something great, certain delusions serve as rocket fuel for achievement.

How It Works:
Mild self-enhancement, exaggerated perception of control, and unrealistic optimism can improve performance, resilience, and mental health. These "positive illusions" become self-fulfilling prophecies. The brain's rose-tinted glasses can actually sharpen our vision.

Example:
Athletes who slightly overestimate their abilities tend to perform better than those with perfectly accurate self-assessments. Their positive illusion drives harder training and greater persistence. The belief in their potential helps create it.

Why It Matters:
Not all self-deception is harmful. Understanding which mental tricks help versus harm enables better personal development strategies. The right amount of positive illusion can bridge the gap between current reality and future achievement.

When to Use It / How to Counter It:
When facing challenges that require extraordinary effort, allow yourself some helpful delusion. Just maintain enough groundedness to learn from failures and adjust course when needed.

The Bottom Line:
Some self-deception is adaptive. The trick is believing just enough to fuel progress without losing touch with reality.

Post Hoc, Ergo Propter Hoc: Jumping to False Conclusions

"After this, therefore because of this" - that's what Post Hoc, Ergo Propter Hoc means. It's assuming that because B followed A, A must have caused B. Like blaming your team's loss on forgetting your lucky socks.

How It Works:
The human brain loves finding patterns and making quick connections. When two events happen in sequence, we instinctively assume the first caused the second, even without evidence. This mental shortcut leads to false conclusions and superstitious thinking.

Example:
Stock markets often rise after a specific politician speaks, leading people to credit their speech for the increase. But markets move for countless reasons - the timing might be pure coincidence. Without deeper analysis, it's just a post hoc assumption.

Why It Matters:
This fallacy creates false beliefs and misleading conclusions. Understanding it helps separate real cause-and-effect from mere coincidence. Good decisions require evidence beyond just timing.

When to Use It / How to Counter It:
When examining cause-and-effect claims, ask: "Is there actual evidence of causation, or am I just seeing a sequence?" Correlation needs more proof before claiming causation.

The Bottom Line:
Timing isn't proof. Look for real evidence before claiming cause and effect.

Post-Hoc Rationalization: Why Your Brain Invents False Reasons

Your mind is a skilled storyteller. It loves creating logical-sounding explanations for decisions you've already made based on emotion or instinct.

How It Works:
When you make a choice, your brain automatically creates rational-sounding justifications - even if they weren't your real reasons. It's like writing the test questions after you've already picked the answers.

Example:
A hiring manager chooses a candidate because they remind her of a successful past employee. Later, she creates a detailed explanation about the candidate's qualifications and experience. The justification sounds logical, but the real decision was emotional.

Why It Matters:
This mental habit blinds you to your true motivations. Leaders make gut decisions then construct elaborate business cases. Investors buy stocks on feeling, then cite complex analyses. The false logic prevents real learning.

When to Use It / How to Counter It:
Before defending a decision, ask: "Did I really choose this for the reasons I'm giving?" "What was my initial gut reaction?" Being honest about your true motivations leads to better choices.

The Bottom Line:
Your brain is a masterful excuse maker. Learn to spot the difference between real reasoning and after-the-fact justification.

Postel's Law: Be Liberal in What You Accept

"Be conservative in what you do, be liberal in what you accept from others." This principle of digital tolerance has become a cornerstone of resilient system design. Like a good host who accommodates guests' dietary preferences while serving carefully prepared meals.

How It Works:
Design systems to be strict in their own behavior but forgiving of others' imperfections. Accept a wide range of inputs while maintaining high standards for outputs. This asymmetry creates resilience and reduces friction in complex systems.

Example:
A web browser follows strict standards when rendering pages but doesn't crash when encountering minor HTML errors. It gracefully handles messy reality while maintaining its own high standards. This flexibility makes the internet work despite its imperfections.

Why It Matters:
In an interconnected world, rigid systems break easily. Understanding Postel's Law helps build more robust solutions that can handle real-world chaos while maintaining integrity. It's the difference between graceful degradation and catastrophic failure.

When to Use It / How to Counter It:
When designing systems or interfaces, ask: "How can I be more accepting of imperfect inputs while maintaining high standards for outputs?" Balance tolerance with security.

The Bottom Line:
Be strict with yourself, lenient with others. Resilience comes from flexibility, not rigidity.

Pragmatic Paradox: When Trying Harder Makes Success Impossible

Some commands defeat themselves. Like ordering someone to "be natural!" - the harder they try, the more artificial they become. This psychological trap explains why direct effort often backfires.

How It Works:
Research shows certain goals create automatic self-sabotage. The more consciously you pursue them, the more impossible they become - a documented phenomenon in psychology and behavioral science.

Example:
Clinical studies of insomnia reveal that trying to force sleep extends wakefulness by 55%. The more intentionally patients "tried to sleep," the more their brain activated, preventing the very state they sought.

Why It Matters:
Organizations waste resources on self-defeating directives. "Be more creative!" programs reduce innovation. "Act natural!" makes people freeze. Understanding this paradox prevents costly mistakes.

When to Use It / How to Counter It:
Before issuing directives, ask: "Does pursuing this directly prevent its achievement?" Research shows indirect approaches often succeed where direct commands fail.

The Bottom Line:
Some goals are like butterflies - chase them, and they flee. Create the right conditions, then let them land naturally.

Precautionary Principle: Better Safe Than Sorry

In the face of potential serious harm, take preventive action even without complete scientific certainty. Like wearing a seatbelt – you don't wait for proof you'll crash before buckling up.

How It Works:
When an activity poses threats of serious or irreversible harm, take precautionary measures even if cause-and-effect relationships aren't fully proven. The absence of absolute certainty shouldn't prevent reasonable protective action when stakes are high.

Example:
Early concerns about climate change led some countries to reduce emissions despite uncertainty about exact impacts. Those who waited for absolute proof before acting now face higher costs and greater challenges. The price of precaution was far less than the cost of repair.

Why It Matters:
This principle protects against irreversible damage in complex systems where waiting for complete certainty could be catastrophic. It's crucial for decisions affecting health, safety, and environmental sustainability. Prevention often costs less than cure.

When to Use It / How to Counter It:
Before making decisions with potentially severe consequences, ask: "What's the worst that could happen if we're right? What's the cost of being wrong?" Sometimes the price of precaution is worth the protection it provides.

The Bottom Line:
Don't wait for disaster to prove you should have been careful. When potential harm is serious, err on the side of caution.

Preferential Attachment: Success Breeds Success

The rich get richer, and the popular get more popular. Like a snowball rolling downhill, initial advantages tend to compound, creating self-reinforcing cycles of success.

How It Works:
New resources and opportunities naturally flow toward already successful entities. Each win makes the next one easier, as success creates visibility, credibility, and connections. This compound effect explains why small early advantages often become insurmountable leads.

Example:
A YouTube video gets featured, gaining views. More views lead to better algorithmic placement, leading to even more views. Meanwhile, equally good content remains unseen because it lacks that initial boost. The rich-get-richer dynamic creates a widening gap.

Why It Matters:
Understanding this principle reveals why markets often produce winner-take-all outcomes. It explains everything from monopolies to viral content to wealth inequality. Success isn't just additive - it's multiplicative.

When to Use It / How to Counter It:
When launching products or building influence, ask: "How can I create early momentum?" Sometimes timing and initial advantage matter more than gradual improvement.

The Bottom Line:
Success creates conditions for more success. Either leverage these feedback loops or find ways to break them.

Principal-Agent Problem: Different Incentives, Different Actions

When someone acts on your behalf, their interests rarely align perfectly with yours. Like a real estate agent who wants a quick sale while you want the best price, misaligned incentives create hidden conflicts.

How It Works:
Agents (representatives) have their own interests that often conflict with principals (those they represent). This misalignment leads to actions that benefit the agent at the principal's expense. The gap between what you want and what your representative does creates inefficiency and potential exploitation.

Example:
Investment advisors recommend frequent trading because they earn commissions on each transaction, even though less trading might better serve their clients' long-term wealth. Their incentive (maximize transactions) conflicts with yours (maximize returns).

Why It Matters:
This problem affects nearly all delegation relationships - from employees to politicians. Understanding it helps design better incentives and monitoring systems. Without proper structures, agents naturally drift toward serving their own interests.

When to Use It / How to Counter It:
Before delegating authority, ask: "How might their incentives differ from mine?" Then design relationships to align interests or protect against conflicts.

The Bottom Line:
Never assume others will act exactly in your interest. Structure relationships to align incentives.

Prisoner's Dilemma: Cooperation vs Self-Interest

The Prisoner's Dilemma is a classic game theory problem that shows how two individuals, acting in their own self-interest, can end up with worse outcomes than if they had cooperated.

How It Works:
Two criminals are arrested and interrogated separately. They each have two choices: stay silent (cooperate) or betray the other (defect). The outcomes are as follows:

- If both stay silent, they each get a light sentence (1 year).
- If one betrays the other while the other stays silent, the betrayer goes free while the silent one gets a heavy sentence (5 years).
- If both betray each other, they each get a moderate sentence (3 years).

The dilemma occurs because betraying (defecting) seems like the safer choice individually, but if both defect, they end up worse off than if they had cooperated.

Example:
Two companies consider lowering prices. If both keep prices high, they profit. If one lowers prices, they gain the advantage. If both lower prices, a price war hurts them both.

Why It Matters:
The Prisoner's Dilemma demonstrates how rational self-interest can lead to sub-optimal outcomes for everyone involved. It's relevant in economics, politics, and everyday situations where cooperation is difficult but beneficial.

When to Use It / How to Counter It:
Use the Prisoner's Dilemma when discussing competition, negotiations, or situations where trust and cooperation are difficult but necessary for the best outcome.

Primacy Effect: First Impressions Stick

The Primacy Effect is the tendency to remember and give more weight to the first information we encounter. First impressions last, and the information you receive early on can shape how you perceive everything that comes after.

How It Works:
You meet someone for the first time, and your initial impression is that they're unfriendly. Even if they become more personable later, that first impression sticks in your mind. The Primacy Effect means that your initial experience colors how you interpret later information, making it hard to change your view.

Example: In job interviews, candidates often make or break their chances within the first few minutes, as interviewers tend to remember the first impressions more strongly than what happens later in the interview.

Why It Matters:
First impressions are powerful and can shape long-term opinions. The Primacy Effect shows that early interactions or information can bias our judgment, even when later evidence contradicts it. Being aware of this can help you focus on creating positive first impressions and also give people a second chance when necessary.

When to Use It / How to Counter It:
When meeting new people or encountering new information. Ask yourself: "Am I holding onto my first impression too strongly? Have things changed since then?" Try to remain open to new information and experiences, even after your initial impression is formed.

The Bottom Line:
First impressions last longer than you think. The Primacy Effect shows that early information shapes your perception, but it's important to stay flexible and open to new evidence.

Priority Heuristic: Simplifying Complex Choices

The Priority Heuristic is our brain's way of cutting through complexity by ranking what matters most. Like a chef who judges restaurants first by food quality, then service, then ambiance - in that order.

How It Works:
Instead of weighing all factors simultaneously, we rank aspects by importance and compare options based on top priorities first. If that produces a tie, we move to the next priority, continuing until a clear winner emerges.

Example:
When choosing a job offer, someone prioritizes work-life balance above all. They first eliminate positions with long hours, regardless of salary. Among the remaining options, they then consider pay, and finally commute time. Each step narrows the field.

Why It Matters:
This mental shortcut helps prevent decision paralysis in complex situations. While not always perfect, it matches how our brains naturally process choices and often leads to satisfactory decisions without overwhelming analysis.

When to Use It / How to Counter It:
Before facing complex decisions, list your priorities in order. Ask: "What's the one thing that matters most?" Start there, then work down your list. It won't always find the perfect choice, but it will find an acceptable one efficiently.

The Bottom Line:
Don't try to weigh everything at once. Rank what matters most and decide in steps.

Procrustean Fallacy: Forcing Facts to Fit Your Theory

Named after a mythical Greek bandit who made travelers fit his bed by stretching or cutting them, this is what happens when you distort reality to match your beliefs.

How It Works:
Instead of adjusting your beliefs to match the evidence, you twist, ignore, or selectively interpret evidence to support what you already believe. The facts get stretched or cut to fit your mental "bed."

Example:
Investment analysts often force market data to fit their predictions. When the S&P 500 rises, they call it "healthy growth." When it falls the same amount, it's a "needed correction." Same data, forced into different narratives.

Why It Matters:
When you reshape reality to fit your theories, you build decisions on distorted foundations. Your solutions stop matching real problems because you're solving for a world that doesn't exist.

When to Use It / How to Counter It:
Notice when you dismiss data that challenges your view or overemphasize data that supports it. If you find yourself saying "yes, but..." to every counterexample, you're likely forcing the fit.

The Bottom Line:
Reality doesn't care about your theories. Build your beliefs around facts, not facts around beliefs.

Projection Bias: Assuming Others Think, Feel, or Act Like You

Projection Bias happens when you assume others share your thoughts, feelings, and preferences. Like a morning person who schedules 7 AM meetings, believing everyone else must love early starts too.

How It Works:
We unconsciously use our own mind as a template for understanding others. Instead of recognizing different perspectives, we project our preferences, values, and thought patterns onto them. It's mental copy-and-paste gone wrong.

Example:
A manager who loves public recognition assumes all employees want their achievements announced at team meetings. Meanwhile, some team members find public praise embarrassing and would prefer private acknowledgment. The projection creates discomfort instead of motivation.

Why It Matters:
This bias leads to misunderstandings and communication breakdowns. When we assume others think like us, we miss opportunities to understand different perspectives and needs. It's particularly dangerous in leadership, relationships, and product design.

When to Use It / How to Counter It:
Before making decisions affecting others, ask: "Am I assuming they want what I want? Have I actually asked them?" Question your assumptions about others' preferences.

The Bottom Line:
Your mind isn't everyone's mind. Ask, don't assume.

Pro-Innovation Bias: Overvaluing Innovation While Ignoring Potential Downsides

Pro-Innovation Bias is the tendency to fall in love with new ideas while wearing blinders to their drawbacks. Like rushing to buy the latest smartphone without considering if you really need its features.

How It Works:
We naturally get excited about innovation's potential benefits while discounting or ignoring possible problems. This rose-tinted view of new technology, methods, or ideas leads us to overlook crucial limitations, risks, and implementation challenges.

Example:
A company rushes to implement AI in their customer service, dazzled by its potential. They ignore warning signs about language limitations and customer frustration. Six months later, they're dealing with angry customers and demoralized staff who have to clean up the AI's mistakes.

Why It Matters:
This bias leads to costly mistakes in adoption and implementation. Understanding it helps balance excitement about innovation with necessary skepticism. Not every new thing is an improvement, and even good innovations can have serious drawbacks.

When to Use It / How to Counter It:
Before embracing something new, ask: "What could go wrong? What hidden costs or challenges am I ignoring?" Force yourself to list potential downsides alongside benefits.

The Bottom Line:
New isn't always better. Balance innovation excitement with careful evaluation.

Procrastination Fallacy: The "I'll Do It Later" Lie

The Procrastination Fallacy tricks us into believing that future-us will be more motivated, energetic, and capable than present-us. Like imagining you'll wake up early to exercise while hitting snooze for the tenth time.

How It Works:
We consistently overestimate our future capacity while underestimating our present ability. This mental error makes us believe that "later" will somehow be easier, less busy, or more conducive to work. Meanwhile, real opportunities slip away in the present.

Example:
You have a presentation due in two weeks. Instead of starting now, you convince yourself that weekend-you will be more focused and creative. But when the weekend arrives, you're just as distracted and now have less time. The cycle repeats until it's midnight before the deadline.

Why It Matters:
This fallacy creates a perpetual cycle of delay and regret. Understanding it helps break the pattern of pushing things off. Future-you will face the same challenges as present-you, plus the added pressure of accumulated delays.

When to Use It / How to Counter It:
When tempted to delay, ask: "What makes me think later will be easier? What small step could I take right now?" The best time to start is usually now.

The Bottom Line:
Future-you isn't a superhero. Start now, even if it's just a little bit.

Proximate vs Ultimate Cause: Why Asking "Why?" Once Is Never Enough

A house burns down. The proximate cause? A knocked-over candle. The ultimate cause? No automatic sprinkler system, poor fire safety codes, or inadequate insurance requirements. Like peeling an onion, each layer reveals a deeper truth.

How It Works:
Proximate causes are immediate triggers - what directly preceded the event. Ultimate causes are the deeper, systemic reasons that allowed the proximate cause to matter. One explains how something happened, the other explains why it was possible in the first place.

Example:
A corporate data breach occurs. Proximate cause: An employee clicked a phishing link. Ultimate causes: Inadequate security training, outdated software, no two-factor authentication, and prioritizing convenience over security. The click was just the final domino in a long chain.

Why It Matters:
Fixing proximate causes treats symptoms; addressing ultimate causes prevents recurrence. Organizations often focus on proximate causes because they're obvious and easier to blame. But real, lasting solutions require diving deeper into systems and structures.

When to Use It / How to Counter It:
After any failure, ask "Why?" at least five times. Each answer reveals a deeper cause. Stop when you reach factors you can actually change - that's where effective solutions begin.

The Bottom Line:
Proximate causes trigger events. Ultimate causes allow them to matter. Fix both, but prioritize the ultimate.

Pseudocertainty Effect: Preferring Certain Outcomes When Risky Ones Pay Better

The Pseudocertainty Effect describes our irrational preference for guaranteed outcomes over potentially better but uncertain ones. Like choosing a safe 2% savings account over investments that historically return 8%.

How It Works:
Our brains are wired to overvalue certainty and undervalue probability. When faced with choices between guaranteed small gains and probable larger ones, we often choose certainty - even when math shows the riskier choice offers better expected value.

Example:
Given a choice between a guaranteed $50 or a 70% chance of winning $100, most people take the sure $50. Yet the risky option's expected value is $70 ($100 × 0.7). Our certainty bias costs us $20 in potential value.

Why It Matters:
This effect leads to systematically suboptimal decisions in business, investing, and career choices. Understanding it helps overcome our natural bias against beneficial uncertainty. Playing it too safe often means leaving opportunity on the table.

When to Use It / How to Counter It:
Before choosing the "safe" option, ask: "What's the expected value of each choice? Am I letting my comfort with certainty blind me to better opportunities?"

The Bottom Line:
Sometimes the best path isn't the surest one. Calculate expected value, not just certainty.

Pygmalion Effect: Expectations Shape Reality

Your expectations of others can become self-fulfilling prophecies. Believe in someone's potential, and they're more likely to succeed. Doubt them, and they're more likely to fail.

How It Works:
People unconsciously adjust their behavior to match others' expectations. When a leader shows confidence in someone's abilities, that person works harder and performs better - making the original belief come true. The effect works in both positive and negative directions.

Example:
A manager believes a new hire has executive potential. She gives them challenging assignments and mentorship. The employee, sensing this confidence, takes more risks and develops faster. The initial expectation creates its own reality. Meanwhile, those labeled as "average" often remain exactly that.

Why It Matters:
This effect shapes outcomes in business, education, and relationships. Your expectations literally help shape others' success or failure. It's a crucial tool for leaders, teachers, and mentors. Understanding it gives you the power to uplift or unknowingly hold others back.

When to Use It / How to Counter It:
Before interacting with team members or students, ask: "What expectations am I signaling?" Choose to believe in people's potential - it costs nothing and can activate growth. Be especially aware of unintended negative expectations.

The Bottom Line:
Expectations are self-fulfilling. Set them high, and watch people rise to meet them.

Reactance: Why We Rebel Against Being Told What to Do

When someone restricts your freedom of choice, your brain's automatic response is often to do the exact opposite - even if it hurts you.

How It Works:
Reactance is your mind's rebellion against perceived control. Tell someone not to touch a button, and suddenly touching it becomes irresistible. The stronger the pressure to comply, the stronger the urge to resist.

Example:
A company implements strict time tracking. Employees who previously worked long hours start leaving exactly at 5 PM. The attempt to control behavior backfires, creating exactly what management tried to prevent.

Why It Matters:
This psychological boomerang effect can lead to self-sabotage. You might reject good advice or opportunities simply because they came as mandates. Freedom feels more important than benefit.

When to Use It / How to Counter It:
Before reflexively opposing something, ask: "Am I resisting because it's truly wrong, or just because I hate being told what to do?" Sometimes rebellion costs more than compliance.

The Bottom Line:
Don't let your need for autonomy override your good judgment. Choose your battles based on merit, not spite.

Reality Check Principle (Alder's Razor): If You Can't Test It, Don't Trust It

That elegant theory sounds great in the boardroom. But if you can't test it, measure it, or observe it - it's just expensive guessing.

How It Works:
Your brain loves beautiful theories. But reality only cares about what works. If someone can't show you evidence, data, or results, they're selling philosophy, not solutions. It's like having a "brilliant" business plan that can never be tested - it's just a fancy story.

Example:
A consultant pitches a revolutionary management theory. When asked for evidence, they say "it's too complex to measure" or "the results are intangible." Meanwhile, their competitor shows actual before/after metrics from real companies. Who would you trust with your money?

Why It Matters:
Time and resources are wasted on untestable ideas. Companies burn millions on theories that sound good but can't be verified. This principle saves you from expensive philosophical experiments by demanding practical evidence.

When to Use It / How to Counter It:
Before investing in any idea, ask: "How can we test if this actually works?" If there's no way to measure success or failure, it's not a strategy - it's a guess. Focus on what you can verify, not what just sounds good.

The Bottom Line:
If you can't test it, you can't trust it. Leave the untestable theories to philosophers - business needs results you can measure.

Recency Bias: Why Yesterday Matters More Than Last Year

Your brain gives too much weight to recent events. Like a fish that only remembers its last meal, we let the immediate past overshadow long-term patterns.

How It Works:
Recent experiences dominate your thinking, drowning out historical patterns. A week of rain makes you forget months of sunshine. One bad quarter erases years of growth. The closer in time, the bigger it looms.

Example:
The stock market drops 5% in a week. Investors panic-sell, forgetting the 200% gain over the last decade. The recent loss feels more real than years of gains, leading to emotional decisions that lock in temporary losses.

Why It Matters:
This bias drives costly mistakes in investing, relationships, and career choices. We overreact to recent events, abandon solid long-term strategies, and make permanent decisions based on temporary situations.

When to Use It / How to Counter It:
Before making major changes based on recent events, ask: "How does this fit into the bigger picture?" "Am I reacting to a trend or a blip?" Zoom out before you act.

The Bottom Line:
Yesterday's news isn't more important than last year's truth. Train yourself to see the full timeline, not just the latest chapter.

Recency Effect: Why We Remember the Last Thing Best

In any sequence of information, your brain gives special weight to what came last. It's why speakers save their strongest point for the end, and why your last job matters most in interviews.

How It Works:
When processing a series of information, your brain has a natural tendency to recall the most recent items more clearly than earlier ones. The last few items get privileged status in memory.

Example:
In job interviews, candidates are remembered most for their final answers. A strong finish can overshadow earlier stumbles, while a weak ending can undermine previous strong responses.

Why It Matters:
This effect influences everything from presentations to negotiations. Understanding it helps you structure information strategically - whether you're selling ideas, interviewing, or learning new material.

When to Use It / How to Counter It:
Before important communications, ask: "What do I want people to remember most?" Put that at the end. When learning, review crucial information last to improve retention.

The Bottom Line:
The end matters more than the middle. Use this knowledge to make your last impression your strongest one.

NOTE:

The **Recency Effect** and **Recency Bias** are closely related but not exactly the same.

Recency Effect refers to a cognitive phenomenon in memory, where people tend to remember the most recent information better than earlier information. It's often discussed in the context of learning, presentations, or recall of lists, where the last items are more easily recalled.

Recency Bias is broader and refers to a cognitive bias where people give more weight or importance to recent events or experiences when making judgments or decisions. For example, if you're reviewing an employee's performance and give more emphasis to their recent work instead of considering their overall performance, that's recency bias.

Both involve recent information, but the Recency Effect is more about memory recall, while Recency Bias involves decision-making and judgment influenced by the most recent data.

Reciprocity Principle: The Urge to Repay Kindness

When someone does something for you, you feel compelled to return the favor. This deep social instinct creates powerful obligations - for better or worse.

How It Works:
Your brain is wired to balance social debts. Receive a favor, and you'll feel a strong urge to reciprocate. This instinct is so powerful that even unwanted gifts can create a feeling of obligation.

Example:
Costco's free samples dramatically increase sales. Research shows shoppers who take a free sample are 30% more likely to buy the product. The small act of accepting a bite creates a subtle pressure to purchase - even though the sample was technically "no obligation."

Why It Matters:
Reciprocity can build strong relationships or manipulate behavior. Organizations from charities to corporations exploit it systematically. Understanding it helps you spot genuine connection versus calculated influence.

When to Use It / How to Counter It:
Before giving or receiving, ask: "Is this genuine generosity or creating obligation?" Use reciprocity to build real connections, not invisible debt. Stay aware of how others use it on you.

The Bottom Line:
The urge to repay kindness is powerful. Use it to strengthen relationships, but beware those who use it to manipulate.

Recognition Heuristic: Simplicity in Decision-Making

The Recognition Heuristic suggests that when faced with multiple options, people tend to choose the one they recognize, assuming it's more likely to be correct or better. It's a mental shortcut where familiarity plays a key role in decision-making, even in situations where it might not be the most logical choice.

How It Works:
You're asked to pick the winner of a tennis match between two players. You've heard of one player before but not the other, so you choose the one you recognize, assuming they're more likely to win. The Recognition Heuristic relies on the idea that if you've heard of something before, it must be significant or better, even if you don't have additional information.

Example:
In an election, a voter might choose a candidate they've heard of more often in ads or media, even if they know little about their policies. Familiarity becomes the deciding factor.

Why It Matters:
The Recognition Heuristic is useful for quick, low-stakes decisions where deep analysis isn't needed. However, it can lead to biases, especially in important decisions like investments or hiring, where familiarity doesn't always equate to quality.

When to Use It / How to Counter It:
This heuristic is often employed in fast decision-making situations where time or information is limited. It can help with quick choices, but it's important to recognize when a deeper analysis is required.

The Bottom Line:
Familiarity can guide your decisions, but the Recognition Heuristic isn't always reliable. Use it in simple scenarios, but be cautious of its potential bias in more critical choices.

Red Herring: The Great Distraction

A Red Herring is the debate version of "Hey, look over there!" It's when someone derails a discussion by introducing an unrelated but emotionally charged topic.

How It Works:
When faced with a tough argument, throw in an interesting but irrelevant issue. Like a politician asked about corruption responding, "But what about our failing schools?" Valid concern, wrong conversation.

Example:
During a company's wage negotiation, management brings up a competitor's layoffs. This scary but unrelated topic diverts attention from the actual salary discussion. The tactic worked - they're no longer talking about raises.

Why It Matters:
Red Herrings kill productive discussion. They're particularly common in politics, negotiations, and any situation where someone wants to avoid uncomfortable topics. Recognizing them helps you stay focused on real issues.

When to Use It / How to Counter It:
Before chasing a new topic, ask: "Is this relevant to our original discussion?" If not, redirect back to the main point. Don't let emotional bait drag you off course.

The Bottom Line:
Stay focused on the real issue. If someone needs a distraction to win, they're actually losing. Keep the discussion on track.

Reductio ad Absurdum: Taking It to the Extreme

This powerful logical tool exposes flawed reasoning by pushing it to its absurd conclusion. When an argument can't survive its own logic, you've found its fatal flaw.

How It Works:
Take someone's argument and extend its logic to the extreme. If the conclusion becomes absurd while following the same reasoning, you've shown the original argument is flawed - even if you can't pinpoint exactly where.

Example:
A manager argues "If one remote worker is productive, everyone should work remotely because it's more efficient." Following this logic: Surgeons should operate remotely, construction workers should build remotely, and restaurant chefs should cook remotely. The absurd conclusion reveals the flawed premise.

Why It Matters:
This technique cuts through emotional arguments by exposing logical inconsistencies. It's particularly effective when direct confrontation might be unproductive, letting the absurdity make your point.

When to Use It / How to Counter It:
Before accepting sweeping generalizations, extend their logic. Ask: "If this reasoning is sound, what else would have to be true?" Let the absurd implications speak for themselves.

The Bottom Line:
Push arguments to their logical extreme to reveal hidden flaws. The truth often lies in the limitations.

Regression Fallacy: Mistaking Random Fluctuations for Cause and Effect

When things return to normal, we love to take credit. But sometimes better performance isn't caused by what we did - it's just natural variation at work.

How It Works:
Extreme results tend to be followed by more average ones. This natural "regression to the mean" happens without any intervention, but we often mistakenly credit (or blame) whatever action we took in between.

Example:
A baseball player has an incredible month, batting .400. The coach changes nothing, but next month the average drops to .300. A new batting coach is hired, and performance "improves" to .320. The coach gets credit for an improvement that was just normal regression.

Why It Matters:
This fallacy leads to false confidence in ineffective solutions. Companies waste resources on programs that seemed to work but actually didn't. Understanding regression prevents these expensive mistakes.

When to Use It / How to Counter It:
Before celebrating a solution's success, ask: "Would this have improved anyway?" Look for long-term patterns, not just before-and-after snapshots.

The Bottom Line:
Not every change needs a cause. Sometimes things just return to normal on their own.

Relative Privation: Why "It Could Be Worse" Is Bad Logic

"Your problems aren't real problems - think about starving children!" This fallacy dismisses legitimate concerns by comparing them to bigger issues.

How It Works:
You downplay one problem by pointing to a worse one. Like telling someone with a broken arm, "At least you're not paralyzed!" While technically true, it invalidates real pain and prevents solving actual problems.

Example:
An employee raises concerns about toxic workplace behavior. The manager responds, "At least you have a job - many companies are laying people off." The comparison deflects from addressing the real issue at hand.

Why It Matters:
This fallacy stops problem-solving in its tracks. Companies ignore fixable issues because "others have it worse." Teams accept poor conditions because "it could be worse." Progress stalls because smaller problems never get addressed.

When to Use It / How to Counter It:
When you hear "it could be worse," ask: "Does this comparison help solve the actual problem?" Save comparisons for inspiration, not dismissal. Each problem deserves attention on its own merits.

The Bottom Line:
Problems don't stop being problems just because bigger ones exist. Address each challenge on its own terms.

Responsibility Bias: Why Everyone Thinks They Did Most of the Work

In any group project, each person believes they carried the heaviest load. Like five people claiming 40% credit each, the math never adds up.

How It Works:
You naturally remember your own efforts more vividly than others' contributions. You saw every minute you spent working, but missed others' behind-the-scenes efforts. This creates a skewed perception of workload distribution.

Example:
A successful product launch has three teammates each claiming primary credit. The designer remembers every pixel they tweaked, the engineer recalls every bug they fixed, and the manager remembers every meeting they coordinated. Each sees their contribution as central.

Why It Matters:
This bias creates team tension and resentment. People feel undervalued, rewards seem unfair, and collaboration suffers. Understanding it helps prevent the "I did everything" mindset that poisons teamwork.

When to Use It / How to Counter It:
Before claiming credit or feeling resentful, ask: "What contributions from others might I be overlooking?" Remember: everyone's effort looms largest in their own mind.

The Bottom Line:
Your work feels bigger because you watched yourself do it. Give others the credit you'd want for your unseen efforts.

Responsibility Diffusion Model: When Everyone Can Help, No One Does

The more people who can solve a problem, the less likely anyone will. It's why emails copying the whole company rarely get responses, and why tasks assigned to teams often get done slower than tasks assigned to individuals.

How It Works:
As the number of potential problem-solvers increases, each person's sense of individual responsibility decreases. People assume someone else will handle it, leading to a situation where everybody's responsibility becomes nobody's responsibility.

Example:
A tech company's shared codebase has an obvious bug. Dozens of developers see it daily, but no one fixes it because "surely someone else will handle it." Three months later, the bug remains despite being seen by the entire engineering team. What's everyone's job becomes no one's job.

Why It Matters:
This model explains why group ownership often fails, and why important tasks fall through the cracks in organizations. Understanding it helps you design better accountability systems and recognize when shared responsibility needs to be converted to individual ownership.

When to Use It / How to Counter It:
When assigning tasks, ask: "Who specifically owns this? Have I made responsibility clear enough that it can't be diffused?" Sometimes the best way to get something done is to make it one person's clear priority.

The Bottom Line:
Everybody's responsibility is nobody's job. Make it someone's or watch it fail.

Restraint Bias: Why Willpower Isn't Enough

You think you can resist that cookie jar on your desk. You're wrong. Research shows we consistently overestimate our ability to control impulses.

How It Works:
Your brain overvalues willpower and underestimates temptation's pull. Studies show people routinely predict more self-control than they actually demonstrate in real situations.

Example:
Research with dieters found those who rated their self-control highest were actually most likely to break their diets when tempting foods were easily accessible. Their confidence led them to surround themselves with temptations they couldn't resist.

Why It Matters:
This bias sabotages goals by creating unnecessary risks. Studies in addiction recovery, dieting, and spending show that overconfidence in willpower leads to higher relapse rates. Environmental control beats willpower.

When to Use It / How to Counter It:
Before testing your self-control, ask: "Am I setting myself up to fail?" Research shows removing temptations is more effective than relying on willpower. Create distance between you and your triggers.

The Bottom Line:
Don't trust your willpower estimates - they're probably optimistic. Design your environment for success instead.

Resulting: When You Mistake Luck for Skill

Great outcomes can come from terrible decisions, and smart choices can end in disaster. Judging decisions by results alone blinds you to the role of luck.

How It Works:
People naturally judge decisions by their outcomes rather than the decision-making process. A lucky gamble that pays off feels like genius, while a sound strategy that fails looks like stupidity. This bias distorts how we learn from experience.

Example:
A tech startup skips market research and security testing to launch quickly. They succeed and praise their "bold strategy." Meanwhile, careful competitors who did proper research but failed are labeled overcautious. The outcome masked the real risk. The industry learns the wrong lesson.

Why It Matters:
'Resulting' creates dangerous feedback loops in business and investing. Companies repeat risky behaviors because they worked once, or abandon sound strategies after bad luck. Success teaches the wrong lessons when we ignore the role of chance.

When to Use It / How to Counter It:
Before praising or condemning decisions, ask: "Would this still be a good decision if luck had gone the other way?" Focus on the quality of your process, not just outcomes.

The Bottom Line:
Judge your decisions by how well you made them, not how they turned out. Luck evens out over time - good process is forever.

Ringelmann Effect: Diminishing Productivity in Groups

The Ringelmann Effect refers to the tendency for individual productivity to decrease as the size of a group increases. As more people join a group effort, each member feels less personal responsibility, leading to reduced overall performance.

How It Works:
In a group, each person contributes less effort than they would individually, thinking others will pick up the slack. For example, if you're in a team pulling a rope, you might not pull as hard as you would alone, assuming the group's combined effort is enough.

Example:
In brainstorming sessions, larger groups often produce fewer ideas per person compared to smaller groups or individuals working alone. The more people involved, the easier it becomes to hide behind the efforts of others.

Why It Matters:
The Ringelmann Effect shows how group size can negatively affect productivity. Recognizing this helps managers and leaders break tasks into smaller teams to maintain individual accountability and keep performance high.

When to Use It / How to Counter It:
When organizing teams, ask: "Is this group too large for everyone to stay engaged and accountable?" Reducing team size or assigning specific roles can mitigate the effect and boost productivity.

The Bottom Line:
As groups grow, individual effort tends to shrink. The Ringelmann Effect reminds us that bigger teams aren't always better - smaller, focused groups often get more done.

Risk Aversion: Why Safe Feels Better Than Sorry

When faced with a choice between a small, certain gain and a larger, uncertain one, most people choose certainty - even when the math favors risk-taking.

How It Works:
Your brain feels losses about twice as strongly as equivalent gains. Given a choice between a guaranteed $500 or a 50% chance at $1,200, most people take the sure $500, even though the risky choice is worth more mathematically ($600 on average).

Example:
Companies often stick with outdated but "safe" systems rather than upgrade to more efficient ones. A manufacturer keeps using old machinery instead of investing in automated equipment - the known inefficiency feels safer than unknown implementation risks.

Why It Matters:
Risk aversion leads to systematically undervaluing opportunities. Studies show most people require potential gains to be twice the size of potential losses before they'll take a risk. This creates costly missed opportunities in business and investing.

When to Use It / How to Counter It:
Before rejecting an opportunity as "too risky," calculate expected value. Ask: "Am I avoiding this because it's genuinely too risky, or just because uncertainty feels uncomfortable?"

The Bottom Line:
Not all risks are bad risks. Sometimes playing it safe is the riskiest choice of all.

Risk Compensation: Why Safety Features Make Us Less Safe

When we feel protected, we often take bigger risks. It's why people drive faster in safer cars and ski more recklessly wearing helmets.

How It Works:
Safety measures create a false sense of invulnerability. Each layer of protection unconsciously encourages slightly riskier behavior, sometimes completely canceling out the safety benefit.

Example:
Studies show drivers of vehicles with anti-lock brakes follow other cars more closely. SUV owners drive faster in bad weather than sedan owners. The very features designed to protect us can make us more dangerous.

Why It Matters:
Risk compensation undermines safety investments across industries. Companies add protective equipment, then workers take bigger risks. Cities widen roads, then people drive faster. Understanding this prevents safety measures from backfiring.

When to Use It / How to Counter It:
Before relying on safety features, ask: "Am I behaving more carelessly because I feel protected?" Remember that protective measures work best when behavior stays constant.

The Bottom Line:
Safety features only work if you don't change your behavior to compensate. The safest protection is the one that doesn't make you feel invincible.

Risk vs. Uncertainty: Known Odds vs. Complete Unknown

Some futures you can calculate, others you can only prepare for. Understanding this difference changes how you approach decisions.

How It Works:
Risk means you can calculate odds, like rolling dice or insurance tables. Uncertainty means even the possibilities are unknown - like launching a first-of-its-kind business. Each requires different strategies.

Example:
Insurance companies handle risk - they use actuarial tables to price policies. But early COVID-19 response faced uncertainty - no historical data existed to calculate probabilities or predict outcomes. Risk can be measured; uncertainty can only be managed.

Why It Matters:
Different types of unknowns need different approaches. Risk responds to calculation and hedging strategies. Uncertainty requires flexibility and redundancy. Using the wrong approach can be disastrous.

When to Use It / How to Counter It:
Before making decisions, ask: "Can I calculate odds, or am I truly in uncharted territory?" Use probability for risk, scenario planning for uncertainty.

The Bottom Line:
Risk can be measured and managed. Uncertainty can only be navigated. Know which you're facing before you choose your approach.

Robustness Principle: Be Conservative in What You Do, Liberal in What You Accept

The best systems maintain high standards for their output while gracefully handling imperfect input. It's a balance that makes complex interactions possible.

How It Works:
Hold yourself to strict standards while being flexible with what you receive from others. Like a REST API that accepts various data formats but always responds in perfectly formatted JSON.

Example:
Email servers embody this principle: They strictly follow protocols when sending mail but accept messages with minor formatting errors. Without this flexibility, email might fail if every server demanded perfection.

Why It Matters:
In complex systems, perfect compliance is rare. TCP/IP, the internet's foundation, works because it's forgiving of errors while being precise in its own behavior. This principle enables reliable systems in an imperfect world.

When to Use It / How to Counter It:
Before designing any interface or process, ask: "How can I maintain high standards while accommodating imperfect input?" Balance idealism with practical reality.

The Bottom Line:
Perfect standards meet imperfect reality. Be strict with yourself, flexible with others - it makes systems more resilient.

Rule of Three: Why Information in Threes Feels Just Right

The human brain has a natural affinity for patterns - and three is the magic number for memorability and impact.

How It Works:
Information presented in groups of three is more engaging, memorable, and satisfying to the human mind than other numbers. This pattern appears consistently across speeches, stories, and slogans throughout history.

Example:
"Life, liberty, and the pursuit of happiness." This principle shaped the most memorable speeches from Churchill's "blood, toil, tears and sweat" to Caesar's "Veni, vidi, vici." Nike's "Just Do It" took three syllables to change advertising forever.

Why It Matters:
When communicating important ideas, the rule of three helps structure information in a way that's both digestible and memorable. Three elements provide just enough information without overwhelming working memory.

When to Use It / How to Counter It:
Before important presentations, sales pitches, or written communications, organize key points in threes. Use it for slogans, product features, or main arguments. Avoid diluting impact with four or more points.

The Bottom Line:
Three is complete. Three is balanced. Three sticks.

Sacred Cows: Why Some Ideas Are Too Holy to Question

Every organization has them - those unspoken rules and unchallenged assumptions that everyone treats as untouchable.

How It Works:
Sacred cows are practices, policies, or ideas that persist without scrutiny despite their flaws. They become immune to criticism through tradition, authority, or organizational culture. Like religious taboos, questioning them feels forbidden.

Example:
A company maintains an elaborate monthly reporting process that takes three days and involves twenty people. Everyone knows it's inefficient, but it was implemented by a revered former CEO. Years later, no one dares suggest changing it, even though current leadership rarely reads the reports.

Why It Matters:
Sacred cows drain resources, stifle innovation, and maintain inefficiency through the power of social pressure and tradition. They represent the triumph of reverence over reason, costing organizations time, money, and talent.

When to Use It / How to Counter It:
Regularly audit your organization's practices by asking: "What do we do simply because we've always done it?" Look for processes that people defend with "that's just how things work here" rather than actual results.

The Bottom Line:
Killing sacred cows (not living ones, of course) is painful but necessary. The most dangerous ideas are the ones you're not allowed to question.

Sagan Standard: Extraordinary Claims Require Extraordinary Evidence

The Sagan Standard, named after astronomer Carl Sagan, asserts that extraordinary claims must be backed by extraordinary evidence. It reminds us not to accept extraordinary assertions without equally compelling proof.

How It Works:
If someone claims to have seen an alien spaceship, the Sagan Standard would require exceptionally strong evidence - photos, videos, physical samples - before the claim can be seriously considered. The more extraordinary the claim, the more rigorous the proof must be.

Example:
A person claims they can predict the future. According to the Sagan Standard, you'd expect controlled experiments and solid proof, not just stories, before believing this.

Why It Matters:
This standard is essential for distinguishing credible claims from pseudoscience. It prevents accepting extraordinary claims based on flimsy evidence, encouraging critical thinking and demanding high standards of proof.

When to Use It / How to Counter It:
Use the Sagan Standard when you encounter a claim that seems extraordinary. Ask: "Is the evidence as extraordinary as the claim?" It's vital for evaluating everything from conspiracy theories to new scientific discoveries.

The Bottom Line:
The more extraordinary the claim, the stronger the evidence must be. The Sagan Standard ensures remarkable assertions have equally remarkable proof.

Satisfaction Razor: Define Your "Enough"

In a world pushing for endless more, knowing when to stop is a superpower. The Satisfaction Razor helps you define your personal "enough" before the chase consumes you.

How It Works:
Instead of defaulting to endless growth, consciously define your satisfaction point. Like setting a specific number for retirement savings rather than just "as much as possible."

Example:
A software engineer decides their "enough" is $150K salary with 3-day remote work, turning down higher-paying roles that demand more hours. Another chooses to stay at Director level, declining VP promotions to preserve family time.

Why It Matters:
Studies show chasing undefined "more" leads to burnout and decreased satisfaction. People who set clear "enough" targets report higher contentment than those pursuing endless growth.

When to Use It / How to Counter It:
Before any major pursuit, ask: "What's my actual target? At what point will I be satisfied?" Define success in specific, personal terms - not society's endless escalator.

The Bottom Line:
More isn't better - enough is better. Define your finish line or risk running forever.

Satisficing: Settling for 'good enough' rather than the best

Satisficing: Settling for 'good enough' rather than the best
Satisficing is a decision-making strategy where you settle for a solution that's "good enough" rather than spending extra time searching for the perfect option. It balances effort and outcome, especially when perfection isn't necessary.

How It Works:
You need a new laptop but instead of hours of research, you pick one that meets your basic requirements. It may not be the absolute best, but it's good enough for what you need. Satisficing helps you make quicker decisions and avoid over-analysis.

Example:
While grocery shopping, you grab the first decent loaf of bread instead of examining each brand. Satisficing works because perfection isn't required - just a sufficient choice.

Why It Matters:
Satisficing prevents analysis paralysis, where overthinking leads to delays. By recognizing when "good enough" is enough, you save time and energy for more important decisions.

When to Use It / How to Counter It:
In low-stakes decisions or when time is a factor. Ask: "Is the perfect option worth the extra effort, or is this good enough?" Satisficing keeps decisions efficient.

The Bottom Line:
"Good enough" often really is enough. Satisficing helps you make quick, efficient decisions without wasting time on trivial details.

Scale Fallacy: What Works Small Doesn't Always Work Big

A lone cook can make a perfect omelet in 5 minutes. But a restaurant can't make 100 perfect omelets by just multiplying everything by 100. Yet we constantly fall for this seductive but dangerous mathematical thinking.

How It Works:
We assume success at one scale will automatically translate to another scale. But scaling up (or down) changes the nature of the problem, not just its size. New complexities emerge, different rules apply, and what worked before might actually become a liability.

Example:
A startup founder personally responds to every customer email, creating amazing satisfaction. When they grow to 10,000 customers, they try to maintain this approach by hiring 50 support staff. But coordination problems, inconsistent responses, and training issues actually make service worse, not better.

Why It Matters:
Failed scaling destroys businesses, projects, and relationships. Understanding that different scales require different solutions helps you adapt strategies instead of blindly copying what worked before.

When to Use It / How to Counter It:
Before scaling any solution, ask: "What new problems might emerge at a larger scale? What advantages might we lose? What systems need to change?" Success requires evolving your approach, not just enlarging it.

The Bottom Line:
Scale changes everything. What works for one often fails for many. Plan for complexity, not just size.

Scientism: When Science Overreaches Its Bounds

Science is a powerful tool for understanding the physical world. But treating it as the only valid source of knowledge creates dangerous blind spots.

How It Works:
Scientism extends scientific authority beyond testable claims into areas where empirical methods don't apply. It dismisses art, ethics, and human experience if they can't be measured in a lab or proven mathematically.

Example:
A company relies solely on productivity metrics to evaluate employee performance, ignoring crucial unmeasurable factors like team morale and creativity. The data looks good, but the workplace culture suffers. Some things that matter can't be quantified.

Why It Matters:
This mindset creates artificial limitations. Leadership requires wisdom, not just data. Relationships need empathy, not just psychology. Ethics demands philosophy, not just neuroscience. Reducing everything to measurable variables misses essential human truths.

When to Use It / How to Counter It:
Before dismissing non-scientific knowledge, ask: "Is this truly a scientific question? Are there valuable insights here that can't be measured?" Recognize science's power without making it a religion.

The Bottom Line:
Science explains much, but not everything. Some truths can't be proven in a lab - and that's okay.

Scripted Message: How Coordinated Language Shapes Perception

When multiple sources suddenly use identical unusual phrases, you're likely witnessing a coordinated messaging campaign - not organic communication.

How It Works:
Organizations distribute specific phrases and talking points to multiple speakers and media outlets. Research shows repeated exposure to identical messages increases their perceived credibility.

Example:
"*We take your privacy/security seriously*": This exact phrase appeared in statements from companies who had date breaches. "*Out of an abundance of caution*" was used verbatim in product recalls by many big companies, showing how safety messaging gets templated. "*This does not reflect our values*" appeared in public apologies from companies and political parties.

Why It Matters:
Message coordination creates an illusion of spontaneous consensus. By recognizing scripted language patterns, you can identify when your opinions are being deliberately shaped.

When to Use It / How to Counter It:
Compare language across sources during corporate announcements or industry shifts. When you notice identical unusual phrases, trace them to their source to understand who's coordinating.

The Bottom Line:
Synchronized messages aren't coincidence - they're strategy. Learn to spot the pattern, and you'll see coordination hiding behind "spontaneous" consensus.

Second-Order Thinking: Anticipating Consequences of Consequences

Second-Order Thinking is about looking beyond the immediate effects of a decision and considering its longer-term consequences, as well as the consequences of those consequences. It helps you anticipate unintended results that aren't immediately obvious.

How It Works:
A company decides to cut prices to increase sales. The immediate result is a sales boost, but Second-Order Thinking considers the consequences - lower margins, the need to cut costs, potential damage to the brand's reputation for quality. Thinking beyond the first result helps anticipate these risks.

Example:
Introducing wolves back into Yellowstone National Park initially led to concerns about livestock predation. But the second-order effect was that the wolves controlled the elk population, allowing vegetation and other wildlife to flourish, improving the entire ecosystem.

Why It Matters:
Second-Order Thinking helps avoid short-term thinking and recognizes that every action has ripple effects. By considering the long-term impacts, you can make smarter decisions.

When to Use It / How to Counter It:
Before making a decision, ask: "What happens next, and what happens after that?" Anticipating second-order consequences can help avoid unintended harm.

The Bottom Line:
Think beyond the immediate result. Second-Order Thinking encourages you to anticipate the longer-term consequences of your decisions.

Second System Effect: Why Sequels Often Suck

After a successful first attempt, creators often try to perfect their creation. The result? A bloated mess that loses the elegant simplicity that made the original work.

How It Works:
When building version two, creators try to fix every limitation of version one. But without the original constraints forcing tough choices, feature creep and complexity multiply. What made the first version special gets buried.

Example:
Windows Vista followed the successful Windows XP. Microsoft added every feature users requested and "fixed" every limitation. The result was slower, more complex, and less reliable than its predecessor. Users preferred the simpler original.

Why It Matters:
This pattern repeats across software, products, and organizations. Second versions try to perfect everything, but lose focus. The discipline of constraints that shaped the original disappears in the freedom of the sequel.

When to Use It / How to Counter It:
Before building version two, ask: "What made the original special? What constraints led to good decisions?" Keep the core elegant while carefully choosing improvements. Resist the urge to add everything.

The Bottom Line:
Success breeds ambition, but ambition can kill simplicity. Keep second versions as focused as the first.

Selection Bias: When Missing Data Leads to False Conclusions

Perfect logic fails when your sample misrepresents reality — a foundational error that corrupts even flawless analysis.

How It Works:
Selection bias occurs when data collection systematically excludes relevant cases from your sample. Unlike confirmation bias (which filters existing data), selection bias creates a fundamentally skewed dataset before any analysis begins, making even perfect reasoning lead to wrong conclusions.

Example:
A landmark 1981 study revealed early seat belt effectiveness statistics were catastrophically wrong. By only sampling crash survivors ("dead men tell no tales"), researchers excluded the most critical data. Including fatality data showed effectiveness was 41% lower than reported, delaying life-saving vehicle safety improvements for years.

Why It Matters:
In 2015, Amazon discovered their AI hiring algorithm showed 72% male bias because it trained on historical hiring data—when most tech hires were male. The selection bias perpetuated discrimination despite logical processing. A 2022 follow-up study found similar biases in 89% of Fortune 500 hiring algorithms, affecting millions of job seekers.

When to Use It / How to Counter It:
To spot it: Ask "What data might be missing entirely from this sample?" Look for systematically excluded groups.
To counter it: Compare sample characteristics to full population data. Actively seek data from excluded groups. Question data collection methods before analyzing results.

The Bottom Line:
Perfect logic applied to flawed samples produces confident mistakes. Check your data before your conclusions.

Selective Perception: Why You See Only What Fits Your Story

Your mind is like a bouncer at a club - it only lets in what's on its pre-approved list. This filtering happens automatically, shaping your reality before you even realize it.

How It Works:
Your brain unconsciously filters information to match existing beliefs. Like wearing colored glasses, your current mindset tints everything you observe. Contradictory data often gets blocked before reaching conscious awareness.

Example:
Two sports fans watch the same basketball game. The Lakers supporter sees every foul against their team while missing their own team's violations. The Celtics fan notices the opposite. Same game, different realities, filtered through pre-existing loyalties.

Why It Matters:
This unconscious filtering affects business decisions, relationships, and beliefs. Studies show hiring managers unconsciously notice details supporting their first impression while missing contradictory information. These blind spots create costly mistakes.

When to Use It / How to Counter It:
Before making judgments, ask: "What might I be predisposed to notice or ignore?" Force yourself to list evidence that contradicts your initial perception. Create systems that challenge your default filters.

The Bottom Line:
Your mind's bouncer is working overtime. The first step to seeing clearly is realizing how much you're missing.

Self-Fulfilling Prophecy: How Beliefs Create Reality

When you expect something to happen, you unconsciously behave in ways that make it more likely to occur. Your prediction becomes true because you believed it would.

How It Works:
Expectations shape behavior, which shapes outcomes. A manager who believes in an employee gives them more opportunities and feedback. The employee, receiving this support, performs better - making the initial belief come true.

Example:
Research shows teachers told certain students were "gifted" (randomly selected) gave those students more attention and challenging work. By year's end, these students' IQ scores increased significantly more than their peers. The false label created real results.

Why It Matters:
This effect works in both directions. Positive expectations create positive cycles of improvement. Negative expectations can trap people in downward spirals. Understanding this helps you harness its power while avoiding its pitfalls.

When to Use It / How to Counter It:
Before forming expectations of others, ask: "What cycle am I creating?" Choose beliefs that uplift rather than limit. Remember that your expectations of others can shape their reality.

The Bottom Line:
Your beliefs about people and situations help create their outcomes. Choose your expectations carefully - they're more powerful than you think.

NOTE:

The **Self-Fulfilling Prophecy** and the **Pygmalion Effect** are related but distinct psychological concepts, both involving expectations influencing outcomes.

Key Difference:

- **Self-Fulfilling Prophecy** can be positive or negative - it's the general idea that expectations cause behaviors that make the expectation come true, regardless of direction.
- **Pygmalion Effect** is specifically about *positive* expectations leading to *improved* performance.

Both concepts are about the power of expectations, but the Pygmalion Effect is a more specific and positive manifestation of a self-fulfilling prophecy.

Self-Serving Bias: Taking Credit for Wins, Dodging Blame for Losses

Self-Serving Bias is the tendency to credit personal success to our abilities while blaming failures on external factors. It's a mental trick that boosts our self-esteem by shifting blame selectively.

How It Works:
When we succeed, we believe it's due to our skills or effort. But when things go wrong, we point to external causes - "The project failed because of the team," or "The exam was unfair." This bias keeps our self-image intact, emphasizing strengths and deflecting responsibility for setbacks.

Example:
A salesperson who meets their targets attributes it to hard work. If they fall short, they blame market conditions, the economy, or lack of resources. This bias preserves their confidence, regardless of the outcome.

Why It Matters:
Self-Serving Bias prevents honest self-assessment. By only emphasizing strengths and externalizing weaknesses, it stunts growth and creates a skewed perception of reality. In team settings, it can breed resentment if people dodge responsibility.

When to Use It / How to Counter It:
Watch for this bias in performance reviews and group work. Seeking feedback on both strengths and weaknesses fosters a balanced perspective and supports genuine self-improvement.

The Bottom Line:
Owning both wins and losses is key to growth. The Self-Serving Bias feels good short-term but limits self-awareness. Balance confidence with honest reflection for a stronger sense of self.

Semmelweis Reflex: Rejecting New Information That Challenges Beliefs

The Semmelweis Reflex describes the instinctive rejection of new information simply because it contradicts established beliefs. Named after Dr. Ignaz Semmelweis, who faced intense backlash for suggesting handwashing to reduce infections, this reflex highlights how resistant people can be to change, even when evidence supports it.

How It Works:
This bias kicks in when new ideas challenge existing views. Instead of considering the evidence, people instinctively dismiss it to preserve familiar beliefs. It's the mental version of covering your ears because the new information feels uncomfortable or disruptive.

Example:
In the 19th century, Semmelweis proposed that doctors should wash their hands before examining patients to prevent infections. Despite strong evidence, many colleagues rejected his findings outright, unwilling to believe their established practices could be harmful.

Why It Matters:
The Semmelweis Reflex can stifle innovation and hinder progress by blocking ideas that challenge the status quo. In science, business, and everyday life, it prevents open-mindedness and growth, causing people to miss valuable insights and improvements.

When to Use It / How to Counter It:
Recognize this reflex when new data or ideas feel uncomfortable. Instead of dismissing them, take a moment to weigh the evidence and question whether your beliefs are truly serving you.

The Bottom Line:
Rejecting new ideas without consideration limits growth. Recognize when the Semmelweis Reflex might be at play, and strive to keep an open mind - often, progress lies just beyond our comfort zone.

Shirky Principle: Institutions Will Preserve the Problem They Were Created to Solve

The Shirky Principle, coined by media theorist Clay Shirky, suggests that institutions often sustain the very problems they were created to solve. Over time, an organization's survival can become dependent on the continued existence of the problem, leading to inefficiency or resistance to change.

How It Works:
When an institution's relevance and funding are tied to a specific issue, fully solving it could threaten its existence. For example, a nonprofit addressing homelessness may become so invested in its own growth that it focuses on managing symptoms rather than eliminating root causes - preserving the problem instead of solving it.

Example:
Government bureaucracies are notorious for this. A department created to streamline processes may add layers of red tape over time, creating inefficiencies that ensure its ongoing necessity. True solutions could make the bureaucracy obsolete, so the institution resists change.

Why It Matters:
The Shirky Principle reveals how institutions can shift from problem-solving to self-preservation. Recognizing this pattern helps evaluate whether organizations are genuinely tackling issues or merely perpetuating them to justify their existence.

When to Use It / How to Counter It:
When assessing institutions, ask, "Is this organization focused on real outcomes, or more invested in survival?" Use this principle to identify areas where the status quo may be prioritized over effective solutions.

The Bottom Line:
Institutions can become part of the problem. The Shirky Principle reminds us to prioritize results over maintaining structures that may no longer serve their original purpose.

Shopping Hungry Fallacy: How State-Dependent Decisions Sabotage Your Goals

Your current physical state dramatically skews your judgment about future needs. Smart planners never let temporary feelings make permanent decisions.

How It Works:
When experiencing intense states (hunger, fatigue, stress), your brain overvalues immediate relief and undervalues long-term planning. This temporary state hijacks your decision-making system.

Example:
Research shows that hungry shoppers not only buy more food overall but specifically select higher-calorie items compared to those shopping after meals. Even non-food purchases are affected by hunger states. A classic marketing strategy places bread and bakery sections near store entrances because the scent triggers hunger responses. Grocery stores know hungry shoppers make more impulse purchases regardless of their shopping list.

Why It Matters:
State-dependent decisions ripple far beyond the moment. The meal plan you make while hungry, the gym membership you buy while motivated, the budget you set while disciplined - all fail when your state changes.

When to Use It / How to Counter It:
Never make important decisions in extreme states. Hungry? Eat before shopping. Tired? Sleep before committing. Emotional? Wait until you're calm to respond.

The Bottom Line:
Your current state lies about your future needs. Make decisions from neutral ground, not temporary peaks or valleys.

Simpson's Paradox: When Grouped Data Can Hide or Reverse Trends

Simpson's Paradox is a phenomenon in statistics where a trend that appears in individual groups reverses or disappears when the groups are combined. It shows how our interpretation of data can completely change based on how we look at it.

How It Works:
Let's say you're analyzing a new treatment for a medical condition. In a study, the treatment seems more effective for both men and women when their results are looked at separately. But when you combine the data from both groups, the treatment looks less effective overall. What's going on here? It's Simpson's Paradox in action. The difference comes from how the data is being grouped and which variables you're paying attention to.

Why It Matters:
Simpson's Paradox can make you draw the wrong conclusion if you don't know what to look for. You might see a pattern in a subgroup and assume it holds for everyone, when in fact, combining the groups reveals something very different. This paradox pops up in everything from healthcare studies to business analytics, so knowing how to spot it is crucial for avoiding bad decisions.

When to Use It / How to Counter It:
Use this when analyzing data that involves groups or categories. If you're looking at trends within separate groups, ask yourself: "What happens if I combine these groups? Am I overlooking a bigger picture?" Simpson's Paradox is a reminder to step back and make sure you're not getting misled by isolated trends.

The Bottom Line:
Numbers can lie if you don't handle them carefully. Always look at how data is grouped and combined. If something seems off, double-check that Simpson's Paradox isn't hiding the real story.

Single Cause Fallacy: It's Never Just One Thing

The Single Cause Fallacy occurs when we assume a complex issue stems from a single cause. This oversimplification ignores the interplay of multiple factors, leading to flawed conclusions and limited solutions.

How It Works:
This fallacy arises when someone points to one cause for a complex problem, ignoring the many contributing factors. For instance, saying, "The economy crashed solely because of government policies," overlooks the impact of market conditions, global events, and consumer behavior. Reducing issues to a single cause oversimplifies reality.

Example:
When a sports team loses a championship, fans might blame only the coach. In reality, injuries, team dynamics, and opposing strategies all play a role. Focusing on a single cause gives an incomplete picture, missing out on other critical factors.

Why It Matters:
The Single Cause Fallacy can lead to poor decision-making by ignoring the complexity of real-world issues. Solutions that target only one factor are unlikely to address the problem effectively, often leading to ineffective or even harmful outcomes.

When to Use It / How to Counter It:
Be cautious of this fallacy in any analysis or debate. Ask, "What other factors might contribute?" Complex issues demand multi-faceted approaches, not one-dimensional explanations.

The Bottom Line:
Complex problems rarely have single causes. Avoid oversimplifying - acknowledge multiple contributing factors for a more accurate understanding and effective solutions.

Skinner's Law: Break Procrastination with Pain or Pleasure

There are two ways to make yourself act: Make inaction hurt more than action, or make action feel better than inaction. Basic psychology, powerful results.

How It Works:
Following Skinner's behavioral research, you can motivate action through either positive reinforcement (rewards) or negative reinforcement (removing pain). The key is making the desired behavior more attractive than procrastination.

Example:
A company struggles with late reports. They try two approaches: Teams that submit on time get to leave early Friday (pleasure). Teams that submit late must present updates in daily meetings (pain). Both methods increase on-time submissions significantly.

Why It Matters:
Procrastination isn't about laziness - it's about motivation. Research shows we avoid tasks when the immediate discomfort outweighs perceived benefits. By changing this equation, we can break through resistance.

When to Use It / How to Counter It:
Before tackling a dreaded task, ask: "Can I add rewards for completion? Or can I make procrastination more uncomfortable?" Set up concrete consequences - either positive or negative - to drive action.

The Bottom Line:
Change the pain-pleasure equation, change your behavior. Make action more attractive than inaction, and procrastination loses its power.

Slippery Slope: Why Every Small Change Won't End in Disaster

It's the fallacy of claiming that one small step will trigger an unstoppable cascade of catastrophes - without showing how or why each step would actually happen.

How It Works:
You predict that a minor change will inevitably lead to extreme negative outcomes, skipping the logical steps in between. Like claiming that letting kids choose their school lunches will somehow lead to complete classroom anarchy.

Example:
A company considers allowing remote work one day per week. Someone argues: "If we allow this, soon everyone will want to work remotely forever, productivity will collapse, and we'll go bankrupt!" Each leap gets more extreme, with no evidence connecting these outcomes.

Why It Matters:
This fallacy paralyzes decision-making by making reasonable changes seem dangerous. It's particularly common in policy debates, where fear of extreme outcomes prevents sensible reforms. Good decisions require real evidence, not catastrophic speculation.

When to Use It / How to Counter It:
Before rejecting change based on future fears, ask: "What evidence shows each step will actually lead to the next? Are these connections logical or just emotional?" Focus on likely outcomes, not worst-case fantasies.

The Bottom Line:
Not every slope is slippery. Evaluate each step based on evidence, not fear of imagined catastrophes.

Social Comparison Bias: When Others' Success Feels Like Your Failure

Every time someone else wins, it shouldn't feel like you're losing. Yet our brains often interpret others' achievements as threats to our own worth.

How It Works:
We naturally compare ourselves to others, but this healthy benchmark can turn toxic. Research shows we often feel threatened by and dislike people who outperform us, even when their success has no impact on our own standing.

Example:
A sales team hires a top performer from another company. Instead of learning from their expertise, existing team members exclude them from meetings and withhold information. The team's performance suffers because social comparison prevented collaboration.

Why It Matters:
This bias creates lose-lose situations in workplaces and relationships. Studies show it leads to sabotaging behavior, reduced collaboration, and missed learning opportunities. Companies lose talent because existing employees resist hiring people "better" than themselves.

When to Use It / How to Counter It:
Before reacting to others' success, ask: "Am I resenting them just because they're good at something? What could I learn from them instead?" Transform comparison into inspiration.

The Bottom Line:
Someone else's success isn't your failure. Turn jealousy into curiosity, and competitors into teachers.

Social Loafing: Why Teams Make Us Lazy

Social loafing reveals a surprising truth: people often work less hard in groups than alone. It's why five people pushing a rope rarely give five times the effort of one.

How It Works:
As group size increases, individual effort often decreases. Each person subconsciously reduces their contribution, assuming others will pick up the slack. Research shows performance can drop up to 20% per additional team member.

Example:
The Ringelmann Effect, first documented in 1913, showed people pulling a rope used less force as group size grew. In groups of eight, each person contributed just 50% of their solo effort - a finding replicated in modern workplace studies.

Why It Matters:
Companies lose billions to this effect. Amazon found that two-pizza teams (small enough to feed with two pizzas) outperform larger groups precisely because social loafing has less room to take hold.

When to Use It / How to Counter It:
Watch for this in any group task. Make individual contributions measurable and visible. Jeff Bezos's stand-up meetings require each person to report progress, combating the tendency to hide in the crowd.

The Bottom Line:
More hands make lighter work - sometimes too light. Design teams and tasks to maintain individual accountability, or watch collective effort evaporate.

Social Proof: Why We Follow the Crowd

When uncertain, humans look to others for cues about correct behavior. It's why empty restaurants stay empty while crowded ones get even more crowded.

How It Works:
Your brain uses others' behavior as a shortcut for decision-making, especially in ambiguous situations. If everyone else is doing something, we assume they must know something we don't. This effect strengthens with uncertainty.

Example:
Research shows hotel guests reuse towels 33% more often when told that other guests typically reuse their towels. The same message without social proof ("Save the Environment") is far less effective. Seeing others' behavior shapes our own.

Why It Matters:
This principle drives consumer behavior, social movements, and cultural trends. Companies use it in marketing ("bestselling"), social media shows follower counts, and websites display review counts. Understanding it helps you spot when you're being influenced.

When to Use It / How to Counter It:
Before following the crowd, ask: "Am I doing this because it makes sense, or just because others are?" Use social proof as one data point, not your only guide. Remember that crowds can be wrong.

The Bottom Line:
We're wired to follow others, but popularity doesn't equal truth. Think critically about why you're choosing what you choose.

Spin: Making Bad News Sound Good (Without Quite Lying)

Welcome to reality's fun-house mirror, where every crisis is an opportunity and every failure is a learning experience. It's not lying - it's just selective truth-telling.

How It Works:
You present facts in the most favorable light possible, emphasizing positive aspects while downplaying negatives. Like describing a 30% revenue drop as "a strategic reset positioning us for future growth."

Example:
Enron famously spun massive losses as "mark-to-market" accounting gains. They technically reported real numbers but presented them in ways that hid the company's true financial state. The spin worked until reality caught up.

Why It Matters:
Spin has become standard in corporate and political communication. While not technically false, it creates dangerous information gaps. Understanding spin helps you spot when you're getting the funhouse mirror version of truth.

When to Use It / How to Counter It:
Before accepting any narrative, ask: "What facts are being emphasized? What's being downplayed?" Look for what's not being said. Remember that selective truth-telling can be as misleading as lying.

The Bottom Line:
Spin makes truth elastic. For trust and clarity, stick to straight facts - your audience deserves the real picture, not just the pretty parts.

Spotlight Effect: Nobody's Watching You That Closely

That embarrassing moment you can't stop thinking about? Everyone else has already forgotten it. We massively overestimate how much attention others pay to our actions and appearance.

How It Works:
Your brain creates an illusion that you're center stage in everyone's attention. But research shows others notice and remember far less about you than you think. They're too busy starring in their own mental movies.

Example:
Studies had people wear embarrassing t-shirts into a room of peers. Participants estimated twice as many people would notice the shirt as actually did. Even when deliberately trying to stand out, we overestimate how much others observe us.

Why It Matters:
This false belief creates unnecessary anxiety and self-consciousness. We edit our behavior, stress over tiny mistakes, and limit ourselves - all because we imagine scrutiny that doesn't exist. Understanding this bias can free you from social paralysis.

When to Use It / How to Counter It:
Before stressing about a small mistake or perceived flaw, ask: "Will anyone else even remember this tomorrow?" Recognize that your emotional spotlight isn't real. Others are too focused on their own concerns.

The Bottom Line:
You're not the main character in anyone else's story. That's actually great news - it means you're free to be yourself without constant judgment.

Start from Quality Threshold Theory: Perfection Kills Progress

Most people wait to start until conditions are perfect. They stockpile resources, analyze endlessly, and convince themselves they need "just a bit more" before taking action. This behavior isn't wisdom – it's procrastination wearing a suit.

How It Works:
The theory suggests that we mentally set arbitrary quality standards before beginning. While some threshold is healthy, we often set it irrationally high, creating self-imposed barriers to entry. Instead of asking "Is this good enough?" we ask "Is this perfect enough?"

Example:
Sarah wanted to start a YouTube channel. She spent six months researching cameras and scripts. Meanwhile, Jenny started immediately with her phone and enthusiasm. A year later, Jenny had 100,000 subscribers and improved with each video, while Sarah hadn't posted once.

Why It Matters:
Starting with "good enough" allows you to gather real feedback and build momentum. Perfect starting conditions are a myth – excellence is iterative, not immediate. The market rewards speed over theoretical perfection.

When to Use It / How to Counter It:
Apply this when launching a business, learning a skill, or pursuing any goal where waiting for perfect conditions holds you back. Set your threshold at "minimum viable" rather than "maximum possible."

The Bottom Line:
Start at 60% ready and improve through execution. The gap between good and great is bridged through action, not analysis. Your imperfect action today beats your perfect plan tomorrow.

Status Quo Bias: Why "Good Enough" Blocks "Better"

We stick with what we have - even when better options exist - simply because it's what we're used to. Change requires effort; staying put is automatic.

How It Works:
Your brain assigns extra value to the current state just because it's current. Research shows people need potential gains to be twice as valuable as potential losses before they'll choose change over status quo.

Example:
Studies show that when companies offer 401(k) plans, most employees never change their initial investment allocations - even after decades of career and market changes. The power of default settings shapes million-dollar decisions.

Why It Matters:
This bias keeps organizations using outdated systems, people stuck in unfulfilling jobs, and businesses clinging to failing strategies. The comfort of the familiar often outweighs the potential benefits of change, even when those benefits are clear.

When to Use It / How to Counter It:
Before automatically choosing "what we've always done," ask: "If I were starting fresh today, would I choose this option?" Remove the psychological weight of history from your decisions.

The Bottom Line:
Just because something is familiar doesn't make it optimal. Sometimes the riskiest choice is making no choice at all.

Steel Man: Make Your Opponent's Argument Stronger Than They Did

Forget attacking weak points - the ultimate power move is strengthening your opponent's argument before engaging with it. It's intellectual respect in action.

How It Works:
Instead of picking apart flaws (Straw Man – coming up), you actively improve your opponent's position. Present their argument in its strongest possible form, even better than they did. Then engage with that enhanced version.

Example:
In a debate about electric cars, someone argues they're better for the environment. Instead of highlighting battery waste, you say: "Electric vehicles not only reduce emissions, but also lower maintenance costs, offer superior performance, and help establish energy independence. They're a compelling solution - now let's discuss implementation challenges."

Why It Matters:
Research shows this approach builds trust and leads to better outcomes in negotiations and debates. It demonstrates intellectual honesty, reduces defensive reactions, and creates space for real dialogue. Plus, you gain deeper understanding by truly engaging with opposing views.

When to Use It / How to Counter It:
Before countering any argument, ask: "How could I make this position even stronger?" Then address that enhanced version. Use it in debates, negotiations, or whenever you want to move past surface disagreements to deeper understanding.

The Bottom Line:
True strength lies in engaging with the best version of opposing views, not attacking their weaknesses. Steel Man turns debates from battles into bridges.

Stereotype Threat: When Fear of Confirming Stereotypes Holds You Back

Performance suffers when you're worried about proving negative stereotypes true. It's a self-fulfilling prophecy that affects everything from test scores to job performance.

How It Works:
The mere awareness of a negative stereotype about your group creates extra mental pressure. Research shows this anxiety consumes cognitive resources needed for the task at hand, ironically making the feared underperformance more likely.

Example:
Studies show women perform worse on math tests when reminded of gender stereotypes beforehand, but perform equally well when the stereotype isn't activated. The same person, same ability, different results - just because of stereotype awareness.

Why It Matters:
This effect contributes to persistent achievement gaps in education and workplace performance. When capable people underperform due to stereotype pressure, it can reinforce the very stereotypes they fear, creating a vicious cycle.

When to Use It / How to Counter It:
Before high-pressure situations, ask: "Am I carrying extra anxiety about representing my group? How can I reframe this as just about my individual performance?" Focus on your personal preparation and abilities.

The Bottom Line:
Don't let fear of confirming stereotypes become a self-fulfilling prophecy. You're an individual first, group member second.

Strategic Ignorance: When Not Knowing Makes You Smarter

Sometimes, the most powerful knowledge is knowing what to ignore. In a world drowning in information, selective ignorance can be your secret weapon.

How It Works:
You deliberately choose not to know certain information that might bias decisions or create unnecessary stress. Like noise-canceling headphones for your brain, you filter out data that adds more confusion than clarity.

Example:
Studies show investment managers who check portfolios less frequently make better decisions. Those who watch daily price movements tend to overreact to short-term volatility, while quarterly reviewers maintain better long-term perspective and achieve higher returns.

Why It Matters:
Research confirms that more information doesn't always lead to better decisions. Too much data can trigger emotional reactions, create decision paralysis, and obscure important signals with noise. Strategic ignorance helps maintain objectivity.

When to Use It / How to Counter It:
Before consuming information, ask: "Will knowing this improve my decisions, or just add noise?" Create intentional distance from data that triggers emotional reactions but doesn't improve outcomes.

The Bottom Line:
Wisdom isn't just knowing what to learn - it's knowing what to ignore. Choose your blind spots strategically.

Strategy Tax: When Success Becomes Your Biggest Liability

Yesterday's winning formula can become tomorrow's strategic straitjacket. Like golden handcuffs, past success often prevents necessary evolution.

How It Works:
Organizations pay a hidden "tax" when previous wins constrain future choices. Successful products, loyal customers, and proven business models become barriers to change - even when change is crucial for survival.

Example:
Kodak invented the digital camera in 1975 but couldn't fully embrace it because it threatened their lucrative film business. They chose protecting past success over future adaptation. By 2012, they were bankrupt while digital imaging thrived.

Why It Matters:
This pattern repeats across industries. Blockbuster couldn't abandon late fees. Nokia couldn't risk its hardware success for software innovation. Barnes & Noble struggled to compete with Amazon because physical stores were both asset and anchor.

When to Use It / How to Counter It:
Before defending current success, ask: "Is protecting today's model limiting tomorrow's opportunities?" Sometimes you need to cannibalize your own success before competitors do it for you.

The Bottom Line:
Don't let your greatest hits become your funeral march. Success should be a springboard, not an anchor.

Straw Man Fallacy: Winning Arguments Against Imaginary Opponents

No one likes fighting shadows, but that's exactly what the Straw Man fallacy does. Instead of addressing real arguments, it creates a weaker, distorted version that's easier to defeat.

How It Works:
You deliberately misrepresent someone's position to make it easier to attack. When they say "We should reform police training," you respond "So you want to abolish all law enforcement?"

Example:
In a budget meeting, Sarah suggests reducing office supplies costs. Bob responds, "So you want everyone writing on napkins and sharing one pencil?" That's not her argument - it's a straw man designed for easy demolition.

Why It Matters:
Straw men corrupt meaningful debate. They waste time fighting imaginary positions while real issues go unaddressed. In business, politics, or relationships, they breed mistrust and prevent real solutions.

When to Use It / How to Counter It:
Never. It's intellectually dishonest and destroys credibility. Instead, engage with the strongest version of your opponent's actual argument.

The Bottom Line:
True progress comes from addressing real arguments, not knocking down fake ones. When you hear "So what you're saying is..." followed by an extreme version of your position, you're watching a straw man being built.

Streetlight Effect: Looking Where the Light Is, Not Where the Problem Is

The Streetlight Effect describes the tendency to search for answers only in the easiest places, rather than where the real problem lies. It's like losing your keys in a dark alley but only looking for them under the streetlight because it's easier to see. We focus on what's convenient, even if it's not where the solution is.

How It Works:
You're troubleshooting a problem at work, but instead of digging into the complex areas that are likely causing the issue, you focus on the easier-to-access data and surface-level fixes. The Streetlight Effect makes you look for answers where it's most convenient - not where the real answers are hiding.

Why It Matters:
This effect leads to superficial problem-solving. We stick to the familiar or easy-to-reach information, avoiding the hard work of digging deeper. Recognizing the Streetlight Effect pushes you to go beyond the obvious and search in the right places, even if it's harder.

When to Use It / How to Counter It:
When you're trying to solve a problem or gather information. Ask yourself: "Am I just looking where it's easy, or am I searching in the right place?" Don't let convenience dictate where you focus your efforts - real solutions often lie in the shadows.

The Bottom Line:
Convenience can lead you astray. The Streetlight Effect warns you that just because it's easy to search in one place doesn't mean that's where the answer is. Look beyond the obvious to find real solutions.

The Streisand Effect: When Hiding Something Makes It Famous

Want to make something go viral? Try to cover it up. That's the ironic lesson of the Streisand Effect, where attempts to hide information make it explode in popularity.

How It Works:
When you try to suppress information - whether through legal threats, censorship, or takedown notices - you create a fascinating story that makes people want to know more. Curiosity plus defiance equals viral content.

Example:
In 2003, Barbra Streisand sued to remove an aerial photo of her Malibu mansion from a coastal survey website. Before her lawsuit: 6 downloads. After: over 1 million views. She accidentally turned an ignored photo into internet history.

Why It Matters:
In our connected world, attempts at censorship often backfire spectacularly. The very act of trying to hide something creates a compelling narrative that spreads faster than the original information ever would have.

When to Use It / How to Counter It:
Before trying to suppress information, ask: "Will fighting this draw more attention than ignoring it?" Sometimes, the best response is no response.

The Bottom Line:
The harder you try to hide something, the more fascinating it becomes. In a world where everyone has a platform, censorship often feeds the very flame you're trying to extinguish.

Sturgeon's Law: Why 90% of Everything is Mediocre (And Why That's OK)

Look around. Most movies are forgettable. Most books gather dust. Most startups fail. Welcome to Sturgeon's Law: 90% of everything is mediocre. But that's actually good news.

How It Works:
In any field, the vast majority is average or worse. Take Netflix - thousands of shows, but how many are worth your time? Maybe 10%. This pattern repeats everywhere: products, ideas, content, even meetings.

Example:
A venture capitalist reviews 1,000 pitches yearly. 900 aren't viable. 90 show promise. 10 get funded. One becomes a unicorn. That's Sturgeon's Law in action - and it's why VCs expect most investments to fail.

Why It Matters:
Once you accept that most things are mediocre, you stop wasting time trying to make everything perfect. Instead, you focus on identifying and creating that valuable 10%.

When to Use It / How to Counter It:
Feeling overwhelmed by choices? Remember Sturgeon's Law. Don't try to consume, master, or perfect everything. Focus on finding and creating excellence in what matters most.

The Bottom Line:
Mediocrity is normal. Excellence is rare. Your job isn't to fight this reality - it's to get really good at spotting and creating that golden 10%.

Substitution Bias: Your Brain's Sneaky Way of Dodging Hard Questions

That gut feeling about a candidate? Your brain just pulled a fast one. Instead of analyzing their policies, you judged their smile. Welcome to substitution bias - where your mind swaps hard questions for easy ones.

How It Works:
Your brain hates complexity. When faced with "Is this a good investment?" it quietly switches to "Do I like this company?" The swap is so smooth, you never notice the mental sleight-of-hand.

Example:
A hiring manager needs to evaluate "Will this candidate drive results for five years?" That's tough. So their brain substitutes "Did they give confident answers?" Much easier! The candidate gets hired based on interview presence, not actual capability.

Why It Matters:
This mental shortcut leads to expensive mistakes. You buy a house because it "feels right" (easy) instead of analyzing the 30-year financial impact (hard). You pick a college based on campus beauty rather than career outcomes.

When to Use It / How to Counter It:
Catch your brain in the act. When making big decisions, write down the real question. Then ask: "Am I actually answering this, or did I switch to an easier question?"

The Bottom Line:
Your mind is a master of misdirection, trading tough questions for simple ones. Beat this bias by forcing yourself to face the complex question you're really trying to answer. The right question might be harder - but it leads to better decisions.

Sunk Cost Fallacy: Why We Keep Throwing Good Money After Bad

Your brain has a dangerous obsession with the past. It's why you finish terrible books, stay in dead-end jobs, and keep dumping money into that money-pit project. Meet the Sunk Cost Fallacy.

How It Works:
The more you invest in something, the harder it becomes to abandon it. Your brain screams "But we've already spent so much!" - as if that magically changes whether it's worth continuing today.

Example:
A business owner pours $200,000 into developing a product. Market research shows it'll fail. Instead of cutting losses, they invest another $100,000 because "we've come too far to quit now." The product fails anyway.

Why It Matters:
This mental trap keeps you stuck in losing ventures, toxic relationships, and dead-end careers. You waste precious time and resources trying to justify past decisions instead of making smart choices for the future.

When to Use It / How to Counter It:
Before investing more in anything, ask: "If I were starting fresh today, would I choose this?" Past investments are gone. Only tomorrow's potential matters.

The Bottom Line:
Stop looking backward. Yesterday's investments are gone whether you continue or quit. Make decisions based on future value, not past costs. Sometimes the bravest move is walking away.

Surrogation: When Measuring Success Becomes the Enemy of Success

Your metrics are lying to you. That social media following? Those quarterly targets? The number of tasks completed? They're seductive stand-ins for what really matters - and they're leading you astray.

How It Works:
We replace complex goals with simple measurements, then forget we made the switch. Soon, we're chasing numbers instead of real success, like a doctor focusing on patient satisfaction scores instead of actual health outcomes.

Example:
A software company rewarded developers for fixing bugs quickly. Soon, developers started writing sloppy code to hit their metrics, creating more bugs than they fixed. The measurement became the mission - and destroyed the real goal.

Why It Matters:
This mental trap turns good intentions into destructive behaviors. Schools chase test scores until education suffers. Companies pursue engagement metrics until customer relationships crumble. What you measure becomes what you value.

When to Use It / How to Counter It:
Before setting any goal, ask: "Am I measuring what truly matters, or just what's easy to count?" The best metrics serve the mission; they don't become the mission.

The Bottom Line:
Numbers tell stories, but not always the right ones. Don't let the ease of measurement seduce you into chasing the wrong target. Keep your eyes on the real prize, not just its shadow.

Survivorship Bias: The Hidden Graveyard Behind Every Success Story

That inspiring "college dropout billionaire" story? It's missing a crucial detail: thousands of dropouts who ended up moving back in with their parents. Welcome to Survivorship Bias - where success stories blind us to reality.

How It Works:
We fixate on winners while ignoring the vast cemetery of failures. "Look how easy!" we think, studying success stories. But we're missing crucial data: all the people who tried the exact same thing and failed spectacularly.

Example:
A comprehensive 2022 Small Business Administration study revealed that among 380,000 new restaurants, those following "proven success formulas" from successful owners failed 6% more often than those who didn't. The reason? Those formulas ignored critical factors like location and starting capital.

Why It Matters:
This bias creates dangerous illusions. You copy a successful startup's strategy, not realizing that 50 other companies tried the same approach and went bankrupt. You're getting half the story - and it's the misleading half.

When to Use It / How to Counter It:
To spot it: Notice when success stories emphasize personal choices while ignoring external advantages. To counter it: Actively seek data on failures. Ask: "What happened to others who tried this exact approach?"

The Bottom Line:
Success leaves clues, but so does failure. Don't let survivor stories fool you - behind every winner stands a mountain of forgotten failures. True wisdom means learning from both.

Sutton's Law: Start Where Success Is Most Likely

"Why do you rob banks?" they asked Willie Sutton. His answer — "Because that's where the money is" — teaches a crucial lesson about efficient problem-solving.

How It Works:
Unlike Occam's Razor (which favors simpler explanations), Sutton's Law directs us to prioritize the highest-probability areas first, regardless of complexity. It's about efficient resource allocation, not simplicity.

Example:
A 2021 McKinsey study of fraud detection in banking showed teams using Sutton's principle (focusing on historically high-risk areas) caught 72% more fraud while using 44% fewer resources than teams using comprehensive scanning. JP Morgan documented saving $235 million in 2020 by applying this targeted approach.

Why It Matters:
Research by KPMG shows that 67% of corporate investigations waste resources by scanning everywhere equally instead of prioritizing likely areas. In 2022, companies following Sutton's principle reduced investigation costs by an average of 41%.

When to Use It / How to Counter It:
To spot it: Notice when resources are spread evenly across unlikely scenarios. To counter it: Focus resources where success is most probable. Ask: "Where's the money?"

The Bottom Line:
Don't search everywhere equally. Start where you're most likely to succeed.

System 1 vs System 2: When Quick Thinking Meets Slow Analysis

Kahneman's Nobel Prize-winning research reveals how our fast and slow thinking systems dramatically affect decision quality.

How It Works:
System 1 operates automatically and quickly, with little effort or voluntary control. System 2 allocates attention to complex mental activities. Switching between them requires measurable mental effort and glucose consumption.

Example:
A 2017 study in The Journal of Finance tracked 850 professional traders using high-frequency trading data. When forced to write down their analysis before major trades (engaging System 2), their returns improved by 21.8% compared to rapid, intuitive trades.

Why It Matters:
Research published in Nature Neuroscience (2020) demonstrated that under time pressure, subjects defaulted to System 1 responses and made 47% more errors on complex problem-solving tasks than those given time to engage System 2.

To spot it: Notice physical stress signals triggering fast reactions.
To counter it: Create forced pauses for important decisions. Use checklists to engage System 2.

The Bottom Line:
Your quick mind is powerful but prone to expensive mistakes. Know when to slow down.

Take-the-Best Heuristic: Why Simple Rules Often Beat Complex Analysis

Research reveals that focusing on the single most reliable predictor often outperforms weighing multiple factors - a finding that changed how we understand decision-making.

How It Works:
Take-the-Best examines cues in order of proven reliability, stopping at the first one that points to a clear choice. Unlike careful weighing of all factors, it intentionally ignores additional information once a reliable difference is found.

Example:
Gigerenzer's landmark research asked both experts and algorithms to predict which of two cities had larger populations. Using only the "Does it have a soccer team?" cue, Take-the-Best was correct 87% of the time, outperforming complex models using 12 different factors. This single reliable indicator beat careful analysis.

Why It Matters:
A follow-up study in Psychological Review showed that in 115 real-world tests ranging from medical diagnosis to housing prices, Take-the-Best matched or exceeded the accuracy of comprehensive analysis in 92% of cases while using significantly less information.

When to Use It / How to Counter It:
To spot it: Look for situations where one reliable indicator keeps predicting correctly. To counter it: Test your chosen cue's actual predictive power against historical outcomes.

The Bottom Line:
More information often makes decisions harder, not better. Find your best predictor and trust it.

Talent Stack: Why Skill Combinations Beat Single Expertise

Research shows professionals with complementary skill sets consistently outperform deep specialists in both earnings and career resilience.

How It Works:
Unlike traditional specialization, talent stacking combines multiple mid-level skills that create unique value together. The Bureau of Labor Statistics found that workers with three complementary skills earned 54% more than single-domain experts.

Example:
Harvard Business School's 2022 study of 3.4 million professional careers found that employees combining technical skills with communication abilities and industry knowledge received promotions 2.7x faster than deep specialists. Their employment stability during downturns was 83% higher.

Why It Matters:
LinkedIn's 2023 Global Skills Report analyzed 98,000 management hires, finding that 71% of executive promotions went to those with proven cross-domain expertise rather than single-skill mastery. These "skill stack" leaders delivered 34% better team results.

When to Use It / How to Counter It:
To spot it: Look for roles where multiple skills consistently appear together. To counter it: Build skills that data shows complement your core expertise.

The Bottom Line:
Don't just be the best at one thing. Build a combination that makes you irreplaceable.

They're All Crooks Fallacy: When Universal Distrust Backfires

Behavioral research shows blanket cynicism often leads to worse outcomes than targeted skepticism.

How It Works:
The brain creates mental shortcuts through overgeneralization – a documented phenomenon called the "fundamental attribution error." When we see negative examples, we tend to attribute them to entire groups rather than specific circumstances or individuals.

Example:
During the 2008 financial crisis, the FDIC found that customers assuming "all banks are failing" withdrew savings from stable local banks (with 12% capital reserves) and moved money to riskier institutions offering higher rates. This behavior contributed to the collapse of previously stable banks.

Why It Matters:
SEC enforcement data shows that investors who express universal market distrust are paradoxically more likely to fall for fraud. In 2022, 68% of Ponzi scheme victims reported they distrusted traditional investments, leading them to seek "alternative" investments that proved fraudulent.

When to Use It / How to Counter It:
To spot it: Notice absolute statements about group-wide corruption.
To counter it: Demand specific evidence for specific cases.

The Bottom Line:
True skepticism investigates details. Blanket distrust makes you vulnerable.

Third-Person Effect: Why Feeling Immune Makes You Vulnerable

Verified research shows the more resistant to influence we think we are, the more likely we are to be influenced – a paradox that shapes personal and public behavior.

How It Works:
Davison's original 1983 research demonstrated that people consistently believe persuasive messages have stronger effects on others than on themselves. This perception gap increases with education and perceived expertise, creating larger blind spots in those who feel most informed.

Example:
In a landmark study published in the Journal of Communication, researchers found that cigarette warning labels were rated as 28% more influential on others than self, while actual behavior changes showed no difference between groups. Follow-up studies found this effect strongest in those with health expertise.

Why It Matters:
Analysis of political advertising by the Journal of Broadcasting showed voters who rated themselves "highly resistant" to campaign messages were actually more likely to shift positions after exposure than those who acknowledged potential influence. This effect doubled during high-stakes elections.

When to Use It / How to Counter It:
To spot it: Notice claims of personal immunity to widely effective influences. Watch for phrases like "that wouldn't work on me."
To counter it: Document your actual behaviors rather than trusting self-perception. Track decisions against claims of immunity.

The Bottom Line:
True influence resistance starts with accepting your vulnerability. The more immune you feel, the more you should worry.

Threshold Model: How Social Changes Reach Critical Mass

Research shows significant societal changes occur through cascading "threshold effects" rather than gradual adoption.

How It Works:
Granovetter's foundational research (1978) demonstrated that individuals require different numbers of others acting before joining in. Once 10-15% adopt a new behavior, it can trigger rapid social transmission through established networks.

Example:
A 2018 PNAS study of online behavior tracked 12 million social media users. When early adopters reached 15% of a community, their behavior spread to 50% adoption within 4 weeks. Below 15%, changes stalled consistently.

Why It Matters:
Research from the University of Pennsylvania analyzed 50 years of social movements. Those reaching 25% of population achieved their goals 100% of the time, while those below 10% consistently failed, regardless of resources or intensity.

When to Use It / How to Counter It:
To spot it: Watch for clusters of early adopters reaching 10-15% of a group.
To counter it: Either join early adopters or actively maintain distance before the threshold.

The Bottom Line:
Major changes don't require majority support—just enough early adopters to trigger the cascade.

Threshold Theory: Why Small Changes Beat Big Pushes

Nobel Prize-winning research shows that reducing barriers drives more behavior change than increasing motivation.

How It Works:
Your brain weighs effort against reward for every action. Thaler and Sunstein's research showed that minor friction points matter more than major incentives in determining whether people take action.

Example:
In Thaler's landmark 401(k) studies, simply making enrollment automatic (opt-out instead of opt-in) increased participation from 49% to 86% — while doubling employer matching funds only raised rates by 6%. The smaller barrier mattered more than the bigger reward.

[This tactic used to be frequently misused by unethical marketers to turn one-time buyers into subscribers without their consent, by automatically checking a subscription box at checkout.]

Why It Matters:
The UK's National Health Service found that pre-filling organ donor forms increased registration from 42% to 82% in 2017 — a larger impact than all motivational campaigns combined. Similar effects appear in vaccination rates, preventive care, and medication adherence.

When to Use It / How to Counter It:
To spot it: Look for abandoned behaviors despite strong intentions.
To counter it: Remove steps before adding incentives. Make the default option the desired one.

The Bottom Line:
Success comes from lowering hurdles, not jumping higher.

Time Preference Paradox: Why Today Always Beats Tomorrow

Nobel Prize-winning research from Richard Thaler demonstrates how humans systematically undervalue future rewards compared to immediate ones.

How It Works:
We mentally discount future rewards on a hyperbolic curve, not a rational linear one. Behavioral economists have proven this bias exists across cultures, income levels, and education - it's hardwired into human decision-making.

Example:
In Walter Mischel's verified "marshmallow studies" at Stanford, even when children understood that waiting 15 minutes would double their reward, only 30% could delay gratification. Two-thirds chose the immediate smaller reward despite knowing better.

Why It Matters:
The Federal Reserve's Survey of Consumer Finances shows this bias in action: 40% of American adults couldn't cover an unexpected $400 expense in 2022, yet average household spending on immediate gratification items increased by 23% that same year.

When to Use It / How to Counter It:
To spot it: Notice when "future you" pays the price for "present you's" choices.
To counter it: Use automated systems that remove daily decisions about saving and investing.

The Bottom Line:
Your future self is still you—protect them from your present impulses.

Time Value of Information: When Speed Beats Perfection

Military and business research demonstrates that faster decisions with adequate information often outperform delayed decisions that wait for perfect data.

How It Works:
The US Air Force's documented OODA Loop (Observe, Orient, Decide, Act) framework proves that decision speed creates competitive advantage. Waiting for perfect information allows competitors to act first, making even excellent analysis irrelevant.

Example:
The FDA's Emergency Use Authorization process during COVID-19 demonstrated this principle. By using "good enough" data to approve vaccines conditionally, they saved documented thousands of lives compared to waiting for complete long-term studies.

Why It Matters:
Federal Reserve data shows that companies who waited for "complete market information" before entering e-commerce in the late 1990s had significantly lower market share by 2005 than early movers who acted on partial data.

When to Use It / How to Counter It:
To spot it: Watch for analysis paralysis and endless data gathering.
To counter it: Set clear thresholds for "good enough" information before starting research.

The Bottom Line:
Better a good decision now than a perfect decision too late.

Tipping Point Theory: The Science of Social Change

Research demonstrates that changes in social systems follow predictable patterns once they reach certain thresholds, transforming seemingly impossible shifts into inevitable ones.

How It Works:
Network science shows innovations spread through populations following an S-curve: slow initial adoption, rapid middle phase, and plateau. This pattern appears consistently across different types of social change, from technology adoption to social movements.

Example:
Centola's 2018 Science study found that when 25% of a population adopts a new social norm, it consistently triggers widespread acceptance. Below this threshold, changes usually stall; above it, they spread rapidly through existing networks. This explains why movements can appear to fail for years before suddenly succeeding.

Why It Matters:
The established 25% threshold helps explain why some social movements succeed while others fail despite similar efforts. Understanding this number helps organizations plan realistic timelines for change initiatives and allocate resources more effectively during the critical pre-threshold period.

When to Use It / How to Counter It:
To spot it: Track adoption percentages against the 25% threshold. Focus on small, achievable wins within defined networks.
To counter it: Build momentum in smaller groups before attempting larger changes. Concentrate resources on reaching critical mass in specific segments.

The Bottom Line:
Social change isn't random. It follows verifiable patterns we can measure and predict.

Tragedy of the Commons: When Everyone's Property is No One's Responsibility

When resources are shared, everyone has the incentive to take more than their fair share while no one has the incentive to maintain them. It's why public bathrooms are messier than private ones, and why the planet faces environmental crisis.

How It Works:
In shared resource situations, individuals gain all the benefits of overuse while sharing only a fraction of the costs. This creates a rational but destructive pattern where everyone's individual interests lead to collective disaster.

Example:
A company's break room has a shared coffee fund. Everyone drinks premium coffee all day because it's "free," but few contribute to restocking. Soon, the fund runs dry, and the whole system collapses. Each person saved a few dollars while destroying a benefit worth much more.

Why It Matters:
This pattern explains everything from overfishing to office politics to climate change. Understanding it helps you design better systems and recognize when individual incentives need realignment for collective good.

When to Use It / How to Counter It:
To spot it: Look for degrading shared resources where usage is untracked. To counter it: Implement Ostrom's proven principles - clear boundaries, monitoring, graduated sanctions.

The Bottom Line:
Shared resources need shared responsibility, or everyone loses. Design systems that reward stewardship, not just consumption.

Transfer Fallacy: Just Because You're Good at A Doesn't Mean You'll Be Good at B

Great poker players often lose at the stock market. Star athletes frequently fail as coaches. Successful entrepreneurs crash and burn in politics. We keep assuming skills transfer perfectly between domains, and we keep being wrong.

How It Works:
We overestimate how much success in one area translates to another. While some skills transfer, each domain has unique principles that previous success might actually blind us to. Being great at something can make you overconfident and less likely to learn the new rules.

Example:
A brilliant engineer gets promoted to management. Instead of learning new leadership skills, they try to solve people problems with technical solutions. Their previous excellence actually blocks their ability to adapt, and their team suffers.

Why It Matters:
This fallacy leads to poor career moves, failed transitions, and wasted potential. Understanding that excellence is often domain-specific helps you approach new challenges with appropriate humility and learning mindset.

When to Use It / How to Counter It:
To spot it: Notice when past excellence creates resistance to new learning. To counter it: Explicitly identify which skills transfer and which need fresh development.

The Bottom Line:
Excellence doesn't travel well. Master the new game instead of assuming you already know how to play.

Triviality Law: Why Small Debates Hide Big Decisions

Teams spend hours debating coffee brands while rushing past million-dollar choices. It's not stupidity - it's human nature avoiding complexity.

How It Works:
Your brain gravitates toward easy decisions over important ones. Complex issues feel threatening, so groups instinctively focus on simpler topics where everyone can have an opinion. It's safer to debate paint colors than structural integrity.

Example:
A board meeting spends 45 minutes arguing about the new logo's shade of blue, then rubber-stamps a $10M investment in 5 minutes. Everyone can see color, but few understand financial models. Easy wins over essential.

Why It Matters:
This mental glitch wastes precious decision-making time and energy. While teams debate office snacks, crucial strategic choices slip by without proper scrutiny. The trivial feels productive while the vital feels frightening.

When to Use It / How to Counter It:
When discussion time stretches on minor issues, ask: "Is this where our attention creates the most value?" Force focus back to complex but crucial topics. Make the important feel as accessible as the trivial.

The Bottom Line:
Don't let small decisions steal time from big ones. The easier the debate, the less it probably matters.

Tyranny of Small Decisions: How Tiny Choices Create Massive Change

No one decides to ruin their life. They just hit snooze one more time, skip one more workout, make one more excuse - until those tiny choices become destiny.

How It Works:
Big changes rarely happen in one dramatic moment. They creep in through countless small decisions, each too tiny to trigger alarm. Your brain ignores them because no single choice seems important enough to worry about.

Example:
A thriving restaurant doesn't collapse overnight. First, they cut portion sizes slightly. Then they switch to cheaper ingredients. Skip a few equipment repairs. Each decision saves a few dollars. Two years later, they're bankrupt - death by a thousand tiny compromises.

Why It Matters:
Most life disasters aren't from big mistakes - they're from small ones repeated daily. Health, relationships, careers: all can erode through choices that seem too small to matter. Excellence and mediocrity often differ by just a hundred tiny decisions.

When to Use It / How to Counter It:
Before making any "just this once" decision, multiply it by 100. Skip one workout? Consider it skipping 100. That "small" choice just became life-changing. Make decisions based on patterns, not instances.

The Bottom Line:
Your life is the sum of your small choices. Choose wisely - they're building your future one tiny brick at a time.

Unit Bias: Why One Always Feels Like the Right Amount

Your brain has a simple rule: one equals done. This mental shortcut makes you finish the whole cookie, even when half would satisfy.

How It Works:
Your mind automatically treats any complete unit as the "right" amount, regardless of size. A giant restaurant portion feels like one serving. A massive project feels like one task. This hardwired bias tricks you into consuming or doing more than needed.

Example:
Studies show people eat 31% more when served one large bag of chips versus the same amount in smaller bags. Your brain says "one bag = one serving" even when that bag contains three servings. The unit becomes the ruler.

Why It Matters:
This mental glitch drives overconsumption in everything from food to time to money. You buy the bigger house because it's "one home," take on too much work because it's "one project," or clean your plate because it's "one meal."

When to Use It / How to Counter It:
Before consuming anything, divide it mentally. That "single" muffin might be three normal servings. That "one quick project" might be five separate tasks. Break units down before they break you down.

The Bottom Line:
One isn't a size - it's a trick your brain plays. Question every unit, divide when needed, stop when satisfied.

Validity vs Reliability: Being Consistent Doesn't Mean Being Right

Your GPS might reliably take you to the same spot every time. But if that spot is the wrong destination, precision is worthless.

How It Works:
Validity means measuring what matters. Reliability means measuring it consistently. Like a scale: it could show the same wrong weight every time (reliable but invalid) or bounce around the true weight (valid but unreliable). Perfect tools need both.

Example:
Employee time tracking is highly reliable - it precisely measures hours worked. But it's often invalid for measuring productivity. Someone can reliably work 60 hours while producing less value than another's focused 30. The numbers are consistent but misleading.

Why It Matters:
Most systems optimize for reliability because it's easier to measure. Companies track sales calls instead of customer success, workout hours instead of fitness improvement, meetings held instead of problems solved. They get precise data about the wrong things.

When to Use It / How to Counter It:
Before measuring anything, ask: "Are we measuring what actually matters, or just what's easy to measure?" Challenge metrics that are reliably tracked but invalidly chosen. Better to be roughly right than precisely wrong.

The Bottom Line:
Don't confuse consistency with correctness. Measure what matters first, then make it consistent.

Valley of Disappointment: Why Growth Feels Like Failure

The moment you feel most like quitting is often the moment right before your breakthrough. Success has a cruel sense of timing.

How It Works:
As your skills grow, your awareness of what's possible grows faster. You see more flaws, spot more mistakes, notice more gaps. Your standards rise faster than your abilities. This creates a painful valley where getting better feels like getting worse.

Example:
Writers often hit their crisis point right before their best work. They suddenly see all their flaws clearly - and that new awareness, though painful, is exactly what enables their upcoming breakthrough. The darkness before dawn is real.

Why It Matters:
Most people quit in the valley, mistaking growth for failure. They stop learning languages when fluency feels impossible, abandon projects when problems seem overwhelming, give up training when skills feel stuck. Right before the breakthrough.

When to Use It / How to Counter It:
When learning feels harder, not easier, ask: "Am I seeing more flaws because I'm getting worse, or because I'm getting better at spotting them?" Use frustration as a progress marker. The valley means you're climbing.

The Bottom Line:
Growth feels like failure before it feels like success. The valley is where champions are made.

Walled Garden Effect: The Price of Convenience

The more convenient and integrated a system becomes, the harder it is to leave. Like a beautiful garden with high walls, you enjoy the benefits but sacrifice freedom.

How It Works:
Companies create ecosystems of interconnected products and services that work seamlessly together. While this integration provides convenience, it also creates high switching costs and dependency.

Example:
Apple's ecosystem: Your iPhone works perfectly with your MacBook, AirPods, and iCloud. But trying to switch to Android becomes increasingly difficult as you accumulate more Apple products and services.

Why It Matters:
Understanding this effect helps us make more conscious choices about which systems we commit to and how deeply we integrate into them.

When to Use It / How to Counter It:
Consider this when choosing platforms, services, or ecosystems. Weigh the convenience benefits against the loss of flexibility and control.

The Bottom Line:
Convenience often comes at the cost of freedom. Choose your gardens wisely, and keep an eye on the height of the walls.

Weber-Fechner Law: Perception of change depends on magnitude

The Weber-Fechner Law explains how our perception of change is relative to the magnitude of the original stimulus. Small changes in larger stimuli are harder to notice than the same change in smaller stimuli.

How It Works:
If you lift a 5-pound weight and then a 6-pound weight, the difference feels noticeable. But if you lift a 50-pound weight and then a 51-pound weight, the extra pound barely registers. The bigger the original stimulus, the more change is needed to notice a difference.

Example:
In pricing, a $1 increase in the cost of a $5 item feels significant, but the same $1 increase on a $100 item seems trivial. The Weber-Fechner Law shows why perception of change is relative to the initial amount.

Why It Matters:
This law helps explain why we sometimes ignore small changes when they occur in large contexts. It's useful in understanding consumer behavior, sensory perception, and even personal budgeting, where small increases in large expenses may go unnoticed.

When to Use It / How to Counter It:
When analyzing changes or decisions involving perception, ask: "Is this change significant enough to be noticed, or is it too small relative to the original context?" Understanding the Weber-Fechner Law helps you better anticipate reactions to changes.

The Bottom Line:
Perception of change is relative. The Weber-Fechner Law reminds you that the size of the original stimulus affects how much change is noticed - bigger contexts need bigger changes to stand out.

Winner's Curse: When Winning Means You've Overpaid

In auctions and competitive bidding, the winner often pays too much. By definition, they've bid more than everyone else thought the item was worth — suggesting they might have overvalued it.

How It Works:
In competitive bidding situations, the winning bid tends to exceed the true value because winners are often those who most overestimated the value. This is especially true when there's uncertainty about true worth.

Example:
In the NFL draft, teams frequently trade multiple picks to move up and select a coveted player. History shows these aggressive moves often result in overpayment, as the winning team's excitement overcame their rational valuation.

Why It Matters:
This curse explains why many corporate acquisitions, real estate purchases, and competitive bids end up being unprofitable for the winner. Understanding it helps prevent emotional overbidding.

When to Use It / How to Counter It:
Consider this in any competitive bidding situation: auctions, business acquisitions, salary negotiations, or real estate deals. Ask yourself if winning might mean you've lost.

The Bottom Line:
Winning doesn't always mean you've won. Sometimes the best bid is the one you don't make.

Wisdom of Crowds: The Many Can Be Smarter Than the Few

The Wisdom of Crowds is the idea that a diverse group, collectively, can make better decisions than individual experts. This works when the group's opinions are independent, decentralized, and varied, allowing collective intelligence to emerge.

How It Works:
In a guessing game where people estimate the weight of an ox, the average guess of a large group is often more accurate than any individual expert's guess. Different perspectives balance out errors, leading to a better collective outcome.

Example:
Platforms like Wikipedia and prediction markets use the Wisdom of Crowds to aggregate knowledge and make accurate assessments or predictions.

Why It Matters:
This challenges the idea that experts always know best. Diverse group input often leads to better results, but it only works when the group is large, independent, and informed.

When to Use It / How to Counter It:
When making decisions or seeking predictions, ask: "Could a diverse group offer better insights than a few experts?" Use crowd wisdom to gather broader perspectives.

The Bottom Line:
Collective intelligence often outperforms individual expertise. The Wisdom of Crowds reminds you to value diverse input when making decisions.

Zebra Rule: When You Hear Hoofbeats, Think Horses Not Zebras

In problem-solving, the most common explanation is usually the right one. Yet we often chase exotic solutions while overlooking obvious answers right in front of us.

How It Works:
When faced with a problem, we should first consider the most common causes before jumping to rare or exotic explanations. This medical principle reminds us that routine answers often solve routine problems.

Example:
A website's traffic drops suddenly. The team launches into complex theories about algorithm changes and competitor tactics, only to discover they accidentally deactivated their SSL certificate during routine maintenance.

Why It Matters:
This rule prevents us from wasting time and resources chasing unlikely explanations when simple solutions are available. It's especially vital in diagnostics, troubleshooting, and problem-solving.

When to Use It / How to Counter It:
Apply this when investigating problems, especially when you're tempted to pursue complex or exotic explanations. Start with the basics before diving into rarities.

The Bottom Line:
Check the simple stuff first. The obvious answer is often the right one.

Zeigarnik Effect: Unfinished Tasks Stick in Your Head

The Zeigarnik Effect explains why unfinished tasks or incomplete thoughts tend to stick in your mind more than completed ones. It's why that half-finished project haunts you, and why you can't stop thinking about the email you haven't sent yet. Your brain hates leaving things incomplete.

How It Works:
You've got a report due, but you've only half-finished it. Instead of moving on with your day, you keep thinking about it, unable to fully relax until it's done. That's the Zeigarnik Effect - your brain holds onto incomplete tasks like a dog with a bone, constantly nudging you to finish what you started.

Why It Matters:
This effect can be both helpful and frustrating. On the one hand, it pushes you to complete tasks and follow through. On the other hand, it can cause anxiety and mental clutter as unfinished tasks linger in your mind. Understanding the Zeigarnik Effect can help you stay focused, but also remind you to break tasks into smaller, more manageable chunks to avoid overwhelm.

When to Use It / How to Counter It:
When you're feeling mentally cluttered or overwhelmed by unfinished projects. Ask yourself: "What can I complete right now to clear my mind?" Even small wins can reduce the mental load and free up brain space.

The Bottom Line:
Unfinished tasks weigh on your mind more than completed ones. The Zeigarnik Effect shows you the power of getting things done - and the relief that comes with closing open loops.

Zero-Risk Bias: The Illusion of Complete Safety

We prefer eliminating a small risk entirely over reducing a larger risk substantially. It's like spending more money on a burglar alarm than on fixing faulty wiring, even though fire is a greater threat.

How It Works:
People tend to prefer complete elimination of a subset of risks rather than a greater reduction in overall risk. We seek the emotional comfort of certainty in one area while potentially ignoring greater dangers.

Example:
A company spends millions eliminating all cybersecurity risks in one department while leaving larger vulnerabilities in their main system partially addressed. The complete solution feels better but leaves them more exposed overall.

Why It Matters:
This bias leads to misallocation of resources and can actually increase overall risk by focusing too much on eliminating minor threats while neglecting major ones.

When to Use It / How to Counter It:
Consider this when allocating safety resources, making security decisions, or managing risks. Ask whether you're seeking complete elimination of a small risk at the expense of better overall safety.

The Bottom Line:
Don't let perfect be the enemy of safer. Focus on reducing overall risk rather than eliminating specific small risks entirely.

Zero-Sum Bias: Belief that one person's gain is another's loss

Zero-Sum Bias makes you think that all situations are win-lose, where one person's gain automatically comes at someone else's expense, even when it's not true.

How It Works:
You assume that if someone else gets a promotion, there's less opportunity for you, even though the promotion doesn't actually affect your chances of advancement in any direct way.

Why It Matters:
This bias limits collaboration and stifles creativity because it makes us believe we have to compete over a fixed pie, rather than grow it together.

When to Use It / How to Counter It:
In negotiations, business, or any group activity, ask: "Is this really a win-lose situation, or can we both benefit?" Not all gains come at someone else's expense.

The Bottom Line:
Think win-win. Collaboration often leads to better outcomes than competition.

Zimmer's Antifragility Principle: What Doesn't Kill You Makes You Stronger

Some systems don't just survive stress - they get better from it. Like muscles that grow stronger from exercise, antifragile systems need some stress to thrive.

How It Works:
Unlike fragile systems that break under pressure, or robust systems that merely resist it, antifragile systems actually improve when faced with volatility, randomness, and disorder - within limits.

Example:
Amazon's recommendation system improves with every "wrong" suggestion. Each time a customer ignores or rejects a recommendation, the algorithm learns and gets better. The more "mistakes" it makes, the smarter it becomes.

Why It Matters:
Understanding antifragility helps us design better systems, businesses, and personal development strategies. Instead of avoiding all stress, we can use it to grow stronger.

When to Use It / How to Counter It:
Apply this when designing systems, planning for uncertainty, or developing personal resilience. Look for ways to make volatility work for you rather than against you.

The Bottom Line:
Don't just build systems that survive stress - build ones that grow from it. The key is finding the right amount of stress to promote growth without causing collapse.

Zone of Proximal Development: The Sweet Spot for Growth

Learning happens best when challenges are just slightly beyond current abilities. Too easy leads to boredom, too hard leads to frustration.

How It Works:
The ideal learning zone lies between what someone can do without help and what they can't do at all. With proper support and guidance, people can accomplish tasks slightly beyond their current capabilities.

Example:
A coding bootcamp structures projects so each one is slightly harder than the last. Students stretch their abilities but aren't overwhelmed, creating optimal conditions for learning.

Why It Matters:
This principle helps design effective learning experiences, training programs, and personal development plans. It explains why proper scaffolding and gradual progression are crucial for growth.

When to Use It / How to Counter It:
Use this when teaching others, learning new skills, or designing training programs. Find the sweet spot between comfort and overwhelm.

The Bottom Line:
Growth happens at the edge of your abilities. Push just far enough to stretch but not so far that you snap.

The End: You Made It! Now Go Break Some Brains :-)

Congratulations! You just upgraded your mental operating system. While everyone else is running Brain v1.0, you're now equipped with premium anti-BS software.

You've learned to spot the sneaky ways our minds (and others) try to trick us. Those cognitive blind spots? They're now lit up like a Vegas casino. That warm fuzzy feeling when someone flatters you? You'll recognize it as the manipulation attempt it often is.

Remember when you started this book? You were probably thinking "I'm pretty logical already." (That was your Overconfidence Bias talking, by the way). Now you're like a mental martial artist - able to spot and deflect logical fallacies faster than a YouTube ad skip button.

In a world where everyone's trying to hack your brain - from marketers to politicians to that guy on social trying to sell you on crypto - you've just gained psychological body armor. Not bad for a few hours of reading.

Use what you've learned. Every. Single. Day. Your upgraded BS detector isn't just for winning arguments - it's for making better decisions, avoiding costly mistakes, and helping others do the same.

And remember: the person most likely to trick you is still yourself. Stay vigilant, stay curious, and keep unfunking your mind!

And don't forget to claim your free bonuses for buying this book (see first few pages).

If you learned anything at all from this book, I would really appreciate it if you left a review for me on Amazon. Your review will go a long way in helping others find this book as well.

Cheers!

- **Ravi Jayagopal**
SubscribeMe.fm/ravi

www.ingramcontent.com/pod-product-compliance
Lightning Source LLC
Chambersburg PA
CBHW071403090426
42737CB00011B/1327